Coursebook

Margaret O'Keeffe
Lewis Lansford
Ros Wright
Mark Powell
Lizzie Wright

A2+

Business Partner

FT Publishing
FINANCIAL TIMES

GSE
Global Scale of English

Contents

Introduction for learners

Why … Business Partner?

Our research showed that:

- You study business English in order to communicate better in your workplace.
- To achieve this, you need to improve your knowledge of the English language that is used in the workplace, and also develop key communication skills.
- You need a flexible course which you can adapt to suit your needs.

Business Partner focuses on delivering a balance of language and skills training that you can use to improve your work, studies or job search.

Why … skills training?

Language is only one aspect of successful communication. You also need to understand different business situations and be aware of different ways of communicating, especially when working with people from different cultures.

In *Business Partner*, every unit has a lesson on 'Communication skills' and a lesson on 'Business skills':

- 'Communication skills' (Lesson 3) means soft skills such as *small talk*, *solving workflow problems* and *supporting a colleague*.
- 'Business skills' (Lesson 4) means practical skills such as *starting a meeting*, *presenting results* and *being positive in meetings*.

Why … authentic content?

Business Partner is based on authentic videos and articles with a wealth of international business information as well as real examples of British, U.S. and non-native-speaker English. You can hear and read about the real world to understand better the world of work.

Why … video content?

Business Partner has two videos in every unit:

- an authentic video in Lesson 1, based on real-life video clips and interviews suitable for your level of English. These videos show interesting business documentaries.
- a dramatised Communication skills video in Lesson 3 (see p.6 for more information). These videos show different skills and behaviours in professional situations.

Why … flexible content?

This course can be adapted to your needs.

- Each unit and lesson works independently, so you can focus on the topics, lessons or skills which are most relevant to you.
- You can then use the extra activities and additional materials in MyEnglishLab to work more on the aspects that are important to you.

What's in the units?

Lesson outcome and self-assessment

- Each lesson starts with a Lesson outcome and ends with a short Self-assessment section: this is to help you think about the progress that you have made.
- You can find detailed self-assessment tasks and suggestions for extra practice in MyEnglishLab.

Vocabulary

The main topic vocabulary is presented and practised in Lesson 1 of each unit, building on vocabulary from the authentic video. You will get lots of opportunities to use the vocabulary in discussions and group tasks.

Functional language

Functional language includes phrases to deal with *giving and receiving feedback*, *managing questions* and *making requests*). Learning functional language helps you communicate in real work situations in English. You will practise the language in group speaking and writing tasks.

L There is a Functional language bank in MyEnglishLab. You can quickly look at lists of useful language when preparing for a work situation, such as a meeting, presentation or interview.

Grammar

The approach to grammar is flexible: you can spend a lot of time on grammar or only consolidate when you need to.

- There is one main grammar point in each unit, in Lesson 2.
- There is a link from Lesson 5 to an optional second grammar point in MyEnglishLab – with short video presentations and interactive practice.

There is more information on these grammar points in the Grammar reference section at the back of the coursebook (p.119).

Listening and video

- There are lots of listening activities to help you develop your comprehension skills and to hear language in context.
- All of the video and audio material is available in MyEnglishLab and includes a range of British, U.S. and non-native-speaker English.
- Lessons 1 and 3 are based on video.
- In four of the eight units, Lesson 2 is based on audio.
- In all units, you also work with audio recordings in Lesson 4 and the Business workshop.

Reading

There are authentic texts and articles, mainly from the *Financial Times*. Every unit has a main reading text with comprehension tasks. This appears either in Lesson 2 or in the Business workshop.

L There is also a Reading bank in MyEnglishLab, with a longer reading text for every unit and comprehension activities.

Speaking

There are collaborative speaking tasks at the end of Lessons 1, 3, 4 and the Business workshop in every unit. You can practise the language and the skill of the lesson. There are lots of opportunities to personalise these tasks to suit your own situation.

Writing

- Lesson 5 in every unit has a model text and practice in a business writing skill. There is a wide range of genres such as emails, short messages or presentation slides.
- There are also short writing tasks in Lesson 2 with grammar practice.

L There is also a Writing bank in MyEnglishLab, with models of different types of business writing and useful phrases.

Pronunciation

- There are two pronunciation points in every unit. Pronunciation points are linked to the content of the unit – usually to a video/audio presentation or to a grammar point.
- The pronunciation presentations and activities are at the back of the coursebook (p.112), with signposts from the relevant lessons. This section also includes an introduction to pronunciation with British and U.S. phonetic charts.

Reviews

There is a one-page review for each unit at the back of the coursebook (p.104). The review recycles and revises the key vocabulary, grammar and functional language presented in the unit.

Signposts, cross-references and MyEnglishLab

T **Signposts for teachers** indicate that there are extra activities in MyEnglishLab which can be printed or displayed on-screen. These activities can be used to extend a lesson or to focus in more depth on a particular section.

L **Signposts for learners** indicate that there are additional interactive activities in MyEnglishLab.

→ page 000

Cross-references refer to the Pronunciation bank and Grammar reference pages.

MyEnglishLab

There is a code on the inside cover of this book. Use it to access MyEnglishLab.

There are two versions of the course (look on the front cover to see which one you have):

Digital Resources powered by MyEnglishLab including: downloadable coursebook resources, all video clips, all audio recordings, Lesson 3 additional interactive video activities, Lesson 5 interactive grammar presentation and practice, Reading bank, Functional language bank, Writing bank and My Self-assessment.

Full content of MyEnglishLab: all of the above, plus the full self-study interactive workbook with automatic gradebook. Teachers can assign workbook activities as homework.

The Global Scale of English (GSE) is a standardised, granular scale from 10 to 90 which measures English language proficiency. The GSE Learning Objectives for Professional English are aligned with the Common European Framework of Reference (CEFR). Unlike the CEFR, which describes proficiency in terms of broad levels, the Global Scale of English identifies what a learner can do at each point on a more granular scale – and within a CEFR level. The scale is designed to motivate learners by demonstrating incremental progress in their language ability. The Global Scale of English forms the backbone for Pearson English course material and assessment.

GSE	10	20	30	40	50	60	70	80	90
CEFR	<A1	A1	A2 +	B1 +		B2 +	C1	C2	

Learn more about the Global Scale of English at english.com/gse

Video introduction

Introduction

The Communication skills videos (in Lesson 3 of each unit) show the skills you need to work in teams, especially with people from different cultures.

In each Communication skills lesson, you will:

1 watch a set-up video which introduces the main characters and challenge of the lesson.

2 watch different approaches to a situation (Video A and Video B).

3 answer questions about each approach before watching the conclusion.

There is a storyline running through the eight units, with the main characters appearing in different situations. However, you can watch each clip separately and do each lesson independently; you will still understand the story.

Communication skills video storyline

TGC is an Irish HR consultancy firm. They advise companies on different aspects of their business: recruitment, learning and development and company strategy. The company is growing and recently hired four new people. In the eight units of the book we see the characters in various work-related and social situations.

Characters

Jasmine Wilson (American) Associate Consultant (units 1, 4, 5, 6, 7, 8)
Azra Kaya (British) Consultant (units 1, 3, 5, 6, 7)
Alex Schmidt (German) Consultant (units 1, 2, 5, 6)
Shaun Kelly (Irish) Senior Consultant (units 1, 2, 3, 4, 5, 7, 8)
Thiago Silva (Italian) Associate Consultant (units 1, 3, 4, 5, 6, 7, 8)
Orla Murphy (Irish) Senior Consultant (units 1, 4, 5, 7, 8)
Graham O'Brien (Irish) Managing Director (units 1 and 4)
Ethan Firth (British) Recruiter (units 1 and 4)
Della O'Reilly (Irish) Office Manager (unit 8)
Nick Walsh (British) Head of HR at Zapna Clothing, TCG's client (unit 2)
Michael (or 'Mike') Hammond (British) Recruiter (unit 4)
Caroline Smith (British) Recruiter (unit 7)

Video context by unit

1 **Small talk**
Video synopsis: *Senior management have invited new starters to a welcome dinner.*

2 **Checking and clarifying**
Video synopsis: *Shaun and Alex are meeting a client, Zapna Clothing.*

3 **Solving workflow problems**
Video synopsis: *Thiago is late with a report for Shaun.*

4 **Making group decisions**
Video synopsis: *Shaun is trying to persuade the team to get involved in reverse coaching.*

5 **Negotiating team roles**
Video synopsis: *Orla is building a team to work on a new project.*

6 **Supporting a colleague**
Video synopsis: *Thiago, Azra and Alex try to encourage and motivate Jasmine.*

7 **Giving explanations**
Video synopsis: *The company is introducing a new procedure for claiming expenses.*

8 **Giving and receiving feedback**
Video synopsis: *Thiago has his mid-year review meeting with Orla.*

Travelling for work

1

> 'Travel makes one modest. You see what a tiny place you occupy in the world.'
>
> Gustave Flaubert, novelist

Unit overview

1.1	**Business travel** **Lesson outcome:** Learners can use vocabulary related to business travel.	**Video:** Business travel **Vocabulary:** Transport, accommodation and travel **Project:** Helping a business traveller
1.2	**Events management** **Lesson outcome:** Learners can make simple comparisons.	**Listening:** Interview with an Events Manager **Grammar:** Comparatives and superlatives **Speaking and writing:** Choose a venue for a party
1.3	**Communication skills:** Small talk **Lesson outcome:** Learners can make small talk using a simple model.	**Video:** Making small talk **Functional language:** Making small talk **Task:** Practise making small talk with colleagues
1.4	**Business skills:** Dealing with problems **Lesson outcome:** Learners can use a range of expressions to explain and solve problems with IT.	**Listening:** Talking about problems **Functional language:** Explaining and solving IT problems **Task:** Practise explaining and solving an IT problem
1.5	**Writing:** Email – Asking for information **Lesson outcome:** Learners can organise information in a work-related email and write an email to ask for information.	**Model text:** Email asking for information **Functional language:** Phrases for writing an email **Grammar:** *can* and *could* to ask for information **Task:** Write an email asking for information

Business workshop 1: p.88 | **Review 1:** p.104 | **Pronunciation:** 1.2 The letter 'r' 1.3 Showing interest in small talk p.114 | **Grammar reference:** p.119

1.1 Business travel

Lesson outcome Learners can use vocabulary related to business travel.

Lead-in

1 Tick (✓) the types of transport and accommodation you use when you travel to another country. Then compare with the class.

Transport

boat bus car coach motorcycle plane taxi train

Accommodation

bed and breakfast (B&B) budget hotel business hotel holiday resort home of friend or family luxury hotel rented apartment youth hostel

2 Work in groups. When you travel, how do you choose which transport to use? Price? Speed? Comfort? How easy it is to use? What about accommodation? Price? Comfort? Location? Something else?

VIDEO

3 1.1.1 **Watch the video about business travel. Which topics do the speakers talk about?**

a Why they travel
b Where they travel
c Who they travel with
d Types of transportation
e Accommodation
f The cost of travel
g Advice for travel
h How to pack a suitcase

4 Watch the video again and choose the correct option.

1 Which type of travel do they talk about?
- **a** travel to cities in their own country
- **b** travel to other countries
- **c** going to and from work

2 What does Alex talk about?
- **a** using his laptop for video chats
- **b** problems with travelling a lot
- **c** travelling by plane

3 For a hotel, what's important to Alessio?
- **a** It needs to be near his job.
- **b** It should have free breakfast.
- **c** He likes to be able to book it online.

4 How does Amira feel about talking with local people?
- **a** She worries about it a lot.
- **b** She never tries it.
- **c** She likes it because they help her.

5 What problem did Amira have at the airport?
- **a** She didn't arrive at the airport on time.
- **b** She made a mistake about the time.
- **c** The time of her plane was changed.

6 What does Alessio's advice include?
- **a** an idea for having more free time
- **b** an idea for saving money
- **c** tips for good communication

T Teacher's resources: extra activities

5 Work in pairs or small groups. Do you think each speaker enjoys travelling for work? Why? / Why not?

Vocabulary Transport, accommodation and travel

6 Complete the sentences with these words from the video.

flight gate location
lounge public transportation
reservation ridesharing app
stay vehicle

1 They made a ___________ for two rooms, but when they arrived, only one was available.
2 I took a thirteen-hour ___________ from Madrid to Buenos Aires.
3 We need to hire a ___________ to take ten people from the airport to the conference centre.
4 He usually uses a ___________ to get a car from one meeting to the next.
5 I arrived at the ___________ five minutes after the plane had left.
6 We had a comfortable ___________ in Vietnam because the resort was very modern.
7 They waited in the departure ___________ until it was time to get on the plane.
8 The ___________ of the apartment is perfect – near the office and the station.
9 I like to take ___________ so I can see what life in the city is like.

7A Match the words in bold with the definitions.

1 I go **abroad** for work trips quite often.
2 I take several **short-haul** flights each year.
3 The flight was **delayed** by two hours.
4 The captain said that we were ready for **landing**.
5 The **departure** was a few minutes late.

a a flight or plane that travels a short distance
b the action of bringing a plane down to the ground after being in the air
c to or in another country
d the action of leaving a place, especially at the start of a journey
e late, usually because of a problem

B Write the words in bold in Exercise 7A with their opposites.

1 long-haul ___________
2 take-off ___________
3 arrival ___________
4 on-time ___________
5 local ___________

T Teacher's resources: extra activities

8 Work in pairs or small groups. Use adjectives to make sentences about business travel.

Making a hotel reservation
Waiting in a lounge
Travelling abroad
Using a ridesharing app
A delayed train or flight
Driving when you're abroad
A long-haul flight

is ___________ because ...

*Travelling abroad **is** interesting **because** you see new places.*

PROJECT: Helping a business traveller

9A Work in pairs or small groups. Imagine you need to give advice about your town to a visitor from abroad. For each category, decide what advice you would give and explain why.

- Travel – how to arrive in your town: by plane, bus, train, etc.
- Accommodation – where to stay
- Travelling around town – transportation
- Other useful information – the sights to see in free time, the foods to try, etc.

The City Hotel is quiet and is in a good location. It's a great place to stay.

B Roleplay a conference call with your colleague. Explain the plans for the visit. Remember to talk about all four categories in Exercise 9A.

A: *How do I get to your city?*
B: *Take a flight. Then take a train from the airport to the Central Rail Station.*
A: *OK. Where can I stay?*
B: *The City Hotel is quiet and ...*

Self-assessment

- How successfully have you achieved the lesson outcome? Give yourself a score from 0 (I need more practice) to 5 (I know this well).
- Go to My Self-assessment in MyEnglishLab to reflect on what you have learnt.

1.2 Events management

Lesson outcome Learners can make simple comparisons.

Lead-in

1 **Work in pairs. Which of these events have you been to?**

an anniversary celebration	a conference	a graduation party
the grand opening of a new business	the launch of a new product	
a special meal with colleagues from work	a wedding	

2A **Which of the skills and personal qualities below are useful for planning events? Why?**

You need to be: organised / able to cook food for a lot of people / good at telling jokes / able to pay attention to details / good with budgets.

B **Would you enjoy planning a big event, for example a company's tenth anniversary celebration? Why? / Why not?**

Listening

3 **You are going to listen to an interview with an Events Manager. Think of one or two things she will talk about for each category.**

- The types of events she plans
- Important things to think about
- Important skills for an Events Manager

4 1.01 **Listen to the interview. Did Alicia talk about any of your ideas from Exercise 3? Did you hear any other ideas?**

5 **Listen again and decide if these sentences are *true* (T) or *false* (F). Correct the incorrect sentences.**

1 She helps people plan weddings.
2 Most of her clients are businesses.
3 In the first meeting, she never talks to clients about money.
4 She says that planning a big event is like planning a circus.
5 She believes that getting details right is very important.
6 She says her job is to make her clients happy.

T Teacher's resources: extra activities

6 **Would you enjoy being an Events Manager? Why? / Why not?**

Grammar

Comparatives and superlatives

7A **Look at the sentences from the interview. Which sentences are comparatives? Which are superlatives?**

1 Weddings are **harder than** business lunches.
2 I try to find **the best** location for each event.
3 I can't choose **the most expensive** hotel in town for an event for someone with a small budget.
4 For a cheap event, we choose **the least expensive** venue possible.
5 And for you, are some venues **better than** others?
6 Planning an event outdoors is always **the biggest** challenge.
7 Was the circus event **more difficult than** your usual events?
8 And for you, are any of the skills more important – or **less important**?

B Complete the sentences with *comparative*, *superlative* or *irregular*.

1 To form the __________ of most adjectives, we use *the* before the adjective and *-est* or *most/least*.

2 To form the __________ of most adjectives, we use *-er* or *more/less* and *than*.

3 Some common adjectives are __________ , e.g. *good – better than – the best*.

→ page 119 See Grammar reference: Comparatives and superlatives

8 Choose the correct option in italics to complete the sentences.

1 The steak is *the most / more* expensive meal on the menu.

2 Organising a lunch is *difficult less / less difficult* than organising a trip.

3 Planning a party for 200 people is *the hardest / harder* than planning a party for 20.

4 Some people think that this is *the worst / worse* hotel in town.

5 A circus theme is *the most / more* fun than just having a meal.

6 Managing an informal event is *the easiest / easier than* managing a formal event.

7 *The best / Better* option is a big tent in the park.

8 *The least / Less* popular time for a party is during the work day.

9 Complete the sentences with the comparative or superlative form of the word in brackets. Use *the* and *than* where necessary.

1 The Metropole Hotel has __________________ (big) dining room.

2 Today's weather is __________________ (bad) yesterday's weather.

3 Is a phone call __________________ (easy) a face-to-face meeting for you?

4 We don't have much money, so we want to choose __________________ (expensive) option.

5 We need to choose __________________ (cheap) venue, because we don't have much money.

6 For a small group, a restaurant party is __________________ (good) an office party.

7 With ten tables, the Grey room is __________________ (small) the Blue room, which has twenty tables.

8 I think __________________ (good) day for our party is Friday.

T Teacher's resources: extra activities

Speaking and writing

10A Work in pairs. Look at the information about event venues. Make sentences comparing the venues.

Barbecue in the park	Lakeside restaurant	Hotel ballroom
• food (€€): meat on the grill • entertainment: country band • up to 200 guests • staff: 12	• food (€€€): fish • entertainment: singer with guitar • up to 150 guests • staff: 15	• food (€€€€): a choice of meat, fish or vegetable pie • entertainment: jazz band • up to 300 guests • staff: 20

The barbecue is cheaper than the restaurant.

The restaurant is the smallest.

The ballroom is probably more formal than the other rooms.

B Which location would be the best choice for a party with your English class? Why?

11 Think of three possible event venues in your town, or imagine them. Write three comparative sentences and three superlative sentences about them.

→ page 114 See Pronunciation bank: The letter 'r'

Self-assessment

- How successfully have you achieved the lesson outcome? Give yourself a score from 0 (I need more practice) to 5 (I know this well).
- Go to My Self-assessment in MyEnglishLab to reflect on what you have learnt.

COMMUNICATION SKILLS
Small talk

Lesson outcome Learners can make small talk using a simple model.

Lead-in

'Small talk' is an unimportant conversation about unimportant things, usually with people you don't know very well.

1A Work in pairs. Read the comment on the left about small talk and discuss whether you agree or disagree.

B Discuss the questions.

1 In which situations and places can small talk take place? Make a list.
2 Why do people make small talk?
3 What do you usually talk about when you meet someone for the first time?

C In small groups, discuss where on the line you would put these small talk topics. Explain your choice.

I definitely would talk about this. ⟷ I definitely wouldn't talk about this.

family health home town music personal finances the place you are in politics religion sports travel the weather

VIDEO

2 ▶ 1.3.1 **Watch the video as Jasmine arrives at The Gallagher Consultancy dinner and answer the questions.**

1 What is Jasmine's new job?
2 What does The Gallagher Consultancy (TGC) do?
3 Who are the people in the restaurant? Why are they meeting?
4 Why is Jasmine late?

Video A ▶ 1.3.2

3A Watch Video A.

1 Which topics in Exercise 1C do Orla and Azra talk about?
2 Where is Azra from originally? Where does she live now?
3 What do we learn about:
   a Shaun's typical journey home?
   b Shaun's trips to Los Angeles and Bangkok?

B In pairs, decide which sentence best describes how Shaun speaks.

a He asks Jasmine a number of questions and listens carefully to her answers.
b He doesn't really listen to Jasmine, but prefers to talk about himself.

Video B ▶ 1.3.3

4A Watch Video B. What do you learn about:

1 Jasmine? 2 Thiago? 3 Azra? 4 Alex?

B Watch Video B again and tick (✓) the things the speakers do as they make small talk.

	Thiago	Jasmine	Alex	Azra
Ask a question				
Answer the question				
Add new information				
Show interest (lean forward, use eye contact, smile)				

5 ▶ 1.3.4 **Watch the Conclusions section of the video. What is the AAA model?**

Reflection

6 Think about how good you are at making small talk. In pairs, discuss how you could improve your skills.

Functional language

Making small talk

7A Match the questions (1–8) with the answers (a–h).

1 **Where do you** come from?
2 **What do you think about** this restaurant?
3 **How long was your** trip?
4 **What do you know about** working at TGC?
5 **Do you know** Turkey?
6 **Which do you prefer**, London or Istanbul?
7 **Do you know** Orla?
8 **What are you doing** in Dublin?

a It's very nice.
b Not much.
c Yes, I met her at the interview.
d About an hour.
e I'm starting a new job on Monday.
f A little. I went there on holiday about three years ago.
g I'm from Turkey.
h I love them both.

B Match words from the box with the expressions in bold in Exercise 7A to make more small talk questions. There may be more than one possible answer.

Angelina's Pizzeria	the company	David	fashion	flight	the food
in Boston	~~live~~	Prague or Barcelona	the project	the town	

1 Where do you live?

C Write eight more small talk questions using the phrases in bold from Exercise 7A.

8A Complete the extract from the video using the phrases in the box.

I'd like to	that's right	to university	you from	you know it

Thiago: Shaun says you're American. Where are [1]___________ ?
Jasmine: [2]___________ . I'm from Boston. I went [3]___________ there. Do [4]___________ ?
Thiago: No, I've never been, but [5]___________ .

B Look at Jasmine's response in Exercise 8A.

1 Does she use the AAA (answer, add, ask) model? Explain your answer.
2 Could Thiago also use the AAA model and continue the conversation? What could he say?

C Watch Video B again and find two more examples of the AAA model.

9 Work in pairs. Use the AAA model and the question forms in Exercise 7A to practise making small talk.

Where do you come from?
Answer: Italy. Add: I live in Trieste. Ask: Do you know it?

T Teacher's resources: extra activities

→ page 114 See Pronunciation bank: Showing interest in small talk

TASK

10A Work in pairs. Choose one of the situations below to practise making small talk.

• at the coffee machine • on an aeroplane • during a conference
• in the staff canteen • at a train station

B Practise making small talk using the AAA model and the expressions in Exercise 7A to discuss two or more of these topics. Remember to show interest as you speak.

• food • holidays • home town • music • sports • the weather

C Work with a different partner. Choose a different situation and topic(s) from the list in Exercises 10A and 10B.

D Tell the class what you learnt about your partners.

Self-assessment

• How successfully have you achieved the lesson outcome? Give yourself a score from 0 (I need more practice) to 5 (I know this well).
• Go to My Self-assessment in MyEnglishLab to reflect on what you have learnt.

1.4 BUSINESS SKILLS
Dealing with problems

Lesson outcome Learners can use a range of expressions to explain and solve problems with IT.

Lead-in

1A Look at the photo. How did you feel on your first day at a new college or job?

B Work in pairs. Note down 3–4 pieces of advice for someone's first day in a new job.

Take notes during the day. Arrive at your new workplace 10 minutes early.

Listening

2 1.02 **It's Jakob's first day in a new job. Laura, the HR Manager, is explaining the schedule. Listen and number Jakob's tasks in the correct order (1–4).**

- Set up his email account
- Go to the induction briefing
- Do the health and safety training
- Meet the team

3A 1.03 **Jakob is speaking to Sue, the IT Technician. Listen and tick (✓) the things Jakob is having problems with.**

1 his password ☐
2 his user name ☐
3 his email address ☐
4 the company phone number ☐
5 connecting to the company intranet ☐

B Listen again and answer the questions.

1 What is Jakob's user name?
2 Why couldn't Jakob log on to the intranet?
3 How do you spell Jakob's family name?
4 What is Jakob's extension number?

Teacher's resources: extra activities

Functional language

Explaining and solving IT problems

4A Listen again and complete the expressions from the audio using the phrases in the box.

a company email address | connect to the intranet | finding my extension number | 'intern32' | log on | logging on | set that up | set up my email account | ~~the IT~~ | use your login details

1 I'm having problems with *the IT* .
2 I can't __________ .
3 I don't know how to __________ .
4 You need to __________ .
5 Can you try __________ again?
6 Try __________ .
7 I need to get __________ .
8 How do I __________ ?
9 I'll __________ for you.
10 I'm having trouble __________ .

B Put the expressions in Exercise 4A into the correct section in the table.

Explaining a problem	Solving a problem
I'm having problems with the IT.	*You need to use your login details.*

Teacher's resources: extra activities

Tip

Explain a problem using *I'm having problems/trouble (with)* + the *-ing* form of a verb, OR *with* + a noun. *I'm having problems connecting to the intranet / with the intranet.*

Solve a problem using *You can try / Try* + the *-ing* form of a verb, OR *You need to* + the infinitive form of a verb. *Try logging on again. / You need to log on again.*

5A Match the IT problems (1–4) with the solutions (a–d). There may be more than one possible answer.

Problems		Solutions	
1	connecting to the network printer	a	search for his surname in the online phonebook
2	finding Dan's extension number	b	check your wi-fi settings
3	logging onto the intranet	c	restart your computer
4	can't access the internet	d	go to the printer settings and select printer 004AC

B Work in pairs. Use the expressions in Exercise 4A to practise explaining and solving the problems in Exercise 5A.

A: *What's the problem?*
B: *I'm having trouble finding Dan's extension number.*
A: *You need to search for his surname in the online phonebook.*
B: *OK, thanks.*

TASK

6A Work in pairs. You are going to take turns to explain and solve an IT problem.

Student A: Read the information below. **Student B:** Look at page 127.

You are working on an important document but are experiencing some IT problems. Choose three problems from the list below or think of your own problem and call Student B for help.

You have incorrect login details.
Your password has expired.
You can't connect to the network printer.
You can't connect to the internet/intranet.
You are locked out of your computer.
Your computer screen freezes every few minutes.

B Take a few minutes to prepare, then roleplay the situation. Swap roles.

C When you have finished, discuss how easy or difficult it was to explain and/or solve an IT problem in English. Share your experience with the class.

Self-assessment

- How successfully have you achieved the lesson outcome? Give yourself a score from 0 (I need more practice) to 5 (I know this well).
- Go to My Self-assessment in MyEnglishLab to reflect on what you have learnt.

1.5 WRITING
Email – Asking for information

Lesson outcome

Learners can organise information in a work-related email and write an email to ask for information.

Lead-in

1 Read the email asking for information from a hotel. Complete it with the words and phrases in the box. Then compare in pairs.

book city centre conference facilities desk five nights lunch price two large rooms walk 50 people

To: Hotel Manager
From: Ananya Chadha
Subject: Conference facilities

Dear Sir/Madam,

I am writing to ask for information about the [1] ___________ at your hotel.

We are looking for a venue which has at least [2] ___________ and which can each accommodate [3] ___________ . We need to have a hotel near the [4] ___________ so please can you confirm how long it takes to [5] ___________ to the centre from your hotel? We would like to [6] ___________ 100 rooms for all the delegates for [7] ___________ and we would also like each room to have a [8] ___________ and wi-fi. We are planning to have breakfast and [9] ___________ at the hotel each day. The conference lasts for five days so could you tell me what your best [10] ___________ for this is?

I look forward to hearing from you.

Kind regards,

Ananya Chadha, Conference Manager

Functional language

2 Complete the table using words and phrases from the email.

Greeting/Opening
1 ___________
Dear Mr Zhao,
Reason for writing
2 ___________ information about ...
I am writing to enquire about ...
Giving information
3 ___________ for a venue ...
4 ___________ to have a hotel near the city centre.
5 ___________ book 100 rooms.
We 6 ___________ each room to have a desk and wi-fi.
Asking for information
7 ___________ how long it takes ... ?
8 ___________ me what your best price is?
Please can/could you let me know what/if ... ?
Can/Could you confirm that you have my booking, please?
I would like to know how far it is to the city centre.
We would also like more information about ...
Concluding email
9 ___________ hearing from you.
I hope to hear from you soon.
Closing
10 ___________
All the best,

T Teacher's resources: extra activities

L The email contains examples of *can* and *could* to ask for information. Go to MyEnglishLab for optional grammar work.

→ page 119 See Grammar reference: *can* and *could* to ask for information

TASK

3A Work in pairs. Look at the questions on page 127. Write questions asking for this information using the structures in the table in Exercise 2.

B Look at the notes about a hotel booking on page 130. Write an email of about 120 words asking for information about the hotel.

C Exchange emails with your partner. Which functional language phrases did your partner use? How many were different from the ones you used?

Self-assessment

- How successfully have you achieved the lesson outcome? Give yourself a score from 0 (I need more practice) to 5 (I know this well).
- Go to My Self-assessment in MyEnglishLab to reflect on what you have learnt.

Business location

2

> *'Be sure you put your feet in the right place, then stand firm.'*
>
> Abraham Lincoln

Unit overview

2.1	**Dovetailed in Cambridge** **Lesson outcome:** Learners can use vocabulary related to places of work and business locations.	**Video:** Choosing a business location **Vocabulary:** Location **Project:** Researching the location of a company
2.2	**Visiting Singapore** **Lesson outcome:** Learners can use *enough* and *too* to express sufficiency and insufficiency.	**Reading:** Singapore creates a tropical wildlife paradise **Grammar:** *enough* and *too* **Speaking and writing:** Describing problematic situations
2.3	**Communication skills:** Checking and clarifying **Lesson outcome:** Learners can check, confirm and clarify information using a range of expressions.	**Video:** Clarifying information **Functional language:** Checking and clarifying **Task:** Checking and clarifying information in a meeting
2.4	**Business skills:** Starting a meeting **Lesson outcome:** Learners are able to use a variety of expressions to open meetings.	**Listening:** A meeting **Functional language:** Opening a meeting, referring to the agenda and stating purpose **Task:** Opening a meeting
2.5	**Writing:** Short communications **Lesson outcome:** Learners can communicate by text message, write short emails and use abbreviations and shortened forms appropriately.	**Model text:** Short messages **Functional language:** Abbreviations **Grammar:** Present Continuous **Task:** Informal and formal messages

Business workshop 2: p.90 | **Review 2:** p.105 | **Pronunciation:** 2.1 Syllables and stress 2.2 Stress in noun phrases p.114 | **Grammar reference:** p.119

2.1 Dovetailed in Cambridge

Lesson outcome Learners can use vocabulary related to places of work and business locations.

Lead-in

1 Discuss these questions.

1 What is good or bad about the location where you live, work or study? Use some of the expressions in the box to help you.

I (don't) really like (my town) because ... It's (not) a very (interesting, nice, etc.) place. It's full of (parks, etc.). There are lots of good (shops, etc.). I think it's very (quiet, noisy, etc.). It's near (the station, etc.).

2 Which factors are most important to you when choosing a place to live, work or study?

VIDEO

2 2.1.1 **Watch the video interview with Dr Vaiva Kalnikaitė about her company, Dovetailed. Tick (✓) the five reasons she says Cambridge is a good location for her business.**

- ☐ cheap location
- ☐ international city
- ☐ can work with other companies
- ☐ good public services (schools, hospitals, etc.)
- ☐ can work with the university
- ☐ salaries lower than other places
- ☐ nice place to live
- ☐ easy to travel to London

3 Watch the video again and answer the questions.

1 When did Dr Kalnikaitė start her company?
2 Which company did she work for as an intern in Cambridge?
3 What help does she get from her business contacts? *funding / products / advice*
4 What help does she get from Judge Business School? *funding / products / advice*
5 How long does it take Dr Kalnikaitė to get to work?
6 How long does it take to get to London by train? And by car?

Teacher's resources: extra activities

4 Based on what you saw in the video, would you like to live and work in a city like Cambridge? What would you like most? What would you like least?

Vocabulary

Location

5 Look at these extracts from the video. Match the words in bold with the definitions.

1 where to **locate** the business
2 **access to** skilled staff
3 good **transport links**
4 reasonable **rents** for **factory** or office space
5 a technology design **studio** and innovation **lab**
6 it's very **close to** London
7 drive to London on a **motorway**

a a special room or building in which a scientist does tests
b a room where an artist, photographer or designer regularly works
c a very wide road for travelling fast over long distances, especially between cities
d something that makes travel between two places possible
e a building in which goods are produced in large quantities, using machines
f put or build something in a particular place
g how easy or difficult it is for people to enter a public building, to reach a place or to talk to someone or contact them
h money that is paid regularly to use office buildings, etc.
i not far from something

→ page 114 See Pronunciation bank: Syllables and stress

6 **Replace the underlined phrase in each sentence using the words and phrases in the box.**

car park	convenient	facilities	headquarters (HQ)	port	warehouse

1 This is the place where we store large quantities of our products.
2 The transport company is close to the place where the ships arrive and leave.
3 The place with spaces for people to leave their vehicles outside the office is very small.
4 The train station is very close and easy to reach.
5 Google's main offices are in Mountain View, California.
6 The conference rooms, equipment and services at the hotel are excellent.

7 **Match the facilities with the examples. Can you think of another example for each?**

1 office facilities
2 hotel facilities
3 sports and leisure facilities

a 24-hour reception, car park, room service, free wi-fi
b swimming pool, gym, football stadium, park
c car park, printers, meeting rooms, staff kitchen

8A **Choose the correct option in italics to complete the sentences.**

1 Where are the most expensive *rents* / *locate* for office space in your town or city? Where are the cheapest? Why is this?
2 Which part(s) of your town or city have good *access* / *close* to an airport / a port / a motorway? How does this help a business?
3 What are the best *headquarters* / *facilities* where you work or study?
4 What sports and leisure facilities are there *close* / *access* to your home?
5 Where would you *locate* / *convenient* a new hotel in your town or city? Why?
6 How good are the transport *links* / *ports* in your town? What would make them better?

B **Work in pairs or small groups. Discuss the questions in Exercise 8A.**

T Teacher's resources: extra activities

PROJECT: Location, location, location

9A **Work in pairs or small groups. You are going to research the location of a company in your town or city. Choose from one of these options or use your own idea.**

an airport a bank a factory a gym
the headquarters of a company a hospital
a luxury hotel a restaurant a shop
a transport company a university a warehouse

B **Find out why the company chose that location. Describe the advantages of the location. Are there any disadvantages?**

C **Present what you found out about the location to another pair or group.**

Self-assessment

- How successfully have you achieved the lesson outcome? Give yourself a score from 0 (I need more practice) to 5 (I know this well).
- Go to My Self-assessment in MyEnglishLab to reflect on what you have learnt.

2.2 Visiting Singapore

Lesson outcome Learners can use *enough* and *too* to express sufficiency and insufficiency.

Lead-in

1A Work in pairs or small groups. Do you ever visit any of these places?

aquarium | bird park | city zoo | ski resort | theme park | wildlife park

B Tell each other about a visit to one of these places.

→ page 114 See Pronunciation bank: Stress in noun phrases

Reading

2 Read the article quickly and choose the best headline.

1. Singapore opens more parks in the city centre
2. Singapore creates a tropical wildlife paradise
3. Singapore offers more shopping experiences

3 Read the article again and answer the questions.

1. What are the names of the five parks in the Mandai project?
2. Which of the Mandai parks are already open?
3. How long do tourists usually stay in Singapore?
4. Why is the government creating the Mandai project?
5. What type of rooms will the Banyan Tree resort offer?
6. Why does Singapore want to change its image?
7. What type of tourists will go to Mandai?

T Teacher's resources: extra activities

NIKKEI ASIAN REVIEW

JUSTINA LEE, Nikkei staff writer

Singapore is creating an eco-tourism hub* with five wildlife parks in Mandai, in the northern part of the country. Mandai is already home to the Singapore Zoo, the Night Safari and the River Safari, which opened in 2014. The famous Jurong Bird Park in the southwestern side of the country is now [1]too small. It will soon relocate to a site in Mandai, which is [2]big enough for the 5,000 birds that come from 400 species. In addition the new Rainforest Park will open in a few years. Within the hub, there will also be conservation projects for endangered species.

Singapore is a stopover for visitors going to other parts of Asia or travelling from Europe to Australia. Most holidaymakers feel three or four days is [3]enough time to see the country. The government wants to attract tourists to less visited parts of the city and get them to stay longer. It hopes the Mandai project will receive more than 10 million visitors each year.

Luxury resort operator Banyan Tree will open its eco-resort with around 400 rooms in Mandai by 2023. Apart from the standard and family rooms, visitors will also be able to stay in treehouses and cabins that will provide a unique experience. Visitors can also go on nature walks.

The government wants Singapore to offer more than the usual shopping and dining experiences to attract tourists. Today there is [4]too much competition from online shopping and bigger destinations in Asia.

Seshan Ramaswami, associate professor of marketing education at Singapore Management University, said the Mandai project and Banyan Tree resort will appeal to travellers who want 'to experience nature in a sophisticated urban environment.'

*hub: the most important part of an area, system or activity that other parts are connected to

Grammar *enough* and *too*

4 Look at the underlined phrases (1–4) in the article. Match them with the meanings (a–d).

a it is as big as it needs to be
b it is more than needed or wanted
c it is not as big as it needs to be
d it is a good amount of time to do what is needed or wanted

5 Look at these comments on a review site about a theme park. Which visitors were satisfied? Which visitors were not? Why?

1 Great theme park with enough attractions for all ages!

2 There are too many people in summer! It's too hot to queue for hours.

3 A day isn't long enough to do and see everything. Fantastic!

4 Too many shops and not enough rides!

5 My children weren't tall enough to go on the best rides.

6 Look at the underlined phrases in the article and the sentences in Exercise 5. Choose the correct options.

1 (**not**) *adjective / noun* + **enough**
2 (**not**) **enough** + *adjective / noun*
3 **too** + *adjective / noun*
4 **too many** + *countable / uncountable* noun
5 **too much** + *countable / uncountable* noun

→ page 119 See Grammar reference: *enough* and *too*

7 Put the words in the correct order to complete the sentences.

1 This office ___________ for six people.
enough / big / isn't
2 The station ___________ to walk.
too / is / far
3 Are there ___________ everyone?
attractions / for / enough
4 There ___________ to finish the presentation.
time / wasn't / enough
5 There are ___________ waiting.
customers / many / too
6 It's ___________ for one person.
too / work / much

8A Complete the dialogue with *(not) enough*, *too*, *too many* and *too much*.

A: Is there [1]___________ space in this room for the meeting?
B: Yes, but I think there are [2]___________ chairs.
A: You're right! I'll move some next door.
B: And it's [3]___________ hot in here, isn't it? Let's open the windows.
A: Oh no! There's [4]___________ noise from outside. I'll put the air conditioning on.
B: OK! I see there are [5]___________ glasses. I'll get some more from the kitchen.
A: Is there [6]___________ time to make some photocopies?
B: Yes! We have lots of time. It's still [7]___________ early for people to arrive.

B 2.01 **Listen and check your answers to Exercise 8A.**

T Teacher's resources: extra activities

Speaking and writing

9 Work in pairs or small groups. What would you say in these situations? Use *too* and *(not) enough*.

1 You went to bed at 2 a.m. last night and got up at 7 a.m. this morning. You are having difficulties concentrating on your work/studies now.

2 You arrived late for lunch in the canteen. There was one person serving a long queue of customers. The only dessert option was apples. All the tables were occupied or had dirty plates on them.

10 Choose one of these options. Write 80–100 words and use *too* and (*not*) *enough*. 1) Write an email complaining to the canteen manager at work. Explain some recent problems with the canteen. 2) Write a short online review for a tourist attraction (e.g. a park or museum), hotel or restaurant.

Self-assessment

- How successfully have you achieved the lesson outcome? Give yourself a score from 0 (I need more practice) to 5 (I know this well).
- Go to My Self-assessment in MyEnglishLab to reflect on what you have learnt.

2.3 COMMUNICATION SKILLS
Checking and clarifying

Lesson outcome Learners can check, confirm and clarify information using a range of expressions.

Lead-in

1A Work in pairs. Think about the last meeting or discussion you took part in at your place of work or study. How many of these people attended your meeting? Think of two or three more.

1 The person who always arrives late.
2 The person who talks a lot but is very unclear.
3 The person who takes lots of notes.
4 The person who spends a lot of time looking at their mobile phone.

B In small groups, discuss where on the line you would put the people in Exercise 1A. Explain your choice.

Least annoying ⟷ Most annoying

VIDEO

2A ▶ 2.3.1 Watch the video as Shaun and Alex prepare to meet their client, Nick from Zapna Clothing. Answer the questions.

1 What is the purpose of the meeting?
2 What type person in Exercise 1A does Shaun say Nick is?

B How easy do you think it will be for Shaun and Alex to get the information they want from Nick?

Video A ▶ 2.3.2

3A Watch Video A and complete as much of the information sheet as you can. How do you think Shaun and Alex feel about the meeting now? Why?

Candidate Profile Form	TGC THE GALLAGHER CONSULTANCY	
Company name	Zapna Clothing	
Job title	Assistant Manager	
Location	Poznań, Poland	
Contract type	1 *replacement / maternity cover / new post*	(circle)
Contract length	2 ____________ months	
Experience	3 ____________ , ____________	
Language(s) spoken	English and 4 ____________	
Language level	5 *basic knowledge / working knowledge / fluent*	(circle)
Package offered	bonus scheme subsidised staff canteen gym membership private healthcare pension	6 (tick) ☐ ☐ ☐ ☐ ☐
Relocation package	7 *Yes / No / Needs further discussion*	(circle)
No. of candidates for interview	6 maximum	

B What can Shaun and Alex do to get the information they need from Nick?

Video B ▶ 2.3.3

4A Watch Video B and complete the rest of the information sheet in Exercise 3A. How do you think Shaun and Alex feel about the meeting now?

B What did Shaun and Alex do to improve their communication with Nick? Compare your answers with your ideas in Exercise 3B.

5 ▶ 2.3.4 Watch the Conclusions section of the video and note the main points the speaker makes about checking and clarifying information.

Reflection

6 Think about how you check and clarify information in English. In pairs, discuss how you could improve your skills.

Functional language

Checking and clarifying

7A Watch Video B again and complete these expressions for checking and clarifying.

1 So Nick, ___ ___ ___ ___ you want someone with logistics experience?
2 And ___ ___ ___ ___, you're looking for someone with a good language level?
3 ___ ___ ___ you want to hire someone locally?
4 Yes, you said that, but ___ ___ ___ ___ ___?
5 There's an international airport not far from Poznań, ___?
6 ___ ___ ___ ___, it's a sensitive topic.

B Match the responses (a–f) with the correct questions in Exercise 7A.

a No, not necessarily, but they must be prepared to move.
b Exactly; fluent in English and Polish.
c That's right, Poznań has its own airport.
d Yes, of course. We understand.
e Correct, but they also need a diploma in management.
f I mean there's a good bonus scheme and a subsidised staff canteen.

Tip

You can use *Right*, *That's right*, *Correct* and *Exactly* to confirm information.

8 Put the words in the correct order to make sentences.

1 you / for / confirm / us / just / can / that / ?
2 I / what Tim / think / means / is / the best candidate / that / won't live locally
3 relocation / what / package / you / by / do / mean / ?
4 right / that / is / ?
5 you say / it's a / what / sensitive topic / when / you / do / mean / ?

T Teacher's resources: extra activities

TASK

9A Work in two groups. Group A: Look at page 128; Group B: Look at page 138. Read your scenario and prepare for the meeting in your group.

B In pairs, roleplay Scenario 1 using expressions from Exercises 7 and 8 to check, clarify and confirm information. Student A, take the role of the client. Student B, take the role of the TGC staff member and complete the Candidate Profile Form. Exchange roles and roleplay Scenario 2.

C When you have finished, discuss how easy or difficult it was to check, clarify and confirm information in English. Share your experience with the class.

Self-assessment

- How successfully have you achieved the lesson outcome? Give yourself a score from 0 (I need more practice) to 5 (I know this well).
- Go to My Self-assessment in MyEnglishLab to reflect on what you have learnt.

2.4 BUSINESS SKILLS
Starting a meeting

Lesson outcome Learners are able to use a variety of expressions to open meetings.

Lead-in

1A In pairs, discuss the questions.

1 What kind of meetings do you attend at your place of work or study?
2 What topics do you usually discuss during meetings in your place of work or study?
3 Are your meetings always successful? Why? / Why not?

B Look at the list of reasons why meetings are sometimes unsuccessful. Discuss whether you agree or disagree, and why. Add two or three more reasons.

1 The meeting doesn't have a clear purpose.
2 Some people are not invited to the meeting.
3 The chairperson has no control over who speaks, or for how long.
4 People are not prepared for the meeting.

C Discuss your ideas in Exercise 1B with another pair. What can make meetings more successful?

Listening

2A Josh and Samia are discussing the next staff meeting. Before you listen, match the words and phrases (1–6) with the correct definitions (a–f).

1 action point
2 agenda item
3 AOB (Any Other Business)
4 deadline
5 minutes
6 matters arising

a a written record of what people say during a meeting
b the time when something must be finished by
c something that will be discussed during the meeting
d the time when you can ask questions about the previous meeting
e a task for someone to do after the meeting
f things that need to be discussed but are not included on the agenda

B 2.02 Listen to Josh and Samia discussing the meeting and complete the agenda (a–f). How do you think they feel about the meeting?

Staff Meeting
8 December (15.00–16.30) Room 2. Chair: Don A.

DRAFT AGENDA

Item	Responsible	Time
1 Matters arising		15.00–15.10
2 Staff reports	All	15.10–15.25
3 a ______________	Mike	15:25–15.35
4 b ______________	c ______________	15.25–15.45
5 Micro-kitchen	Deirdre	15.45–16.00
6 d ______________	e ______________	16.00–16.15
7 AOB		16.15–16.30
8 f ______________		16.30

3A 2.03 **Listen to part of the meeting and decide if the sentences are *true* (T) or *false* (F). In pairs, correct the incorrect sentences.**

1 Everyone is on time for the meeting except Josh.
2 Harry has just joined the team.
3 Harry agrees to manage the timing of the meeting.
4 Ellen doesn't want to take the minutes.
5 The team discussed the micro-kitchen idea during the last staff meeting.
6 The budget for the micro-kitchen is more than 500 pounds a month.

B Listen again and complete the expressions.

1 Right, so let's ___________ .
2 Does anyone want to add anything ___________ ?
3 Harry, ___________ you to be time-keeper?
4 And could I have a volunteer to ___________ ?
5 So, ___________ to item 5: this is Deirdre's point, I think.
6 The reason ___________ discuss this ___________ agree on a budget.

Functional language

Opening a meeting, referring to the agenda and stating purpose

4A Look at these expressions from the meeting. Match the beginnings (1–8) with the endings (a–h).

1 I'd like to start
2 Nice to see everyone, and
3 So, one reason for meeting is to
4 Does everyone have
5 The main aim today is to
6 Could I have a volunteer
7 Let's look at
8 Sorry, can we just go back

a item 1, Matters Arising.
b to item 2?
c introduce you all to Harry.
d on time.
e a copy of the agenda?
f catch up before the holidays.
g welcome back to Ellen.
h to take the minutes?

B Complete the table with the expressions from Exercise 4A.

Opening a meeting	Stating purpose	Giving tasks	Referring to the agenda
I'd like to start on time.			

Teacher's resources: extra activities

C Add the expressions in Exercise 3B to the correct section of the table.

TASK

5A Work in groups of four. Write up an agenda for a meeting.

B Work in different groups of four. You are going to take turns to chair the opening of a meeting. Use your agendas from Exercise 5A to chair your meetings.

- Open the meeting
- Welcome and introduce everyone
- Give roles – minute-taker, time-keeper
- Discuss the agenda
- Explain the purpose of the meeting and/or one or two agenda items

C When you have finished, discuss how easy or difficult it was to open a meeting in English. Share your experience with another group.

Self-assessment

- How successfully have you achieved the lesson outcome? Give yourself a score from 0 (I need more practice) to 5 (I know this well).
- Go to My Self-assessment in MyEnglishLab to reflect on what you have learnt.

Short communications

Lesson outcome

Learners can communicate by text message, write short emails and use abbreviations and shortened forms appropriately.

Lead-in

1A Read the messages between an estate agent and his secretary and answer the questions.

1 What is the problem?

2 Why does Jeff, the estate agent, want to contact his client, Dana, urgently?

Hi Jeff. Where are you?

Waiting outside Duke St offices for Dana Matthews.

FYI Dana sent email last night to cancel. She's in Rome. Didn't you see it?

No. She needs to see offices ASAP. Other companies interested, appointment times TBC. Emailing her now.

Are you coming back now?

Yes. With you in 20.

B Read the email reply to Jeff from Dana. What does she want to do?

Hi Jeff,

Thanks for your email and sorry I had to cancel our meeting today. I'm working in Rome at the moment. Back tomorrow, ETA 1800 hrs, so can we rearrange the appointment for Thurs? About 4 p.m.? I'm WFH that day and Duke Street is very close to my apartment.

I hope this is OK for you.

Regards,

Dana Matthews

Functional language

2A What do you think the underlined abbreviations in Exercises 1A and 1B mean?

B Match the abbreviation in each sentence to the meaning in the box.

by the way close of business end of day to be announced

1 We should get an answer by COB.

2 Will complete report by EOD.

3 Product ready for markets. Launch date TBA soon.

4 Thanks for finishing presentation. BTW, it looks good.

C Look at the table and complete the gaps. Use two to three words in each gap.

Formal	Informal
Use full forms 1 __________ outside the Duke St offices. Other companies 2 __________ .	**Use shortened forms** Waiting outside Duke St offices. Other companies interested.
Use pronouns Sorry I had to cancel.	**Don't use pronouns** 3 __________ to cancel.
Use articles She sent 4 __________ last night.	**Don't use articles** Sent email last night.
Use all words I will be with you 5 __________ .	**Don't use unnecessary words** With you in 20.

T Teacher's resources: extra activities

L The text messages and email contain examples of the Present Continuous. Go to MyEnglishLab for optional grammar work.

page 120 See Grammar reference: Present Continuous

TASK

3A Work in pairs. Read the email on page 127. Discuss how you could shorten it.

B Look at the notes on page 127 and write both an informal text message and a more formal email. Use no more than 50 words for the text and 80 for the email. Abbreviations like BTW (*by the way*) count as one word.

C Exchange text messages and emails with your partner. Did your partner use the same abbreviations as you? Did your partner use all the techniques in Exercise 2C?

Self-assessment

- How successfully have you achieved the lesson outcome? Give yourself a score from 0 (I need more practice) to 5 (I know this well).
- Go to My Self-assessment in MyEnglishLab to reflect on what you have learnt.

Retail 3

'Whoever said money can't buy happiness didn't know where to shop.'

Gertrude Stein, novelist, poet, playwright

Unit overview

3.1	**The Ziferblat café** **Lesson outcome:** Learners can use vocabulary related to shops and shopping.	**Video:** An unusual café **Vocabulary:** Shops and the shopping experience **Project:** A survey about shopping habits
3.2	**The retail experience** **Lesson outcome:** Learners can tell a simple story about past events and activities.	**Listening:** Shopping experiences **Grammar:** Past Simple and Past Continuous **Writing:** Writing a tweet
3.3	**Communication skills:** Solving workflow problems **Lesson outcome:** Learners are aware of different decision-making styles and can use a range of expressions to facilitate a decision-making meeting.	**Video:** Dealing with a problem **Functional language:** Solving problems **Task:** Dealing with a workflow problem
3.4	**Business skills:** Presenting results **Lesson outcome:** Learners are aware of the importance of structuring a presentation and can use a range of phrases to present results in an organised way.	**Listening:** A presentation **Functional language:** Signposting a presentation **Task:** A presentation
3.5	**Writing:** An online review form **Lesson outcome:** Learners can complete a simple online review form about a restaurant or hotel.	**Model text:** An online review **Functional language:** Phrases from a review **Grammar:** Types of adverbs **Task:** An online review

Business workshop 3: p.92 | **Review 3:** p.106 | **Pronunciation:** 3.2 Past Simple 3.3 Stress in short sentences p.115 | **Grammar reference:** p.120

3.1 The Ziferblat café

Lesson outcome Learners can use vocabulary related to shops and shopping.

Lead-in

1 Discuss these questions.

1 How often do you go to cafés?

2 Which of these activities do you usually do in cafés? Do you do anything else?

chat to a friend	get something to eat	have a coffee	read the newspaper
use the free wi-fi	watch sport on TV	work on your computer	

3 Which are your favourite cafés and what do you like about them?

BBC VIDEO

2 3.1.1 Watch the video about the Ziferblat café, an unusual retailer. What is special about it?

1 Customers like to spend the day there.

2 It's a very cheap place to eat and drink.

3 You pay for the time you spend there.

3 Watch the video again. Complete the notes about the café. Use only one word in each gap.

Ziferblat is an unusual retailer. Everything in the café is [1]____________. People only pay for the time that they spend there. You check in and out like at a [2]____________, stay as long as you want, use the wi-fi, and eat and drink as much as you like. It costs 6p a [3]____________. The largest café is in Manchester, in northern England. Ziferblat means 'clock face' in Russian and [4]____________.

The shortest time one person spent there was [5]____________ minutes, and the longest time was eleven hours. That was a man who was [6]____________ a book.

This café in Manchester gets 12,000 people every [7]____________. There is also one Ziferblat in London, but to have to charge 20 or 25 pence a minute it sounds [8]____________.

T Teacher's resources: alternative video and extra activities

4 Work in pairs or small groups. Ziferblat's owner says, 'We like to describe it as home.' In what ways is the café similar to a home or an office?

Vocabulary

Shops and the shopping experience

5 Look at these extracts from the video. What do the words in bold mean? Match them with the definitions (1–8).

Your **bill** is calculated at 6p a minute, including **VAT**.

The largest **branch** of this international retail **chain** is here in Manchester.

... we **charge** 6p a minute ...

The business makes a **profit**.

This branch **serves** 12,000 **customers** each month.

1 people who buy goods or services from a shop, company, etc.

2 list showing how much you have to pay for the food you ate in a restaurant

3 one local business, shop, etc. that is part of a larger business

4 number of shops, hotels, etc. owned or managed by the same company or person

5 to help customers in a shop, restaurant, etc., especially by bringing them the things that they want

6 ask someone for a particular amount of money for something you are selling

7 tax added to the price of goods and services in the UK and the EU

8 money that you gain by selling things or doing business, after your costs have been paid

6 3.01 **Listen to seven extracts. Which shop do the people want to go to? Number the places 1–7.**

bakery ☐ bookshop ☐ butcher's ☐ clothes shop ☐
department store ☐ pharmacy ☐ shopping centre ☐

7 Match the verbs with the correct collocations. <u>All</u> the words in the group must be possible with the verb.

1	charge	**a**	for clothes / at the market / online
2	make	**b**	customers / meals / drinks
3	serve	**c**	6p per minute / customers for the wi-fi / JP¥15,000
4	shop	**d**	a profit / a mistake with the bill / coffee
5	cost	**e**	some food / a coffee / a meal
6	order	**f**	money / time / the day shopping
7	pay	**g**	the bill / in euros / by credit card
8	spend	**h**	a lot of money / me $99 / nothing

T Teacher's resources: extra activities

8 Choose the correct option in italics to complete the questions. Then discuss the questions in pairs or small groups.

1 Do you prefer to *pay* / *shop* at large department stores, smaller shops or online? Why?
2 What are your favourite *branches* / *chains* of clothes shops?
3 When do you prefer to *pay* / *spend* in cash and when by card?
4 Should cafés *cost* / *charge* customers who want to use their wi-fi?
5 Will shopping centres continue to *make* / *serve* a profit in future? Why? / Why not?
6 Do you think High Street *clothes shops* / *bookshops* have a future or will people buy things to read online?

PROJECT: Shopping habits

9A Work in pairs or small groups. You are going to do a survey about each other's shopping habits. Look at the questions in the box. Which questions do you need to complete gaps 1–4 in the survey on page 129?

a What is your favourite day for shopping?
b Where do you prefer to buy clothes?
c What do you enjoy about shopping in High Street shops and online?
d What don't you like about shopping in High Street shops and online?
e Which of these products do you prefer to buy online?
f What do you spend most money on?
g Which is the best description of the way you shop?
h Do you have a discount card for any shops?
i What percentage of your money do you spend shopping online?
j Which of these sentences do you agree with?
k Do social networks / famous people make you want to buy things?

B Write three more questions for the shopping survey. Choose from the options in the box in Exercise 9A or use your own ideas.

C Work in a new group. Conduct your shopping survey.

D Work in the same pair or group as in Exercise 9A. Discuss these questions.

1 What did you learn from the answers to your survey?
2 Do you think customers will still want High Street shops in future or will we all shop online?
3 Which High Street shops do you think will survive?

Self-assessment

- How successfully have you achieved the lesson outcome? Give yourself a score from 0 (I need more practice) to 5 (I know this well).
- Go to My Self-assessment in MyEnglishLab to reflect on what you have learnt.

3.2 The retail experience

Lesson outcome Learners can tell a simple story about past events and activities.

Lead-in

1A Work in pairs. Match the words in the box with the photos.

bazaar	convenience store	covered market	magic mirror	self-service	try something on

1

2

3

B Have you ever shopped in places like these or used augmented reality?

Listening

2 3.02 **Listen to three people talking about recent shopping experiences. Which person do you think had the best retail experience? Which person had the worst?**

3 Choose the correct option. Listen again if necessary.

Extract 1

1 Who was in Istanbul for work?
  a the man **b** the man's wife **c** both of them

2 What does the man say about their visit to the Grand Bazaar?
  a They were there a long time. **b** They visited everything. **c** They didn't buy anything.

Extract 2

3 How does the woman feel about the magic mirror?
  a She likes it. **b** She doesn't like it. **c** It doesn't work very well.

4 Why didn't she buy anything at the store?
  a She didn't have any money. **b** She didn't like anything. **c** She couldn't decide.

Extract 3

5 What does the woman say about ordering food in restaurants in China?
  a Her colleagues help her. **b** It's often difficult. **c** It's not hard.

6 How does she feel about the automated shop?
  a It's a really useful shop. **b** She doesn't like the food it sells or the service. **c** It's too difficult to buy things with the codes

T Teacher's resources: extra activities

Grammar Past Simple

4A 3.03 **Complete the extracts from the dialogues with the correct Past Simple form of the verbs in brackets. Then listen and check.**

1 __________ you __________ (have) a nice holiday?
2 ... the carpet seller __________ (serve) us tea when we __________ (sit) down ...
3 I __________ (can) try on different styles and colours ...
4 ... when I __________ (leave) the store, they __________ (send) me a list ...
5 I __________ (not speak) much Chinese when I __________ (arrive) here ...
6 When I __________ (go) in, I __________ (choose) my food ...

B What word do we use to form negative sentences and questions in the Past Simple?

C Which verbs in Exercise 4A are regular and which are irregular?

→ page 120 See Grammar reference: Past Simple and Past Continuous

5

3.04 Complete the dialogue with the correct Past Simple form of the verbs in the box. Then listen and check.

be get meet not come
not see pay ring say
think write

Tony: So, how was work when I was away last week?

Sonia: We [1]__________ very busy without you. We [2]__________ another big order from Piotr.

Tony: Again? [3]__________ he __________ us for the last order?

Sonia: No, not the full amount. I [4]__________ him an email about it when I received the new order. He [5]__________ me immediately and [6]__________ he'll pay us this week.

Tony: That sounds good. And [7]__________ you __________ the new Marketing Manager when she started last week?

Sonia: No, I [8]__________ her. She definitely [9]__________ to the office. In fact, I think she starts this week.

Tony: Yes, you're right! I [10]__________ it was last week.

Teacher's resources: extra activities

page 115 See Pronunciation bank: Past Simple

Past Continuous

6

Look at these extracts from the dialogues. How do we form positive sentences, negative sentences and questions in the Past Continuous?

*She **was working** Monday to Friday but she **wasn't working** at the weekend.*

*We **were browsing** for hours but we **weren't looking** for anything specific.*

*What **was** I **thinking**?*

*Sorry! Did I interrupt you? **Were** you **eating**?*

page 121 See Grammar reference: Past Simple and Past Continuous

7

Work in pairs. Ask and answer each other's questions.

Student A: Ask your partner:

'What were you doing yesterday at ... ?'

7 o'clock in the morning
10 a.m.
2 p.m.
6 o'clock in the evening
midnight

Student B: Ask your partner:

'What were you doing on Saturday at ... ?'

2 o'clock in the morning
9 a.m.
midday
4 p.m.
7 p.m.

Teacher's resources: extra activities

Writing

8

Write three tweets for your followers on social media. You can invent any details you like. Use a maximum of 280 characters and the Past Simple and Past Continuous. Write about:

1 a recent or memorable shopping experience.
2 what you did at work or college yesterday.
3 what you did last weekend.

I was #shopping @H&M when I saw the cool T-shirts from the new #summercollection. There was a great selection and I bought 3!
Then I went to @Vegan_Paradise for lunch with friends. I tried their special salad and had a banana cake for dessert. It was delicious.

Self-assessment

- How successfully have you achieved the lesson outcome? Give yourself a score from 0 (I need more practice) to 5 (I know this well).
- Go to My Self-assessment in MyEnglishLab to reflect on what you have learnt.

3.3 COMMUNICATION SKILLS
Solving workflow problems

Lesson outcome Learners are aware of different decision-making styles and can use a range of expressions to facilitate a decision-making meeting.

Lead-in

1A In pairs, discuss which of the following people create the biggest problems for others at work.

1 People who don't answer their email.
2 People who don't return phone calls.
3 People who don't meet deadlines.
4 People who don't work well in teams.

workflow (noun) – the steps people in a work-group need to take to complete a task successfully and on schedule

B Read the definition of *workflow*. In pairs, discuss what kind of workflow problems the people in Exercise 1A can cause. The following phrases may help you.

miss deadlines	waste time	fall behind schedule	hold things/people up

VIDEO

2A ▶ 3.3.1 Watch Thiago explaining a problem he's having to Azra and answer the questions.

1 What is Thiago worried about? Why?
2 What does Azra suggest Thiago should do? Does it seem like good advice?
3 How did Shaun react the last time Thiago had a similar problem?

B Why might it not be a good idea for Thiago to avoid Shaun?

Video A ▶ 3.3.2

3A Watch Shaun and Thiago discussing the problem. Answer the questions.

1 Who asks for the meeting – Thiago or Shaun? How does this give him an advantage in the conversation?
2 Thiago tries to explain why his report is late. Does Shaun a) reject his explanations as excuses or b) listen and try to think of ways to help?
3 Does Shaun blame Thiago for creating a workflow problem?
4 How do Shaun and Thiago suggest the report can be finished? Do they agree on how to do this?
5 Who is happier with the final outcome of the meeting?

B What could Thiago and Shaun do differently to get a better outcome?

Video B ▶ 3.3.3

C Watch a different version of the conversation and answer the same questions you answered in Exercise 3A.

4A Think about the two versions of the meeting you just watched. When someone, like Thiago, is causing workflow problems for others in their team, which of the following questions is the most important to ask?

1 What's going wrong?
2 Whose fault is it?
3 How can we fix it?

B Can the other questions in Exercise 4A sometimes be useful, too? If so, when?

5 ▶ 3.3.4 Watch the Conclusions section of the video and compare the advice with your answers in Exercise 4.

Reflection

6 Do you focus more on problems or solutions when you make decisions in life and at work? Would you like to change your approach? What steps could you take to do this?

Functional language

a Get the person's attention.

b Check he/she is free to talk.

c Ask about progress.

Solving problems

7 **The diagram on the left shows three steps for asking someone about their progress with a task. Match 1–6 below with the correct step (a–c).**

1 Have you got a moment?
2 How are you doing with that report?
3 Just the person I was looking for!
4 Do you have a minute?
5 Any progress with that report?
6 Ah, there you are!

8A **Use phrases from the box to complete the sentences.**

How about	I'll see	Let me	What else	What if	Why don't I

1 ___________ deal with Accounts.
2 ___________ if I can get [someone] to share some of your workload.
3 ___________ can we do to get this report finished?
4 ___________ I bring in [someone] to help you out?
5 ___________ asking [someone] to help you with some of the figures?
6 ___________ just write an executive summary of the main points?

B **Use the same phrases from Exercise 8A to make two more sentences.**

1 ___________ **a** see what I can do. **b** try and get you some IT support.
2 ___________ **a** if we can increase the budget. **b** if there's any flexibility in the budget.
3 ___________ **a** can I do to help? **b** do we need to do?
4 ___________ **a** we make the deadline later? **b** I give you an extension?
5 ___________ **a** rethinking the schedule? **b** adding more people to the project team?
6 ___________ **a** get you some help? **b** give you an assistant?

C **Match the responses with the correct suggestions in Exercises 8A and 8B. Some match more than one suggestion.**

1 Thanks, **I'm not great with** numbers!
2 **Someone to assist with** the paperwork **would be a big help**.
3 **Having** a couple more people on the team **would really speed things up**.
4 Good, **I'm having problems with** some of the software.
5 Great, **another** five days **should be enough**.
6 **An extra** 10 percent **would make a big difference**.

T Teacher's resources: extra activities

→ page 115 See Pronunciation bank: Stress in short sentences

TASK

9 **Work in pairs. Read the information and decide which of you is Speaker 1 (S1) and Speaker 2 (S2) in each situation. Roleplay the situations.**

Situation 1 S1 is giving an important conference presentation in Montreal six days from now. Ten days ago S1 asked S2 to prepare some slides for the presentation. The deadline for getting the slides ready is tomorrow, to give S1 time to practise the presentation. Unfortunately, S2 is having problems, so he/she needs to find a solution as quickly as possible.

For details, S1 look at page 133 and S2 look at page 139.

Situation 2 S2 has to complete a sales report six days from now. Ten days ago S2 asked S1 to produce performance charts for each of the company's sales units. The deadline for doing this is tomorrow to give S2 time to add the charts to the report. Unfortunately, S1 is having problems, so he/she needs to find a solution as quickly as possible.

For details, S1 look at page 129 and S2 look at page 131.

10 **When you have finished, discuss how the meetings went. How effectively did you:**

• avoid blaming anyone? • avoid making excuses? • develop a plan of action? • find out what the basic problems are?
• remain calm? • suggest possible solutions?

Share your experience with the class.

Self-assessment

- How successfully have you achieved the lesson outcome? Give yourself a score from 0 (I need more practice) to 5 (I know this well).
- Go to My Self-assessment in MyEnglishLab to reflect on what you have learnt.

3.4 BUSINESS SKILLS
Presenting results

Lesson outcome

Learners are aware of the importance of structuring a presentation and can use a range of phrases to present results in an organised way.

Lead-in

1 Work in pairs. Read the advice to business presenters and discuss the questions.

Giving a presentation is like taking your audience on a journey. To successfully reach your destination, you need to make sure nobody gets lost on the way! So provide them with a clear map of your talk at the start and always tell them where you're going as you speak – moving on, going back, changing direction. Think of it as GPS for presenters!

1 How is a presentation like a journey?
2 What do you need to do at the start of your presentation?

Listening

2A Carl and Inés work for a large chain of mobile phone stores. This morning they gave a presentation to their Regional Sales Managers. In pairs, look at their slides and check any words you don't know. What is their presentation about?

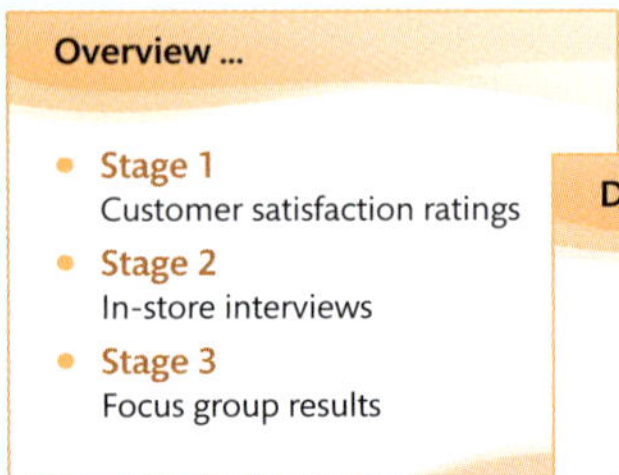

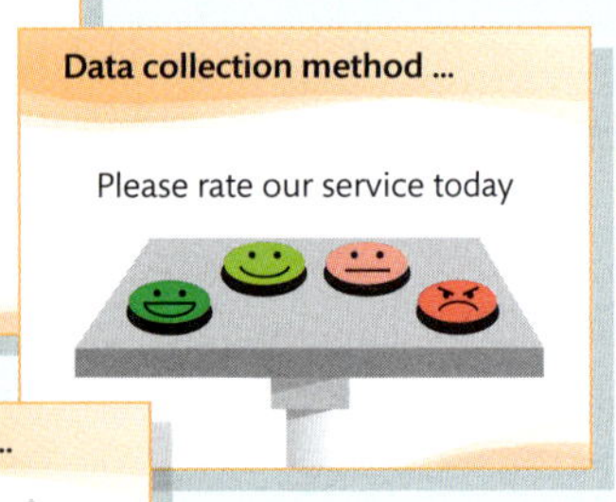

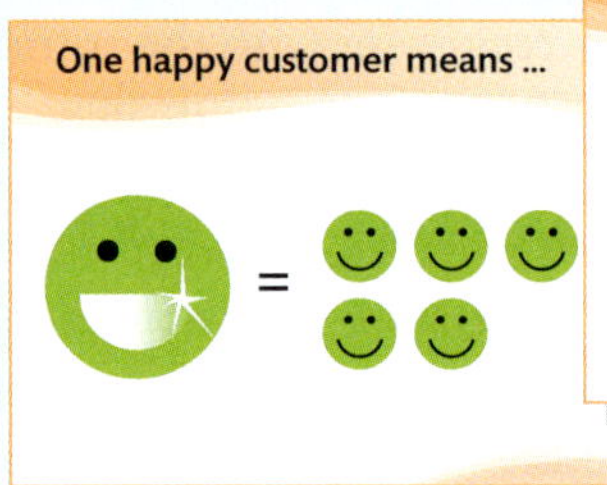

B 🔊 3.05 Listen to the introduction to the presentation and answer the questions.

1 What is the subject of the presentation?
2 Who is going to talk about the following: Carl or Inés?
 a customer satisfaction ratings
 b in-store interviews
 c focus group results
3 When can the audience ask questions: during or after the talk?
4 Where did the data for the customer satisfaction ratings come from?

C In pairs, discuss how clear Carl's overview of the presentation was, and why.

3A 🔊 3.06 Listen to the next part of the presentation and answer the questions.

1 Why was it necessary to do in-store interviews?
2 A happy customer recommends the store to how many people?
3 How many unhappy customers leave feedback? How many don't?

B Listen again and raise your hand every time the presenter pauses for more than a couple of seconds. Why are these pauses helpful?

4 🔊 3.07 Listen to the last part of the presentation and answer the questions.

1 According to Carl, what information do the interviews *not* provide?
2 How many focus groups were there? What did the research team ask them to do?
3 What result did Inés and her team find surprising? Why?
4 What final recommendation does Inés make? Why?

Functional language

Signposting a presentation

5 Put the following words from the presentation in the correct order.

Secondly, … Finally, … Then … First of all, …

1 ___________ 2 ___________ 3 ___________ 4 ___________

6 Complete the phrases and expressions for structuring a presentation using the verbs from the boxes.

brings hand move start sum

look jump recap started wrap

1 I'd like to ___________ off by talking about stage one.
2 Now, let's ___________ on to the in-store interviews.
3 That ___________ me to the end of my part of the presentation.
4 I'll ___________ you over to Inés to talk about stage three.
5 So, just to ___________ up, …
6 OK, let's ___________ at the interview data in more detail.
7 So, to ___________ on the main points so far.
8 So, let's ___________ right in.
9 OK, let's ___________ it up there.
10 OK, let's get ___________ .

T Teacher's resources: extra activities

TASK

7A Work in groups of four. Two of you should read the information on Presentation A below. The other two should look at Presentation B on page 127.

B Read your information and decide who will be Presenter 1 and Presenter 2. Take a few minutes to prepare your presentation. Make some simple slides if you like.

PRESENTATION A

Presenter 1

Introduction and overview

1 Introduce yourself and Presenter 2.
2 Introduce the subject of your talk: 'A comparison of customer satisfaction ratings before and after providing our sales team with people skills training in Q2.'
3 Say who will talk about Parts 1, 2, 3 and 4.

Part 1: Satisfaction ratings for Q1

☺ 61% 😐 25% ☹ 14% (not great!)

Estimated no. of customers not leaving feedback: 47% (we needed more data on this)

Part 2: Customer research in Q1

1 72% of customers who didn't leave feedback were neutral 😐 or dissatisfied ☹
2 91% just wanted simple, friendly advice about the products – not too technical!

Close and hand over to Presenter 2.

Presenter 2 Thank Presenter 1 and move on.

Part 3: People skills training in Q2

Three four-hour face-to-face training sessions:

1 How to explain things in simple English
2 Dealing with difficult customers
3 Building a relationship with the customer

Plus 6 weeks of M-learning using mobile phones – very popular with our sales team!

Part 4: Satisfaction ratings for Qs 3–4

☺ 79% 😐 15% ☹ 6% (very good news!)

Estimated no. of customers not leaving feedback: 16% (significantly better)

Summary and conclusion

1 Training programme was extremely successful.
2 Customer satisfaction was up by almost a third.
3 Satisfaction ratings are now more accurate.

Close and thank audience.

C Take turns to give your presentation to the other pair.

D When you have finished, discuss how the presentations went. How effectively did you:

- introduce yourself and your co-presenter?
- introduce the subject of your talk?
- move on from one point to the next?
- give the audience an overview of your talk?
- use pauses for effect?
- hand over to your partner?
- sum up?
- end your talk?

Self-assessment

- How successfully have you achieved the lesson outcome? Give yourself a score from 0 (I need more practice) to 5 (I know this well).
- Go to My Self-assessment in MyEnglishLab to reflect on what you have learnt.

An online review form

Lesson outcome Learners can complete a simple online review form about a restaurant or hotel.

Lead-in

1 Read the online restaurant review. Complete it with verbs from the box. Then compare in pairs.

ate bring brought changes didn't arrive eat have offers recommend were celebrating

Orchid restaurant review form We value your feedback. Please leave your comments here.

How often do you eat here?	We usually [1]__________ in the Orchid restaurant at least once a week.
When did you last eat here?	We last [2]__________ there yesterday when we [3]__________ some business clients.
What was the purpose of your last visit?	We [4]__________ a sales contract with the clients. We often [5]__________ our clients to the Orchid.
What do/did you like about the restaurant?	The location of the restaurant is perfect for our company. The staff are always friendly and helpful. The 'specials menu', which [6]__________ every day, is always interesting.
Is/Was there anything you aren't/weren't happy with?	Yesterday the food [7]__________ very quickly. Sometimes the service is slow, especially when we [8]__________ a meeting to get to. However, it has never been a big problem.
Would you recommend us?	The Orchid is a lovely restaurant, which [9]__________ a wide range of local as well as international dishes, and we highly [10]__________ it.

Functional language

2A Complete the table below with phrases from the box.

Background Bad points Good points Recommendation

1 __________	We last ate there yesterday with some clients.
2 __________	The location of the restaurant is perfect.
3 __________	Unfortunately, the food didn't arrive very quickly yesterday.
4 __________	We highly recommend it.

B Write these phrases in the correct place in the table in Exercise 2A.

The view from the restaurant is wonderful. We sometimes have company lunches there.
I'm afraid I cannot recommend your restaurant to other people/businesses. It is too expensive.
We had dinner there two days ago. The food is always excellent. The food was terrible.

T Teacher's resources: extra activities

L The review contains examples of adverbs. Go to MyEnglishLab for optional grammar work.

page 121 See Grammar reference: Types of adverbs

TASK

3A Work in pairs. Look at the review form for the Flamingo Palace Hotel on page 130. The comments are all mixed up. Work together to put the comments in the correct place.

B Choose a hotel/restaurant you know. Copy and complete an online review form like the one in Exercise 1 or Exercise 3A.

C Exchange reviews with your partner. Did your partner put the right information in each part of the review form? If your partner wrote about a place you know, do you agree with your partner's review?

Self-assessment

- How successfully have you achieved the lesson outcome? Give yourself a score from 0 (I need more practice) to 5 (I know this well).
- Go to My Self-assessment in MyEnglishLab to reflect on what you have learnt.

4 Work patterns

'Choose a job you love, and you will never have to work a day in your life.'

Confucius, Chinese philosopher

Unit overview

4.1 My working life
Lesson outcome: Learners can use vocabulary related to the working day and their working lives.

Video: The working day
Vocabulary: Describing jobs and contracts
Project: Researching work patterns

4.2 Executives at work
Lesson outcome: Learners can use the Present Perfect Simple to refer to personal experiences in the past.

Reading: Women in Business
Grammar: Present Perfect Simple
Speaking: Asking and answering questions using the Present Perfect Simple

4.3 Communication skills: Making group decisions
Lesson outcome: Learners are aware of different decision-making approaches and can use a range of expressions to facilitate a decision-making meeting.

Video: Approaches to decision-making
Functional language: Facilitating a decision-making meeting
Task: Discussing proposals in a meeting

4.4 Business skills: Phoning to change arragements
Lesson outcome: Learners can use a range of expressions to make or change arrangements and give colleagues updates on the phone.

Listening: Changing an appointment on the phone
Functional language: Rescheduling appointments on the phone
Task: Roleplay a phone call to confirm an appointment

4.5 Writing: Confirming arrangements
Lesson outcome: Learners can write work-related emails to make and confirm arrangements.

Model text: Emails making and confirming arrangements
Functional language: Phrases for confirming, inviting questions, thanking, apologising and concluding in an email
Grammar: Prepositions of time
Task: An email to confirm arrangements

Business workshop 4: p.94 | **Review 4:** p.107 | **Pronunciation:** 4.1 Vowel sounds: British English and American English p.115 4.2 Present Perfect Simple p.116 | **Grammar reference:** p.122

4.1 My working life

Lesson outcome Learners can use vocabulary related to the working day and their working lives.

Lead-in

1 Discuss the questions.

1 How many hours a week do you work and/or study?
2 What would you change about your work or study schedule?
3 What would be an ideal working week for you?

VIDEO

2 4.1.1 **Watch the video. Who has one job? Who has more than one job?**

3 Watch the video again and decide if these sentences are *true* (T) or *false* (F). Correct the incorrect sentences.

1 'Nine-to-five' means the starting and finishing times of work.
2 Companies today want more 'nine-to-five' office staff.
3 Sharni starts and finishes work at the same time every day.
4 The way she works has advantages for her family life.
5 Lauren works for an agency that gets her work.
6 She likes the security the job offers.
7 Laurie says he does the same job for different companies.
8 He likes having free time to work on his own projects.

T Teacher's resources: extra activities

Vocabulary Describing jobs and contracts

4A Complete the sentences from the video with words from the box to make adjective + noun collocations.

day	employees	hours	jobs	lives	patterns	schedule	worker

The way we work is changing fast and one clear example of this is our 1**work** ____________ .
The traditional work pattern was based on 2**permanent** ____________ doing 3**full-time** ____________ .
The typical office worker … had a 4**working** ____________ of nine o'clock to five o'clock.
We talked to some people about their 5**working** ____________ .
I like working 6**flexible** ____________ .
Some people will work better with a 7**fixed** ____________ .
I'm a 8**temporary** ____________ and that basically means that I work for an agency.

B Match the phrases in bold in Exercise 4A with the definitions.

a the part of their lives when people have a paid job
b the time during the day that people spend doing their job
c people who have contracts to work for a long time
d timetable that cannot be changed
e work for all the hours of a normal week at work (e.g. 35–40 hours)
f the different ways people's hours of work can be organised
g when someone can choose when they start and finish work each day, week, or month
h someone who has a job for only a limited period of time

→ page 115 See Pronunciation bank: Vowel sounds: British English and American English

5 **Complete the sentences with words from the box.**

employee	employer	intern	retired	self-employed	staff	unemployed

1 The people who work for an organisation are the ____________ .
2 A person, company or organisation that gives people work is a(n) ____________ .
3 Someone, especially a student, who works for a short time in a job to get experience is a(n) ____________ .
4 Someone without a job is ____________ .
5 When you are working for yourself and you are not employed by a company, you are ____________ .
6 When you stop working, usually because you are old, you are ____________ .
7 Someone who is paid to work for another person is a(n) ____________ .

6 **Look at the description of a company's work patterns. Choose the correct options to complete it.**

Company work patterns

The standard [1]*working day / working lives* for office staff with [2]*full-time / part-time* jobs in the company is Monday to Thursday 9.00 a.m. to 5.30 p.m. and Friday, 9.00 a.m. to 4.30 p.m. Staff with [3]*full-time / part-time* contracts work 22 hours a week.

The production department works 24 hours a day and staff work one of three eight-hour [4]*patterns / shifts*. These are early (6 a.m. to 2 p.m.), late (2 p.m. to 10 p.m.) and nights (10 p.m. to 6 a.m.).

In the summer months, the company employs [5]*permanent / temporary* workers in the factory to cover for [6]*permanent / temporary* employees who are on holiday.

T Teacher's resources: extra activities

7A 4.01 **Listen to three people talking about their work patterns. Make notes about their jobs and working hours.**

B **Work in pairs. Talk about the work patterns of some of your family and friends. Use words from Exercises 4A, 5 and 6 and the models in Exercise 7A to help you.**

PROJECT: Researching work patterns

8A **Work in pairs. Research some of the work patterns in your country. Follow these steps.**

- Choose two or three different companies in which you can interview staff.
- Find out about the typical working patterns in the companies. Choose ideas from the box to help you and use your own ideas.

flexible hours / fixed schedule	full-time/part-time jobs	interns
permanent employees / temporary workers	shifts	working day

- Which company has the best/worst work patterns? Why?

B **When you finish your research, work in groups with students from other pairs. Exchange information about your research. Which companies and industries have the best/worst work patterns?**

Self-assessment

- How successfully have you achieved the lesson outcome? Give yourself a score from 0 (I need more practice) to 5 (I know this well).
- Go to My Self-assessment in MyEnglishLab to reflect on what you have learnt.

4.2 Executives at work

Lesson outcome Learners can use the Present Perfect Simple to refer to personal experiences in the past.

Lead-in

1A Which of these things do you do on an average day? What else do you usually do at work or at university and in your free time? Make a list.

'escape' at lunchtime	get to work/class early	give presentations	have meetings	
listen to music	read a book	sit in heavy traffic	talk to colleagues	use public transport

B Work in pairs. Compare your lists and ask each other some questions.

A: What time do you get to work? *B: About 8 o'clock.*

Reading

2 Work in pairs. Read an interview with a businesswoman and follow the steps below.

Student A: Read the article and complete exercises 2 and 3 on page 132.

Student B: Read the interview with Anne Kiem on this page and put the questions in the correct place. Two questions are not used.

- **a** What is your favourite book?
- **b** What is an average day at work like?
- **c** What is the biggest lesson you have learnt?
- **d** What is the best advice you have ever received?
- **e** What is the worst job you have ever had?

3 Student B: read your article again and answer the questions.

1. What was Kiem's first profession after university?
2. Why does she get to work early?
3. What does an 'open-door' policy mean?
4. How does she relax during the working day?
5. What question does she say is important to ask?
6. What was difficult about her worst job?

4A Tell your partner in your own words about the businesswoman you read about. What similarities and differences between Anne Kiem and Kathryn Bishop can you find? Use the ideas in the box or your own ideas.

city where they work	country of residence	education
number of jobs	previous work experience	working day

T Teacher's resources: extra activities

B Which person do you think has a more interesting professional life?

5 Choose three questions from the interviews in Exercise 2 to ask your partner.

FT

Women in Business: Anne Kiem

Anne Kiem is Chief Executive of the Association of Business Schools in London. Ms Kiem grew up in Australia and then studied to become a teacher and taught maths in London before moving into finance. She has worked at Barclays Bank and the Institute of Financial Services. In her free time, Ms Kiem enjoys listening to live music.

1 ____________

I like to be at my desk by 8 a.m., partly because the tube is less busy at that time, but also because it gives me some quiet time to prepare for the day ahead. I have an open-door policy and anyone can come and speak to me about anything. I want to know what is going on. It means that anything might happen, but I like it like that. I also go and talk to people to see what is going on. I escape the building at lunchtime when I can. I think it is important to try to take some time out during the day to help me not get too stressed by what is going on.

2 ____________

Perhaps the biggest is to never be afraid to ask the question 'Why?' Some of the most intelligent and successful people I know don't mind asking that question over and over again. So many things are as they are because that is the way they have always been.

3 ____________

Delivering newspapers – I was nineteen, studying at university in Australia. We had to do it at 3 a.m. before the traffic became too heavy. It wasn't difficult work, but to then go off to university and study maths was a bit strange, and I admit I sometimes found it difficult to stay awake in lectures.

Grammar

Present Perfect Simple

6 **Look at these extracts from the interviews. Answer the questions.**

a Anne Kiem **has worked** at Barclays Bank.
b What is the biggest lesson you **have learnt**?
c What is the worst job you **have ever had**?
d It **has taught** me to look at a problem in many different ways.
e ... a book that **has helped** me work in boardrooms ...
f What is the best advice you **have ever received**?

1 Do we know exactly when Anne Kiem worked at Barclay's Bank?
2 How are the verbs *learnt*, *had* and *taught* different from *worked*, *helped* and *received*?
3 In extracts c and f, which word can we use in questions to mean 'at any time'?

→ page 122 See Grammar reference: Present Perfect Simple

7 **What is the infinitive form of these common irregular verbs?**

been	bought	given	met	read	seen	sold	spoken	thought	taken	won	written

8A **Complete the dialogue with the Present Perfect Simple form of the verbs in brackets.**

A: [1]__________ __________ __________ __________ (you/ever/buy) a good business book?
B: No, I [2]__________ __________ __________ (never/buy) one but I [3]__________ __________ (read) a few from the library and I [4]__________ __________ (see) some business experts on YouTube, like Daniel Kahneman. He [5]__________ __________ (write) a lot about how we make decisions and how we don't think as clearly as we believe we do.
A: Ah yes! What was the title of that famous book of his?
B: *Thinking, Fast and Slow*. You know, he's a psychologist, but he [6]__________ __________ (win) a Nobel Prize for Economics.
A: Really? That's interesting. I [7]__________ __________ __________ (never/see) him talk. You know, I [8]__________ __________ (start) that book several times, but I [9]__________ __________ __________ (never/finish) it!

B 4.02 **Look at Exercise 8A again and use contractions where possible. Listen and check your answers.**

T Teacher's resources: extra activities

→ page 116 See Pronunciation bank: Present Perfect Simple

Speaking

9A **Complete the questions with the Present Perfect Simple form of the verbs in the box. Some are regular, some are irregular and some are not used.**

be	give	meet	sell	speak	take	think	visit	want	write

Have you ever ...

1 __________ an email in English?
2 __________ another country for work?
3 __________ in English on the phone?
4 __________ late for work or class?
5 __________ something online?
6 __________ a presentation in public?
7 __________ about working abroad?
8 __________ to be self-employed?

B **Work in pairs. Ask and answer the questions in Exercise 9A. If your partner answers *yes*, ask Past Simple questions to get more details.**

What did you ... ?	When did you ... ?	Why did you ... ?	Where did you ... ?

A: *Have you ever sold something online?* ***B:*** *Yes, I have*
A: *Really? What did you sell?* ***B:*** *I sold some books.*

Self-assessment

- How successfully have you achieved the lesson outcome? Give yourself a score from 0 (I need more practice) to 5 (I know this well).
- Go to My Self-assessment in MyEnglishLab to reflect on what you have learnt.

4.3 COMMUNICATION SKILLS
Making group decisions

Lesson outcome Learners are aware of different decision-making approaches and can use a range of expressions to facilitate a decision-making meeting.

Lead-in

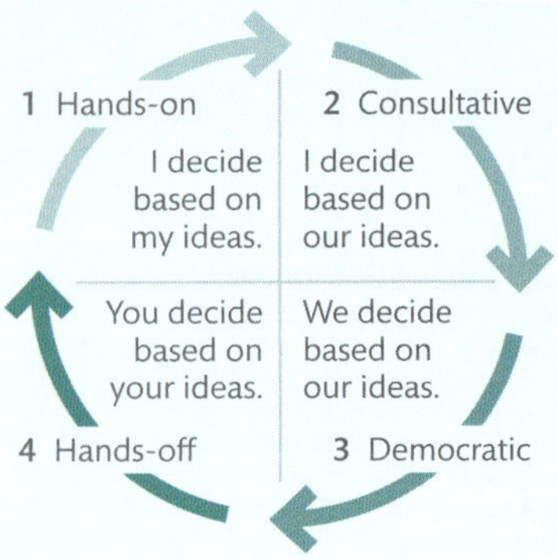

1A The diagram on the left shows four approaches to decision-making from the most hands-on (*I, the boss, decide*) to the most hands-off (*I leave it to you, my team, to decide*). In pairs, discuss which approach is best when:

1 I just need your input before going ahead with my decision.
2 there's nothing much to discuss.
3 I trust you to make the decision without any input from me.
4 I want to share full responsibility for the decision with you.
5 I've decided, but I don't want to leave you out of the process completely.
6 I am the only one with all the relevant information.

B In small groups, discuss some of the pros and cons of each style.

VIDEO

2A ▶ 4.3.1 Watch the conversation between Shaun and Orla and answer the questions.

1 How was Shaun's meeting with Léana?
2 How does Shaun describe 'reverse coaching'?
3 What does Orla think of the idea?
4 What do the junior staff think about the idea?

B How do you think the meeting will go? What could go wrong?

Video A ▶ 4.3.2

3A Watch Shaun briefing the junior staff and answer the questions.

1 Which approach to decision-making from Exercise 1A does Shaun take?
2 How does Shaun 'sell' his idea to the group? Are they persuaded?
3 Who makes the following points? Write in the names *Ethan* (E), *Jasmine* (J) and *Thiago* (T).
   a We're too busy for this. ____________
   b We're not trained coaches. ____________
   c Can we go away and think about it? ____________
   d Will we get paid extra? ____________
4 How does the meeting end? Is it a satisfactory conclusion?

B What do you think is the main thing Shaun did wrong?

Video B ▶ 4.3.3

4 Watch Shaun taking a different approach and answer the questions.

1 Which approach to decision-making from Exercise 1A does Shaun take?
2 How does he respond to the group's concerns?
3 How can Shaun deal with the concerns that Thiago and Jasmine have?
4 What two new ideas come out of the meeting?

5 Compare Shaun's approach and the group's response in Videos A and B. In what way is the end of the meeting in each version a) the same b) different?

6 ▶ 4.3.4 Watch the Conclusions section of the video and compare the advice with your answers in Exercises 3B and 5.

Reflection

7 Think about how you make decisions that affect others. Which approach(es) to decision-making are you most comfortable with? In pairs, discuss how you could develop your skills.

Functional language

Facilitating a decision-making meeting

8A Look at the expressions for encouraging people to take part in a meeting. Put the words in brackets into the correct order to complete the sentences.

1 I'd like ______________________________ before we finalise anything. (input / to / your / get)
2 So, ______________________________ think? (everybody / does / what)
3 Thiago, you're our tech guru, what ______________________________ this? (on / are / thoughts / your)
4 Mike, ______________________________ so far. (you / anything / said / haven't)
5 I'd like ______________________________ think. (what / hear / to / you)
6 Jasmine, what ______________________________ Mike's idea? (think / you / of / do)
7 Does anyone have anything else ______________________________ before we move on? (like / they'd / add / to)
8 Right, well, ______________________________, everybody. (input / thanks / your / for)

B Which expressions in Exercise 8A can you complete using the following phrases? You can use one of the phrases more than once.

to say	do you think about	to hear your views
to know what you	we haven't heard much from you	

9 What word will complete all three expressions from the meeting? They all mean 'I'm not sure I agree with you, but you may be right'.

OK, it's a fair / Hmm, I take your / Mm, you may have a __________ .

10 Match the beginnings (1–3) with the endings (a–c) to make three expressions to delay making a decision.

1 Let's not rush
2 Can we go away and think
3 We don't have to take

a an immediate decision on this.
b into anything.
c about it?

11 Work in groups. Take turns to lead a short discussion about one of these ideas.

1 A chill-out room where employees can relax and reflect.
2 Free drink-and-snack machines for all employees.

T Teacher's resources: extra activities

TASK

12A Work in groups of three. You are going to take turns to lead a meeting to discuss one of the proposals below using the meeting plan and expressions from Exercises 8–10.

1 Fitness tracking
Proposal to monitor employees' fitness and stress levels. Look at page 133 for details.

2 Third-agers
Proposal to make better use of the experience of older managers. Look at page 136 for details.

3 The human cloud
Proposal to employ a network of remote workers. Look at page 137 for details.

MEETING PLAN

- Outline the proposal.
- Ask for input.
- Discuss the pros and cons.
- Make or delay a final decision.

B Take a few minutes to prepare. Then hold each meeting in turn.

C When you have finished, discuss how the meetings went. Did everyone get a chance to speak? What could you do better next time? Share your experience with the class.

Self-assessment

- How successfully have you achieved the lesson outcome? Give yourself a score from 0 (I need more practice) to 5 (I know this well).
- Go to My Self-assessment in MyEnglishLab to reflect on what you have learnt.

4.4 BUSINESS SKILLS

Phoning to change arrangements

Lesson outcome

Learners can use a range of expressions to make or change arrangements and give colleagues updates on the phone.

Lead-in

1A These days, a lot of business is done online. In pairs, look at the following situations and decide if it's better to phone or send an email.

1 You want to invite a group of people to a teleconference.
2 You need to reschedule an appointment at the last minute.
3 You need to ask a colleague about some figures.
4 You just missed a call from an important client.
5 You're stuck in traffic on your way to a job interview.

B Look at the situations in Exercise 1A where you decided to phone. Do they have anything in common? Compare ideas with the rest of the class.

Listening

2A 4.03 Listen to Lou calling her colleague, Ian, about an appointment she made with him last week.

1 What date did Lou and Ian have an arrangement to meet?
2 Why is that date now not possible?
3 Does Lou want to make the appointment sooner or later? Why?
4 Who's available on the following dates?
   a Wed 10, morning: *Lou / Ian*
   b Wed 10, afternoon: *Lou / Ian*
   c Thu 11, afternoon: *Lou / Ian*
   d Fri 12, afternoon: *Lou / Ian*
5 What does Ian offer to do to help?

B In their conversation, Lou apologises for changing the meeting time, while Ian tries to be helpful. Listen again and note down examples of what they say.

3A 4.04 Ian immediately calls his assistant, James. Listen and note down the changes they make to Ian's schedule.

	AM	PM	AM	PM
Monday	**8** HR conference day 1 – London		**15**	Conference call with Paris @ 16.00
Tuesday	**9** HR conference day 2 – London		**16** Meeting with coach @ 10.00	
Wednesday	**10** Performance reviews @ 11.00 ←	Staff training @ 14.30	**17**	Meeting with Lou & Sally @ 14.30
Thursday	**11** Start L&D report!!!		**18** Budget meeting @ 09.45	Fly to Seoul @ 17.50
Friday	**12** Meeting with IT team @ 09.30		**19**	

B Ian is more direct with James than Lou. Why do you think that is?

4 4.05 Listen to Ian calling Lou back to confirm the details. Make brief notes.

MEETING PLANNER | Ian Henderson

Date: __________ Time: __________ Location: ______________ Attending: ____________________

Arrangements: ____

Functional language

Rescheduling appointments on the phone

5A Match 1–5 with a–e and 6–10 with f–j to make expressions from the phone calls.

1 I'm calling about our
2 Do you mind if we fix
3 Let me just check
4 I'm free
5 How does the

a afternoon suit you?
b on Wednesday morning.
c meeting on Wednesday the 17th.
d another time to meet?
e my schedule.

6 How about
7 Which is better for you:
8 I'm busy all
9 Friday's out for
10 I know it's a

f day Thursday.
g Thursday the 11th?
h morning or afternoon?
i bit short notice.
j me, I'm afraid.

B In pairs, find words or phrases in Exercise 5A which match meanings 1–8.

1 it's impossible
2 is it convenient?
3 I'm not doing anything
4 look at
5 I have a lot to do
6 a plan of what I'm going to do
7 arrange
8 I'm telling you only a short time before it happens

6 Put the expressions (1–8) from the phone calls into the correct section in the table.

Making appointments	Changing appointments
Apologising	**Thanking**

1 Sorry to bother you.
2 So, just to confirm …
3 I appreciate it.
4 We're all set for the 10th.
5 I'm really sorry about this.
6 Do you want to postpone it?
7 Thanks for being so flexible.
8 Can we bring it forward?

Teacher's resources: extra activities

TASK

7A Work in pairs. Decide who is Student A and who is Student B. Read your information below.

Student A
You work at your company's Warsaw office. Today is Friday the 26th of February. On Wednesday the 10th of March you have an important strategy meeting with your partner at your company headquarters in Paris. You are just waiting for him/her to call and confirm your appointment.
Look at page 135 for a copy of your schedule.

Student B
You work at your company's headquarters in Paris. Today is Friday the 26th of February. On Wednesday the 10th of March you have an important strategy meeting with your partner who is flying in from the Warsaw office. He/She is just waiting for you to call and confirm the appointment.
Look at page 131 for a copy of your schedule.

B Take a few minutes to prepare. Then roleplay your phone call.

C When you have finished, discuss how well your telephone conversation went. Did you:
- find a convenient time to meet?
- apologise for any problems caused?
- try to make helpful suggestions?

Self-assessment
- How successfully have you achieved the lesson outcome? Give yourself a score from 0 (I need more practice) to 5 (I know this well).
- Go to My Self-assessment in MyEnglishLab to reflect on what you have learnt.

Confirming arrangements

Lesson outcome Learners can write work-related emails to make and confirm arrangements.

Lead-in

1 **Read the two emails making and confirming arrangements. Choose the correct option in italics. Then compare in pairs.**

Dear Mr Sachs,

This is to [1]*confirm / agree* our meeting on Friday 12th April at 9 a.m. to [2]*talk / discuss* new work patterns. The meeting will take [3]*place / part* in our London office, at the Waterman Building, King's Road. The meeting will last until 12.30 and I would like to [4]*receive / invite* you to stay for lunch. [5]*Feel / Make* free to call me if you have any questions.

I [6]*very / too* much look forward to seeing you next week.

All the best,

Lucia Esposito

Dear Ms Esposito,

[7]*Thank / Thanks* you for your email. I am delighted to confirm that I am able to [8]*attend / come* the meeting on Friday morning at 9 a.m. Could you tell me how far your office is from the train station? Unfortunately, I [9]*am unable / cannot* to stay for lunch as I am flying to Germany in the afternoon and need to leave at 12.30.

I look forward to our [10]*meeting / arrangement* on Friday!

All the best,

Friedrich Sachs

Functional language

2 **Complete the table with the words in the box.**

contact delighted free many meeting seeing this unfortunately

Confirming
[1]__________ is to confirm our meeting next Friday. I am [2]__________ to confirm that I am able to attend the meeting next Friday.
Inviting questions
Please [3]__________ me if you have any questions. Feel [4]__________ to call me if you have any questions.
Thanking
(I'd like to) Thank you for your email. [5]__________ thanks for your email.
Apologising
[6]__________, I am unable to attend the meeting as ... I'm sorry, but I cannot stay for lunch because ...
Concluding
I look forward to our [7]__________ on Friday. I very much look forward to [8]__________ you next week.

T Teacher's resources: extra activities

L The emails contain examples of prepositions of time. Go to MyEnglishLab for optional grammar work.

→ page 122 See Grammar reference: Prepositions of time

TASK

3A **Work in pairs. Read the email making arrangements on page 128. Use the emails in Exercise 1 and the functional language phrases to help you rewrite the email in a more formal style.**

B **Look at John Bankes' diary on page 134. Use the information to write his email reply confirming arrangements with Marco Contini in around 80 words.**

C **Exchange emails with your partner. Look at the five functions in the table in Exercise 2. Which functions did your partner use in the email? Did you both use the same functions?**

Self-assessment

- How successfully have you achieved the lesson outcome? Give yourself a score from 0 (I need more practice) to 5 (I know this well).
- Go to My Self-assessment in MyEnglishLab to reflect on what you have learnt.

Money 5

> 'A bank is a place that will lend you money if you can prove that you don't need it.'
> Bob Hope, comedian

Unit overview

5.1	**Going cashless** **Lesson outcome:** Learners can use vocabulary related to the economy, money and personal finance.	**Video:** Cashless payments **Vocabulary:** Money; Collocations **Project:** Creating an advertising campaign to persuade people to go cashless
5.2	**Consumer spending** **Lesson outcome:** Learners can use the first conditional to talk about likely situations in the future.	**Listening:** Podcast about money **Grammar:** First conditional **Speaking:** Talking about yourself
5.3	**Communication skills:** Negotiating team roles **Lesson outcome:** Learners can negotiate their roles in a project team and use a range of expressions to state their preferences.	**Video:** Negotiating roles **Functional language:** Agreeing on team roles in meetings **Task:** Team Tasks Game
5.4	**Business skills:** Presenting facts and figures **Lesson outcome:** Learners can use a range of expressions to talk about exact and approximate figures and present statistical information effectively.	**Listening:** Presentation about retail banking **Functional language:** Quoting figures in presentations **Task:** Give a presentation on equal pay
5.5	**Writing:** Letter about a price increase **Lesson outcome:** Learners can organise information in a formal letter and write a simple letter to explain a price increase.	**Model text:** Formal letter **Functional language:** Reasons, explanations, enclosures, conclusions **Grammar:** *because, so, so that* **Task:** A letter explaining price increases

Business workshop 5: p.96 | **Review 5:** p.108 | **Pronunciation:** 5.2 Intonation in conditionals 5.4 Numbers and figures p.116 | **Grammar reference:** p.123

5.1 Going cashless

Lesson outcome

Learners can use vocabulary related to the economy, money and personal finance.

Lead-in

1 **Tick (✓) the methods of payment you've used in the past month.**

bank transfer	cash	credit card	debit card	mobile phone payment
online payment	store card	other payment method		

2 **Which type of payment do you use the most often? Which do you use the least often? Why?**

BBC VIDEO

3 **You are going to watch a video about cashless payments in India. Before you watch, answer the questions.**

1 Why do you think some governments want people to stop using cash?

a To save money – making notes and coins is expensive.
b Because it's difficult to steal electronic money – and it can't get lost.
c Almost everyone has a mobile phone – cashless payments are becoming easier for everyone.
d To get more money for the government – electronic payments are easier to track.
e Your own ideas.

2 Could you do these things in your country without cash? Why? / Why not?

buy street food	buy vegetables	lend money to a friend
pay for a taxi	pay in a restaurant	

4 ▶ 5.1.1 **Watch the video. Which ideas from Exercise 3 does it mention?**

5 **Watch the video again. Choose the correct option in italics to complete the sentences.**

1 The reporter is going shopping without *money / cash*.
2 Food sellers often pay for their goods *at the time of delivery / on credit*.
3 The reporter paid for his food by *credit card / mobile phone payment*.
4 Cashless payment has increased *a little / a lot* recently.
5 People usually pay for vegetables *by card / in cash*.
6 The reporter couldn't pay for his taxi fare because he didn't have *cash / a credit card*.

T Teacher's resources: extra activities

6 **How easy is it to go cashless in your country?**

Vocabulary

Money

7 **Match the words and phrases in bold from the video with the definitions (a–g).**

1 I put my credit card information into my **mobile wallet**.
2 On the internet, **payment** by credit card is very easy.
3 The **currency** in most countries in the European Union is the euro.
4 **Tax revenues** increase when more people use banks.
5 In a **cashless economy**, people don't use paper money.
6 I have no money – not even one **penny**.
7 Banks are an important part of **the financial system**.

a the act of paying for something
b software that stores your bank or credit card information on your phone
c a system of buying and selling things without using coins or notes
d the money the government collects from people
e a small unit of money
f the system or type of money that a country uses
g the institutions and organisations that help with the transfer of money between people and businesses

Collocations

8A Look at the sentences. Which word from the video completes all the sentences?

The ________ **crunch** in India caused problems for small businesses.
The business has a ________ **flow** of about $50,000 per month.
Shops usually use a ________ **register** to keep money in.
For small items, I usually **pay** in ________ .
She **withdraws** ________ from the bank every Friday.
We pay our workers ________ **in hand** because many don't have a bank account.
We use **petty** ________ to buy paper and ink for the printer.
We pay ________ **on delivery**, so we don't need credit.
I need to stop at a ________ **dispenser** to get some money.
I'm **short of** ________ this week, so I'm not going out.

B Work in pairs. What does each collocation mean?

9A Complete the questions using the correct form of words and phrases from Exercises 7 and 8A.

1. Do you keep money in a ________ on your phone?
2. How do you usually ________ from the bank? Can you get cash from anywhere else?
3. If you're ________ , do you borrow money from a friend or family member?
4. When you use a ________ to take money out of the bank, do you sometimes have to pay a small charge?
5. What ________ do you use in your country? Whose pictures are on the money?

B Work in pairs or small groups. Discuss the questions in Exercise 9A.

T Teacher's resources: extra activities

PROJECT: Let's go cashless!

10 What are the advantages and disadvantages of cash and cashless payments? Complete the table. Use two of the expressions twice.

convenient | no need for correct change | not every seller accepts it | easy to lose | people can steal it | you know how much you have

	Advantages	Disadvantages
Cash	*convenient* ________	________ ________
Cashless payments	________ ________	________ ________

11A Work in pairs. You're going to create an advert to convince people to stop using cash. Can you think of any more advantages or disadvantages to add to the table in Exercise 10?

B Make a magazine or newspaper advert, a television or radio advert. Agree on how you want to present the information.

Think about:

- making an advert better with an interesting or funny picture.
- using a short story to make your point in a TV or radio advert.
- including an interview with a famous person.
- your own ideas.

C Create your advert.

Remember to:

- give the advantages of going cashless.
- explain the disadvantages of cash.
- make your message better with an interesting picture, story or interview.

D Present your advert to the class.

Self-assessment

- How successfully have you achieved the lesson outcome? Give yourself a score from 0 (I need more practice) to 5 (I know this well).
- Go to My Self-assessment in MyEnglishLab to reflect on what you have learnt.

5.2 Consumer spending

Lesson outcome Learners can use the first conditional to talk about likely situations in the future.

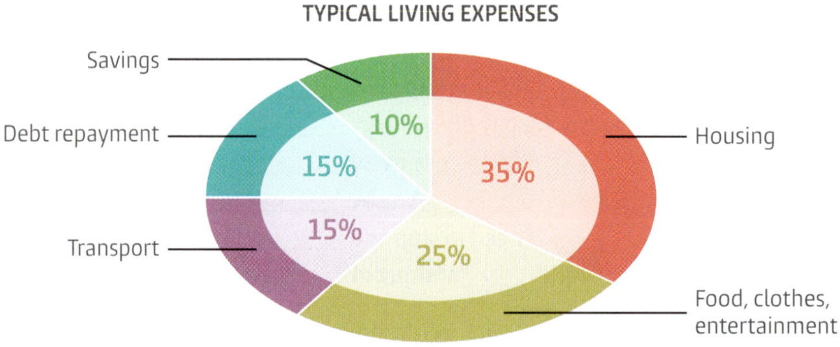

Lead-in

1A Look at the pie chart. Is your own spending similar to this?

B Match the living expenses in the box with a category in the pie chart. Use one of the expenses twice.

bicycle	bus ticket	business suit	cinema ticket	mortgage payment
meals at work	paying a car loan	paying interest on a credit card bill		
pension payment	putting money in the bank for emergencies	rent		

2 What would you like to spend more on? What would you like to spend less on?

Listening

3A 5.01 **Listen to *It all adds up!*, a podcast for consumers on the topic of money. Tick (✓) the topics they speak about.**

- **a** How to borrow money for emergency expenses
- **b** Suggestions for reducing living expenses
- **c** Information about how most consumers save
- **d** What will happen to interest rates over the next few months
- **e** News about currency exchange rates
- **f** Tips for changing money when travelling abroad

B Read about the expression *add up*. Why is *It all adds up!* a good name for a money podcast?

To *add up* means calculate the total of several numbers. For example, 1 + 2 + 3 = 6.

The expression *It all adds up* means that lots of small amounts make a large total. For example, if you save €5 per week, you have €260 after one year.

The expression *It doesn't add up* means that something doesn't make sense. For example, 'I don't understand how I spent so much money! It doesn't add up!'

4 Listen again. Choose the correct option in italics to complete the advice and information from the podcast.

1. It's a good idea to *walk / take your lunch* to work.
2. Don't buy things *with your credit card / that you don't need.*
3. Buy *a used car / cinema tickets* online.
4. In the next few months, *interest rates / borrowing* will go down.
5. *Mortgages / Holidays* will become more expensive.
6. Now is a good time to *visit China / buy Chinese electronics.*

T Teacher's resources: extra activities

5 Which of the tips from the podcast do you think you could easily follow? Which ones would be difficult or impossible for you to follow?

Grammar First conditional

6A Read the sentences from the podcast and answer the questions.

Part a	Part b
If interest rates **increase**,	borrowing **will go down**.
If you **take** your lunch to work,	you **will save** hundreds a year.

1 Which part of the sentence (a or b) is a condition?
2 Which part of the sentence (a or b) is a possible result in the future?

B Look at the structure and complete the rule with the underlined words in Exercise 6A.
We use the first conditional to talk about [1]__________ because of [2]__________ .

C Look at the sentences below. Complete the two possible structures.

If interest rates increase, borrowing will go down. [1]__________ + Present Simple, [2]__________ + infinitive

Borrowing will go down if interest rates increase. *will* + [3]__________ *if* + [4]__________

page 123 See Grammar reference: First conditional

7 Complete the first conditional sentences with the correct form of the verbs in brackets.
1 We __________ (save) more money if I don't have to spend much on transport.
2 If you __________ (not start) saving for a deposit, you'll never buy a house.
3 They'll pay less for their mortgage if interest rates __________ (go down).
4 If I __________ (sell) my car, I'll buy a really nice bicycle.
5 He'll save a lot of money on food if he __________ (stop) eating in restaurants every lunchtime.
6 If she continues using her credit card, she __________ (have) a lot to pay back next month.

T Teacher's resources: extra activities

page 116 See Pronunciation bank: Intonation in conditionals

Speaking

8A Match the beginnings (1–6) with the endings (a–f).
1 If I want to earn more money at work,
2 I'll walk to work or class tomorrow
3 If I have more money in the future,
4 I'll stop using my credit card
5 I won't have any more debt
6 If I buy a car,

a if the weather is fine.
b if I need to spend less money.
c I'll need to improve my English.
d I won't buy a new one, I'll buy a second-hand one.
e I'll move to a bigger house or flat.
f if I pay off my credit card.

B Work in pairs. Are the sentences in Exercise 8A true for you?

C Make first conditional sentences about yourself.
I'll save money if …
If I need to borrow money, …
If I want to go out tonight and not spend too much money, …
If I get a new job, …
I'll buy a new car if …
If I need some financial advice, …

D Work in small groups. Compare your answers to Exercise 8C.

Self-assessment
- How successfully have you achieved the lesson outcome? Give yourself a score from 0 (I need more practice) to 5 (I know this well).
- Go to My Self-assessment in MyEnglishLab to reflect on what you have learnt.

5.3 COMMUNICATION SKILLS
Negotiating team roles

Lesson outcome Learners can negotiate their roles in a project team and use a range of expressions to state their preferences.

Lead-in

1A The chart below shows three different zones of ability. Which zone are you in for each of the skills below? Write the numbers in the chart.

1 planning projects
2 working with figures
3 personal communication
4 leading teams
5 using technology
6 public speaking
7 doing research
8 managing your time
9 making decisions

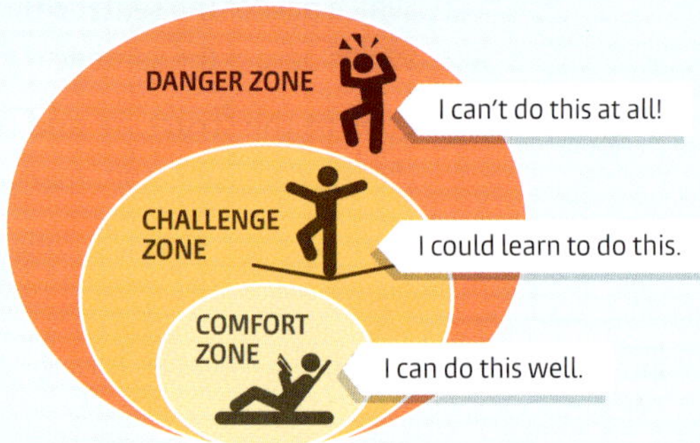

B Good teams need people with *different* skills in them. Compare your chart with other people in your class. Would you make a good team?

VIDEO

client pitch (noun) – a presentation you give to make a customer (or potential customer) want to buy your product or service

2A ▶ 5.3.1 Watch Orla and Shaun discussing a project meeting and answer the questions.

1 How often has Orla's team worked together before?
2 What is the purpose of today's meeting?
3 What is Orla trying to decide?
4 What advice does Shaun give her?

B What do you think of Shaun's advice? Can you see problems with it?

Video A ▶ 5.3.2

3A Watch the meeting and answer the questions.

1 Does Orla take Shaun's advice? Are the responses from the team:
☐ mostly positive? ☐ mostly negative? ☐ mixed (both positive and negative)?
2 Who gets the following team roles, *Alex* (Al), *Azra* (Az), *Jasmine* (J) or *Thiago* (T)?
pitch leader ____ tech support ____ lead presenter ____ learning designer ____
3 Why does Orla decide on the roles in question 2?
4 What are the problems with the roles for each team member?

B What went wrong in the meeting? How could it be improved?

Video B ▶ 5.3.3

4A Watch a more positive version of the meeting and answer the questions.

1 Why does Orla think the team members can decide their own roles?
2 Why doesn't Azra think the pitch is a good opportunity to develop her presentation skills?
3 Why does Orla think Jasmine can manage the learning design role?
4 Why might Thiago be a good presenter?
5 What team role changes are made by the end of the meeting?

B How was the team response in this meeting different from the previous version? What did the team do differently? Think about:

- politeness.
- suggestions not instructions.
- ways of saying 'no'.

5 ▶ 5.3.4 Watch the Conclusions section of the video. Compare the advice with your answers in Exercises 3B and 4B.

Reflection

6 In pairs, discuss saying 'no' in business situations. Are you comfortable saying 'no' to a customer or boss? How can you stay positive when you have to say 'yes' to things you don't want to do?

Functional language

Agreeing on team roles in meetings

7A Match the beginnings (1–8) with the endings (a–h) to make expressions from the video.

1 Is that OK
2 I was thinking you
3 How would you feel
4 If you
5 Perhaps Azra
6 If you're both happy to exchange roles,
7 I'd like you
8 How would you like

a and I could swap roles.
b don't mind.
c could head up the project.
d with everyone?
e then that's fine with me.
f about that?
g to be the learning designer.
h to do the PowerPoint for us again?

B Put the expressions in Exercise 7A into the correct section in the table.

Checking agreement	Making suggestions

8A Use two or more phrases to say 'no' politely.

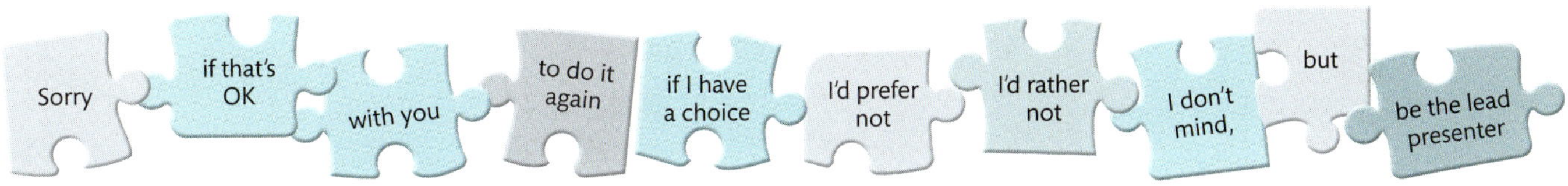

I don't mind, but I'd prefer not to do it again if I have a choice.

B Use two or more phrases to make comments about your strengths and weaknesses.

I'm quite good with technology. Ella is much better at solving problems than me.

T Teacher's resources: extra activities

TASK

9A Work in pairs. You are going to play the Team Tasks Game. Start by completing the grid on page 132.

B When you're ready, politely ask your partner to do one of the tasks on the grid.

- If you ask your partner to do one of his/her comfort zone tasks, you get 2 points and he/she has to agree to do it.
- If you ask your partner to do one of his/her danger zone tasks, you lose 1 point and he/she has to say 'no' politely, explain why he/she's no good at this task, and suggest somebody else for the task (e.g. another class member).
- If you ask your partner to do one of his/her challenge zone tasks, for 2 extra points you must explain why it would be good for him/her to learn how to do it.
- The person with the most points after ten minutes is the winner.

C Discuss how well you both decided who should do each task. Play again if you like, but this time faster.

Self-assessment

- How successfully have you achieved the lesson outcome? Give yourself a score from 0 (I need more practice) to 5 (I know this well).
- Go to My Self-assessment in MyEnglishLab to reflect on what you have learnt.

5.4 BUSINESS SKILLS
Presenting facts and figures

Lesson outcome

Learners can use a range of expressions to talk about exact and approximate figures and present statistical information effectively.

Lead-in

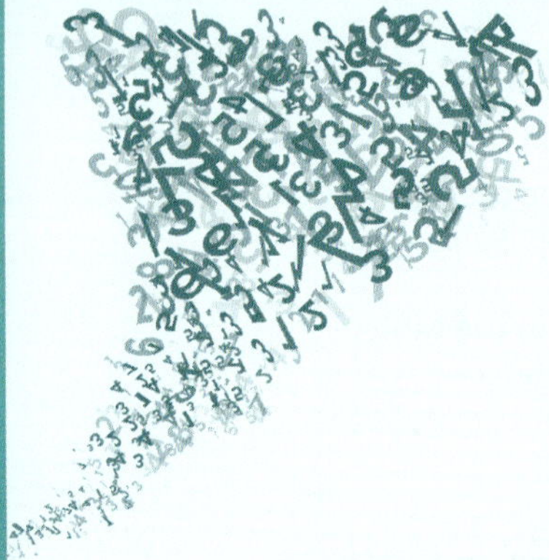

1A Look at three different ways of presenting the same information. Which, for you, is the most effective? Why?

1 There are **a lot of**
2 There are **11.6 million**
3 There are **almost 12 million**

} women business owners in the USA.

B In pairs, look at the following statements. Are they more or less effective than the statements in Exercise 1A? Why?

1 **Approximately one out of every fourteen** American women is the owner of a business.
2 **The number of** women business owners in the USA **is greater than** the whole population of Sweden, Austria or Switzerland.

2A Match the exact figures (1–7) with the approximate figures (a–g).

1 0.95%	a **roughly** a quarter
2 23.5%	b **almost** one in three
3 52%	c **around** two out of (every) five
4 39.4%	d **nearly** three quarters
5 9.867%	e **under** one percent
6 73.9%	f **over** half
7 32.75%	g **about** ten percent

B Label the expressions in bold in Exercise 2A according to their meaning using the following icons.

more than >   less than <   approximately ≈

C You can put the words 'just' and 'well' before 'over' and 'under'. Which means:

a by a large amount?   b by a small amount?

Listening

3A 5.02 **Liz is a Marketing Consultant to the retail banking industry. Listen to the first part of her presentation to a group of clients and answer the questions.**

1 How does Liz get the attention of her audience at the start?
2 Which three generations does she talk about in her introduction? Complete the information in slide 1.
3 Which generation is the main subject of her presentation? Why?
4 How do the audience describe this generation in terms of:
• lifestyle? • technology? • work? • money?

1 Customer age groups

Generation (b. 1964–79) ____________
Generation (b. 1980–94) ____________
Generation (b. 1995–2012) ____________

B Liz used the approximate words *early*, *mid* and *late* to talk about ages and dates. Can you remember the phrases she used for the following? Listen and check.

1 17–19-year-olds *late teens*	3 1964–6 ____________	5 1981–3 ____________
2 21–23-year-olds ____________	4 1977–9 ____________	6 2011–13 ____________

4A 5.03 **Listen to Liz present the financial habits of young adults with approximate figures. What are the *exact* figures? Use the exact figures below and write them on slide 2.**

12   21   29   64   76

2 Financial habits
(16-21-year-olds)

• paid employment *76* %
• own savings account __ %
• account-holders since age 10 __ %
• already saving for retirement __ %
• opposed to all forms of debt __ %

B Listen again and answer the questions.

1 What do the employment figures for 16–21-year-olds show?
2 What does Liz say is the most surprising figure in the chart? Why?
3 What kind of debt are 16–21-year-olds against? Why?
4 What's the good news about 16–21-year-olds for the retail banking industry? What's the bad news?

3 Marketing to young savers

10.6 1bn 53% 42m

5A 5.04 **Listen to the final part of the presentation. What do the figures in slide 3 show?**

1 10.6 = ______________________
2 1 billion = ______________________
3 53% = ______________________
4 42 million = ______________________

B What does Liz say about her client's marketing strategy?

6 What does Liz say to help the audience remember the number of hours spent online?

Functional language

Quoting figures in presentations

7 Complete the expressions using the words in the box.

context figure idea look means see shows summary takeaway terms thing

1 Have a(n) __________ at this chart, which __________ the results of our survey of the financial habits of people aged sixteen to twenty-one.
2 As you can __________, roughly three-quarters of them are already earning their own money.
3 To put that in __________, that's almost the same as the __________ for Generation Y.
4 To give you a(n) __________ of just how much that is … it comes to around a billion hours of online activity every day!
5 Perhaps the most surprising __________ is that over one in ten of them are already saving for retirement.
6 The key __________ here is that Generation Z likes to save, but doesn't like to borrow.
7 So, in __________, if we want to attract this new generation of customers, we need to make sure we connect with them on a personal level.
8 And, in __________ of selling banking services, this clearly __________ that we need to be doing a lot more than just social media marketing.

8 Approximate the following figures in as many ways as you can in under a minute. Compare your performance with a partner.

33.4% 27.8% 99.9 €21m 11% ¥497 48.9% £995bn

T Teacher's resources: extra activities

page 116 See Pronunciation bank: Numbers and figures

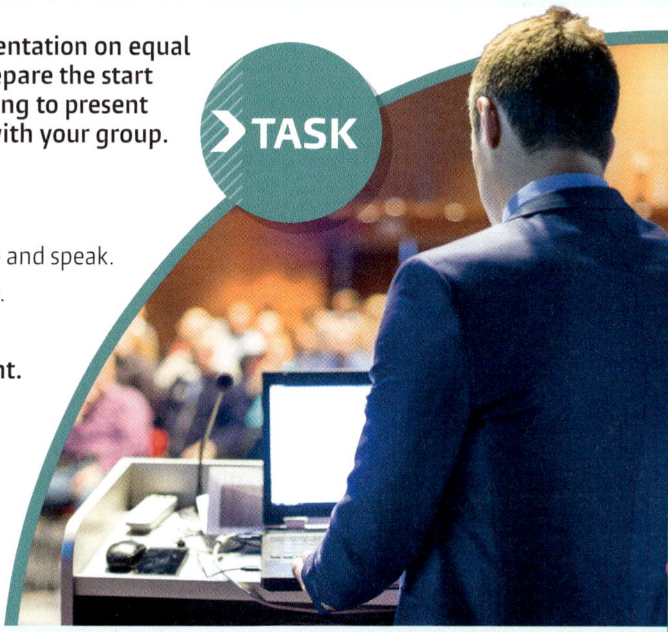

9A Work in pairs or small groups. You are going to give a presentation on equal pay at an HR conference in London. Turn to page 136 to prepare the start of your presentation. Read the notes and decide who is going to present which slides. Then practice your part of the presentation with your group.

B When you are ready, give the presentation.

1 The first time, give the presentation by reading from the notes.
2 Try again, but look down at the notes for each slide, then look up and speak.
3 Present the information once more – this time *without* the notes. Your slides will help you remember what to say!

C When you have finished, discuss how the presentation went. How effectively did you:

- refer to key figures in your slides?
- use approximate figures to make them easier to remember?
- explain why your data is important?
- suggest the action(s) your audience should take in response to your data?

Self-assessment

- How successfully have you achieved the lesson outcome? Give yourself a score from 0 (I need more practice) to 5 (I know this well).
- Go to My Self-assessment in MyEnglishLab to reflect on what you have learnt.

Letter about a price increase

Lesson outcome

Learners can organise information in a formal letter and write a simple letter to explain a price increase.

Lead-in

1 **Read the formal letter explaining a price increase. Complete the text with the phrases in the box.**

if we do not raise prices
increase our prices by 5 percent from 1st October
our prices remain competitive
we will continue to use the best materials

DONAL GORMAN,
UNIT 4 MAGRET INDUSTRIAL CENTRE, ABERDEEN, AB13 4NA

The Purchasing Manager
Greft Engineering
Unit 45 River Trade Park
Salisbury SP7 7SW

13th August 20

Dear Sir/Madam,

As you know, we have not raised our prices for two years. Unfortunately, because of rising costs, we now need to [1]________ .

We tried to avoid any increase but the quality of our products will suffer [2]________ .
We are sure you will agree that quality is very important so [3]________ . We are keeping the rise small so that [4]________ .

We enclose a new price list with this letter. If you have any questions, please do not hesitate to contact us.

We thank you for your business and look forward to supplying you in the future.

Yours faithfully,

Melissa Blanco
Sales Director

Functional language

2A **Look at the letter in Exercise 1 again. Match the sentence halves to complete the rules.**

1 When you don't know the name of the person you are writing to, start the letter with *Dear Sir/Madam,*

2 When you know the name of the person you are writing to, start the letter with *Dear Mr/Ms [surname],*

a and end with *Yours sincerely*.

b and end with *Yours faithfully*.

B **Complete the table using words from the letter.**

Reason for writing (Para 1)
As you know, we have not raised our prices for two years. [1]________ , we now need to increase our prices.
Explanation (Para 2)
We are keeping the [2]________ small so that our prices still [3]________ competitive. [4]________ is very important so we must continue to use the best materials.
Enclosures (Para 3)
We [5]________ a new price list [6]________ this letter. Enclosed with this letter is a new price list.
Positive conclusion (Para 4)
We appreciate your business and hope you will understand our situation. We thank you [7]________ your business and look forward to [8]________ you in the future.

T Teacher's resources: extra activities

L The letter contains examples of the linking words *because*, *so* and *so that*. Go to MyEnglishLab for optional grammar work.

→ page 123 See Grammar reference: *because*, *so*, *so that*

TASK

3A **Work in pairs. Look at page 133 and put the sentences in the letter in the correct order.**

B **Look at the notes on page 135. Write a letter of about 120 words to your customers explaining price increases. Do not include any addresses.**

C **Exchange letters with your partner. Did your partner start and end the letter appropriately? Did your partner organise the letter in four paragraphs?**

Self-assessment

- How successfully have you achieved the lesson outcome? Give yourself a score from 0 (I need more practice) to 5 (I know this well).
- Go to My Self-assessment in MyEnglishLab to reflect on what you have learnt.

Teamwork 6

'Coming together is a beginning, staying together is progress, and working together is success.'

Henry Ford, founder of Ford Motor Company

Unit overview

6.1	**Working together** **Lesson outcome:** Learners can use vocabulary related to teamwork.	**Video:** Teamwork in extreme situations **Vocabulary:** Teamwork; Word building – verbs and nouns **Project:** Plan and make a schedule for a meeting
6.2	**Team building** **Lesson outcome:** Learners can use a range of indefinite pronouns with *some-* and *every-*.	**Reading:** The rise of sport at work **Grammar:** Pronouns with *some-* and *every-* **Speaking and writing:** Describing people, places, things, jobs and studies
6.3	**Communication skills:** Supporting a colleague **Lesson outcome:** Learners can support a colleague who has had a disappointment at work and use a range of expressions to encourage and motivate him/her.	**Video:** Offering support to a colleague **Functional language:** Encouraging and motivating **Task:** Supporting a colleague
6.4	**Business skills:** Being positive in meetings **Lesson outcome:** Learners can contribute to meetings in a positive and constructive way and use a range of expressions to support and build on ideas.	**Listening:** A recruitment problem **Functional language:** Supporting, building on and questioning ideas **Task:** Supporting, building on and questioning ideas in a meeting
6.5	**Writing:** Making requests **Lesson outcome:** Learners can write a simple email making requests to team members.	**Model text:** Email making requests **Functional language:** Making requests **Grammar:** Linking words for sequence **Task:** An email making a request

Business workshop 6: p.98 | **Review 6:** p.109 | **Pronunciation:** 6.1 Vowel sounds: /ɪ/, /iː/, /aɪ/ and /ɪə/ 6.2 Linking between words p.117 | **Grammar reference:** p.123

6.1 Working together

Lesson outcome Learners can use vocabulary related to teamwork.

Lead-in

1 Tick (✓) the things you've done with other people.

☐ play sports	☐ clean up a mess	☐ organise an event
☐ give a presentation	☐ play music	☐ attend a meeting
☐ prepare a meal	☐ complete a project	☐ something else

2 Work in groups. Tell each other about what you did and where and when it was.

VIDEO

3 Look at the photo. Have you ever been to this type of place? Would you like to go there? Why? / Why not?

4 ▶ 6.1.1 Watch the first part of the video (0:23–1:08) with the sound off. Choose the correct option.

1 Job:	**a** tour guide	**b** emergency worker
2 Works:	**a** alone	**b** in a team
3 Important activity at work:	**a** giving and following instructions	**b** dealing with customer complaints
4 Skill:	**a** speaking several languages	**b** climbing

5 Watch the complete video. Choose the correct option in italics.

1 Teamwork is very important in *outdoor / dangerous* situations.
2 Walking and climbing on Table Mountain is *simple / difficult*.
3 The team is always *busy / prepared to work*.
4 They're helping someone who is *hurt / lost*.
5 The team must be as *fast / careful* as possible.
6 The team members need *communication skills / more practice and experience*.
7 The team members *don't argue with / trust* each other.
8 The team *relaxes / doesn't relax* together.

T Teacher's resources: extra activities

6 Work in pairs. Do you think the rescue team enjoy their work? Why? / Why not?

→ page 117 See Pronunciation bank: Vowel sounds: /ɪ/, /iː/, /aɪ/ and /ɪə/

Vocabulary Teamwork

7A Read the text. What type of word is needed for each gap: a verb, a noun or an adjective?

People who work together in a team need to [1]___________ with each other. They may sometimes [2]___________ about what to do, but good teamworkers are good at [3]___________. They can solve these problems and reach a(n) [4]___________. When people have [5]___________ for the people they work with, a(n) [6]___________ can, in fact, be a good way of finding the best solution to a problem.

It's important for people who work together to [7]___________ each other – to believe that the others will do a good job. Of course, if you want people to believe in you, you must be [8]___________ and do the things you say you will do.

In a strong team, more [9]___________ people help the younger, newer workers learn the job and give advice about how to [10]___________ issues that come up.

B Complete the text in Exercise 7A using the words and phrases from the video.

Verbs:	cooperate	deal with	disagree	trust
Nouns:	agreement	argument	conflict management	respect
Adjectives:	experienced	reliable		

Word building – verbs and nouns

Verb	Noun
1 ________	agreement
2 ________	argument
3 ________	communication
cooperate	4 ________
disagree	5 ________
6 ________	management
7 ________	respect
trust	8 ________

Teacher's resources: extra activities

8 **Complete the table with the correct word forms.**

9A **Complete the pairs of statements with the correct form of the word in capitals.**

ARGUE

1 If team members __________ with each other, it means there's a problem.

2 Every __________ has a winner and a loser.

COMMUNICATE

3 Good __________ is important for anyone who works in a team.

4 Words aren't the only way we __________ . Things we *don't* say also send a message.

COOPERATE

5 When we __________ with other people, we need to listen to them carefully.

6 __________ usually produces better work than conflict.

B **Work in pairs or small groups. Think about your own experience at work or studying. Do you agree with the statements in Exercise 9A? Why? / Why not?**

PROJECT: Organising a team

10A **Work in pairs or small groups. Read the email from the CEO of a software development company to all employees. Make a list of things that need to be organised for tomorrow's meeting.**

Emergency – Surprise visit from XYQ Global

We've just learnt that Cécile Durant and her team from XYQ Global in Paris are going to be in Singapore tomorrow and they would like to visit us here at ProgramsPro from 11.30 to 1.30. We were not expecting this, but as you know, they are one of the most important clients for our accounting software, and they are unhappy with our product support. We hope to improve the relationship. This is also a great opportunity to give a formal presentation of our new products – we really need to explain these in great detail. We have about 20 hours to plan a two-hour meeting that will include lunch. I'll put together an emergency team to get everything ready. I'll contact everyone shortly!

B **What will the ProgramsPro staff who attend the meeting with XYQ Global need to do? What skills should they have?**

C **Look at page 139 to see the people the CEO has chosen to take part in the planning of the meeting. Only two of them will actually attend the meeting with the CEO and XYQ Global. Decide who should attend and give planning jobs to the other three.**

A: *I don't think the Engineer should go to the meeting. She's afraid of public speaking.*

B: *OK. But she could explain the products to the Sales Manager before the meeting.*

C: *I agree.*

D **Make a schedule for the two-hour meeting. Decide what each part of the meeting will be about, how long it will last, and who will be responsible for that part of the meeting.**

Self-assessment

- How successfully have you achieved the lesson outcome? Give yourself a score from 0 (I need more practice) to 5 (I know this well).
- Go to My Self-assessment in MyEnglishLab to reflect on what you have learnt.

6.2 Team building

Lesson outcome Learners can use a range of indefinite pronouns with *some-* and *every-*.

Lead-in

1A Work in pairs. For each activity, think of one example from sport and one from business.

competing cooperating learning new skills training and practising working in a team

Football players work in teams. People in offices also work in teams.

B For three of the items in Exercise 1A, think of an example from your own life related to sport, work or something else. Try to use these verbs.

challenge develop improve inspire reduce

I'm learning to use AutoCAD. I practise every day, and I'm improving.

Reading

2 Read the article quickly. Tick (✓) the main idea.

1 Some companies are organising events for their employees to compete against workers from other companies.

2 Many companies encourage their employees to get fit and to get to know each other by doing sport together.

3 Read the article again and choose the correct option.

1 Phil Smith started doing triathlons to *become a better manager / get fit*.

2 His company organised a triathlon to *improve employees' fitness / compete with other companies*.

3 At Björn Borg, exercising together encourages workers to *compete with / talk to* each other.

4 An accounting team *became more competitive / improved teamwork* by running together.

5 Carl Cederström says that doing sport develops *some / all* of the qualities that businesspeople need.

T Teacher's resources: extra activities

4 Would you sign up for a university or company triathlon? Why? / Why not?

→ page 117 See Pronunciation bank: Linking between words

FT

Get fit or be fired trying: the rise of sport at work

More companies are encouraging employees to take part in team sports. In a triathlon, racers swim, cycle and run.

Phil Smith, Chairman of Cisco UK and Ireland, started doing triathlons about 10 years ago. He wanted to do something to challenge himself and improve his health. 'It wasn't part of any sort of plan, but I did my first and really enjoyed it.'

So he signed up for more events. Then he began to think about how to inspire people from different parts of the organisation to work together to get fitter. In 2016, in partnership with other companies, Cisco set up its own team triathlon.

A lot of companies have similar ideas. Björn Borg, the Swedish sportswear maker, closes its head office every Friday for an hour of exercise for everyone in the company. The sports events are also social, giving employees somewhere to get together and chat. For Brian Carroll, a New Yorker who plays for his company's baseball team, sport is a chance to meet other people in the firm. 'We've become friends outside of work. I enjoy conversations about different challenges in the workplace.'

However, the result isn't the same everywhere. When one team in an accounting firm went running a couple of times a week together to improve teamwork, it increased competition and reduced cooperation – which wasn't good for the team.

Does being good at sports make you good at business? Carl Cederström, associate professor of organisation studies at Stockholm Business School, says 'There's tonnes of evidence that suggests if you work out, you get healthier and more resilient*', which certainly helps people do their jobs. But it doesn't always develop other qualities that someone in business needs. 'What does it mean to be a good executive? We don't really know.' Many great leaders are not good at sport.

*resilient: able to deal with and survive difficult conditions and situations

Grammar

Pronouns with *some-* and *every-*

5A Complete the sentences from the article using the words in the box.

everyone	everywhere	someone	something	somewhere

1 He wanted to do ____________ to challenge himself and improve his health.
2 Björn Borg closes its head office every Friday for an hour of exercise for ____________ in the company.
3 The sports events are also social, giving employees ____________ to get together and chat.
4 The result isn't the same ____________ .
5 It doesn't always develop other qualities that ____________ in business needs.

B Read the information. Complete the sentences with numbers 1–5.

a We use pronouns with *some-* to talk about 'a thing', 'a person' and 'in a place'. For example: sentences ____ , ____ , ____
b We use pronouns with *every-* to talk about 'all things', 'all people' and 'in all places'. For example: sentences ____ , ____

page 123 See Grammar reference: Pronouns with *some-* and *every-*

6 Match 1–4 with a–d and 5–8 with e–h to make sentences.

1 We can't do all this work ourselves. We need to hire
2 People all over the world drink cola. It's popular
3 The pay rise wasn't just for managers, it was for
4 I don't want to stay home next weekend, I want to go

a everyone.
b someone.
c somewhere.
d everywhere.

5 This isn't a problem for one or two of us, it's a problem for
6 If you don't have time to make lunch, we can buy a sandwich or
7 He said he understood most of the contract, but not
8 If you need help, just ask

e something.
f somebody.
g everybody.
h everything.

7 Complete the conversation with the correct pronoun.

A: Hello, [1]____________ . I'm glad you're all here. Before we start the meeting, let me ask – do you have [2]____________ you need? A copy of the report and [3]____________ to write with – a pen or pencil?
B: Sorry, I left my copy of the report [4]____________ . I've looked [5]____________ for it, but I can't find it!
A: OK, could [6]____________ please print out an extra copy of the report?

T Teacher's resources: extra activities

Speaking and writing

8A Work individually. Use each word below to describe a person, place or thing without saying who, what or where it is.

everyone/everybody   everything   everywhere   someone/somebody   something   somewhere

It's something you use to write text messages and make calls. (a mobile phone)
This is someone who helps us learn English. (the teacher)
It's what you use to carry everything when you travel. (a suitcase)

B Work in pairs or small groups. Take turns saying sentences and guessing the answer.

9 Write six sentences about your job or studies using pronouns with *some-* and *every-*.

Someone always arrives late to English class.
In the building, there are safety notices everywhere.

Self-assessment

- How successfully have you achieved the lesson outcome? Give yourself a score from 0 (I need more practice) to 5 (I know this well).
- Go to My Self-assessment in MyEnglishLab to reflect on what you have learnt.

6.3 COMMUNICATION SKILLS
Supporting a colleague

Lesson outcome

Learners can support a colleague who has had a disappointment at work and use a range of expressions to encourage and motivate him/her.

Lead-in

1A How good are you at understanding and sharing the feelings of other people? Take the quiz below. Then check your score on page 129.

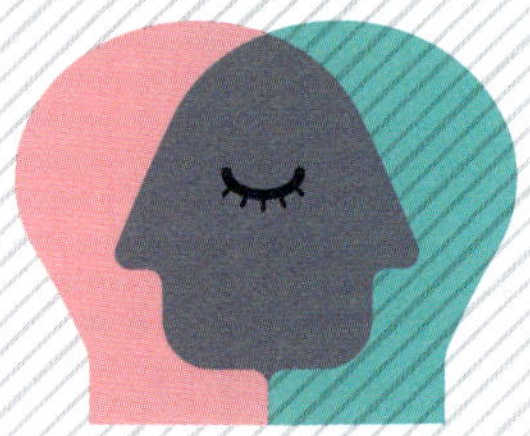

Answer 'Yes', 'No' or 'It depends' to the following questions:

1 Do you usually know when someone is not saying what they really think?
2 Do you generally avoid having emotional conversations?
3 Do people often tell you you're a good listener?
4 Do you find it hard to like someone who has very different views from you?
5 If you can see someone is unhappy, do you often want to help?

B Ask the person with the highest score in the class the question on page 131.

VIDEO

2A 6.3.1 **Watch Jasmine sharing some news with Thiago and answer the questions.**

1 What is Jasmine doing when Thiago brings her a coffee?
2 Who is the email from? Why is it so important to her?
3 What does the email say? How does Jasmine react?

B In pairs, discuss what Thiago a) should say, and b) should *not* say to Jasmine.

Video A 6.3.2

3A Watch both Thiago and Azra trying to say the right thing to Jasmine and answer the questions.

1 Number the things below in the order Thiago does them.
   a He tries to see the positive side. ☐
   b He pretends it isn't important. ☐
   c He changes the subject. ☐
   d He says he's sorry. ☐
   e He says something positive about Jasmine. ☐
2 How successful is he? Which of the things in question 1 works best?
3 How is Azra's approach different from Thiago's? Is it more successful?

B In pairs, discuss what Thiago and Azra are doing wrong.

Video B 6.3.3

4A Watch Jasmine talking with Alex and answer the questions.

1 How does Alex start the conversation positively?
2 What does Alex say about the conference organisers' feedback? What effect does this have on Jasmine?
3 What personal information does Alex share? Why does he do this?
4 What positive things does Alex say about Jasmine? Is this a good idea?
5 What is Alex's main advice to Jasmine? How does she respond?
6 What's the *good* news at the end of their conversation?

B In pairs, discuss how Alex's approach is different from Thiago's and Azra's.

5 6.3.4 **Watch the Conclusions section of the video. Compare the advice with your answers in Exercises 3B and 4B.**

Reflection

6 Think about how you support people who have had a disappointment. In pairs, discuss the questions.

1 Whose style is closest to your own – Thiago's, Azra's or Alex's?
2 How could you become better at this skill? What do you need to learn?

Functional language

Encouraging and motivating

7A Thiago and Azra used a lot of expressions to try to make Jasmine feel better. Choose the correct option to complete the sentences.

1 I know exactly how you *feel / think*! ________
2 Come on, it's no *large / big* deal! ________
3 Look on the *light / bright* side. ________
4 You must be *such / so* disappointed! ________
5 That's too *bad / terrible*! ________
6 Cheer *off / up*! ________

B In pairs, label each of the phrases and expressions in Exercise 7A according to their function.

I feel sorry for you. ☹   Don't worry, be happy. ☺

8 Complete some of the comments Alex made during his conversation with Jasmine using the pairs of words in the box. There is one extra pair.

behind + move	can + try	hope + disappointed	know + important
let + get	look + way	makes + better	question + learn
~~sorry + work~~	sounds + work	understand + feel	

I'm sorry.
1 I'm ___*sorry*___ it didn't ___*work*___ out for you.
2 I ____________ you're not too ____________ .

I understand.
3 It ____________ like you put a lot of ____________ into it.
4 I ____________ how ____________ it was to you.
5 I can ____________ how you ____________ .

Stay positive.
6 You ____________ always ____________ again.
7 If it ____________ you feel any ____________ , I had to apply to engineering school three times before I finally got in.

Learn and look to the future.
8 Put it ____________ you and ____________ on.
9 The ____________ to ask yourself is: What can I ____________ from this?
10 ____________ at it this ____________ : now you'll be free to help me with the Ferguson pitch.

9 In pairs, take turns to share disappointments with each other. Begin with each of the statements below and see how long you can keep the conversations going using some of the expressions in Exercises 7 and 8.

I just failed my driving test for the third time! I'm never going to pass!
I didn't get the scholarship to business school! How will I pay for it now?
My guests are arriving in half an hour and I just burnt the dinner!
My computer just died and I forgot to back up my files!

T Teacher's resources: extra activities

TASK

10A Work in groups of three. You are going to practise supporting a colleague who has had a disappointment at work. Take turns in each of the following roles:

Speaker: Look at page 134 for instructions on how to describe your disappointment to the Helper.

Helper: Look at page 130 for instructions on how to support the Speaker.

Observer: Look at page 135 for instructions on how to take notes on the conversation between the Speaker and the Helper.

B When you have finished, listen to the Observer's feedback. Discuss what went well, what didn't go well, and how you can improve next time.

Self-assessment

- How successfully have you achieved the lesson outcome? Give yourself a score from 0 (I need more practice) to 5 (I know this well).
- Go to My Self-assessment in MyEnglishLab to reflect on what you have learnt.

6.4 BUSINESS SKILLS
Being positive in meetings

Lesson outcome

Learners can contribute to meetings in a positive and constructive way and use a range of expressions to support and build on ideas.

Lead-in

1 In pairs, read the blog post and discuss the questions.

What makes a great team? The answer is surprisingly simple. It's the feeling among team members that it's safe to ask questions, share ideas and even make mistakes without the risk of getting negative reactions from the rest of the team. So, the message is clear. If you want to build a great team, first make it a safe place to be great in.

1 What makes a great team? Do you agree?
2 What's your best team experience? Why was it so positive?
3 What can a team leader do to make a team 'a safe place to be great in'?

Listening

2 6.01 Anatol is head of HR of a large insurance company. Listen to part of a meeting with his two senior recruiters and answer the questions.

1 What recruitment problem is the company currently having?
2 What has happened as a result?
3 What do the team think is causing the problem? Tick (✓) the correct boxes.

a the company's reputation ☐
b the salaries ☐
c the size of the company ☐
d insurance as a career ☐
e employee benefits ☐
f the work culture ☐

3A 6.02 Listen to the end of the meeting and match the suggestions (1–5) with the responses (a–e).

1 Attend more careers fairs.
2 Give talks at universities.
3 Produce a video promotion.
4 Offer training.
5 Sponsor MBA studies.

a No, there's no point.
b We don't have the budget for that!
c Yeah, but we're already doing that.
d No, that's a complete waste of time.
e We tried that before and it didn't work.

B What suggestion does Anatol make at the end of the meeting? Why?

4 Anatol decided to text his team with some 'rules' for their next meeting. Read his text on the left. Can you work out what the missing words are?

1 When someone shares an idea, can we please say at least one pos__________ thing about it before we say anything else?

2 Can we try to build on other people's ideas by considering the poss__________ – what else can we do to make the idea even better?

3 If we can see a pro__________ with an idea, let's not be negative. Let's ask how we could solve it.

5A 6.03 Listen to part of the next meeting and number the suggestions in the correct order.

a Introduce mobile advertising. ☐
b Put trainees into smaller project teams. ☐
c Create more of a fun work culture. ☐
d Offer 12-month internships. ☐
e Provide personal coaching. ☐
f Make job offers a lot faster. ☐

B Compare the second meeting with the first. How have the 'rules' helped?

C Why is each suggestion in Exercise 5A a good idea? Listen again and take brief notes.

a __________
b __________
c __________
d __________
e __________
f __________

D What two possible problems are raised in the meeting? What solutions are suggested?

Functional language

Supporting, building on and questioning ideas

6A Complete the following comments from the second meeting using the pairs of words in the box.

do + can	doing + could	~~like + idea~~	might + idea	problem + about
subject + don't	think + idea	what + idea	wondering + manage	

1 I really ___like___ that ___idea___ !
2 And while we're on the __________ of learning the business, why __________ we provide personal coaching as well?
3 Of course, there *is* the __________ of cost. What can we do __________ that?
4 You know, that __________ not be such a bad __________ .
5 __________ a good __________ !
6 And __________ that means we __________ also make job offers a lot faster.
7 Actually, I __________ that's a great __________ !
8 And if we __________ that, perhaps we __________ also create a bit of friendly competition between teams.
9 I'm just __________ about the amount of reorganisation it'll need. How can we __________ that?

B In pairs, label the expressions in Exercise 6A according to their function, using the following icons.

Supporting an idea ✔ Building on an idea ↔ Questioning an idea ?

T Teacher's resources: extra activities

TASK

7A Work in groups of 3–6. You all work in the creative department of an advertising agency in Los Angeles. Today you received the following email from your Creative Director. Read the email.

Hi team,

As you know, this year is the agency's 50th anniversary and we in the creative department are organising the celebrations. Now, we have a budget of around $150,000, but, no, we won't be spending it all on one big staff party! In fact, I see this as an opportunity to build stronger relationships throughout the year with our key clients, suppliers, possible clients and, of course, each other!

The company has grown so much in the last 50 years, so we want to do something really special. I'd like to hold a discussion meeting at 2 p.m. on Thursday 3rd. Bring your best ideas!

Marc

For instructions on how to run the meeting and some ideas to help you get started, look at the following pages:

Student A: page 138 **Student D:** page 129
Student B: page 133 **Student E:** page 140
Student C: page 131 **Student F:** page 141

B Take a few minutes to prepare. Then hold the meeting.

C When you have finished, discuss how the meeting went. How effectively did you:

- react positively to other people's ideas?
- avoid saying anything negative?
- develop other people's ideas?
- deal with any possible problems?

Share your experience with the class.

Self-assessment

- How successfully have you achieved the lesson outcome? Give yourself a score from 0 (I need more practice) to 5 (I know this well).
- Go to My Self-assessment in MyEnglishLab to reflect on what you have learnt.

6.5 WRITING
Making requests

Lesson outcome Learners can write a simple email making requests to team members.

Lead-in

1 Complete the email with one preposition in each gap. Then compare in pairs.

From: Jason Sparks, Team Leader
To: Product launch team
Re: Next steps for launch

Hi team,

Following the exciting news of our new products, I'm just writing [1]__________ let you know the next steps [2]__________ the product launch [3]__________ two months' time.

Unfortunately, the venue manager emailed yesterday, saying that one [4]__________ the rooms isn't available now. He suggested another room, but first we need to check it has everything we need. If possible, I'd like Ana [5]__________ meet him immediately and see it. Then, if we like it, we'll book it. If we are unhappy [6]__________ it, we will have to find another venue.

Only about 55 percent of guests have replied [7]__________ our invitation. Sarah, would you mind checking the guest list? Please contact everyone who has not replied and remind them. After that, we can inform the catering company of the final numbers.

Finally, we'll need a press release. Gemma and Franz are responsible [8]__________ that. Do you think I could have a copy [9]__________ my desk by the end [10]__________ the week?

Thank you for your hard work. The new schedule is attached.

Best,

Jason

Functional language

2A Complete the phrases in the first column of the table using words and phrases from the email.

Making requests	Alternative wording
If [1]__________ Ana to meet ...	[5]__________ Ana meet ... ?
Sarah, [2]__________ checking the guest list?	Sarah, [6]__________ check the guest list?
[3]__________ contact everyone who hasn't replied.	[7]__________ contact everyone who hasn't replied ... ?
Do you [4]__________ have a copy ... ?	I'd be grateful [8]__________ a copy by the end of the week.

B Complete the alternative in the second column using the phrases in the box.

could   can you   if I could have   would you

page 123 See Grammar reference: Linking words for sequence

T Teacher's resources: extra activities

L The email contains examples of linking words for sequence. Go to MyEnglish Lab for optional grammar work.

TASK

3A Work in pairs. Read the extract from an email on page 139. Rewrite the underlined sections with different ways of saying the same thing.

B Look at the notes on page 129 and write an email of 110–120 words to the conference team.

C Exchange emails with your partner. Which functional language phrases did your partner use? Can you change these for alternative phrases?

Self-assessment

- How successfully have you achieved the lesson outcome? Give yourself a score from 0 (I need more practice) to 5 (I know this well).
- Go to My Self-assessment in MyEnglishLab to reflect on what you have learnt.

Research & development

7

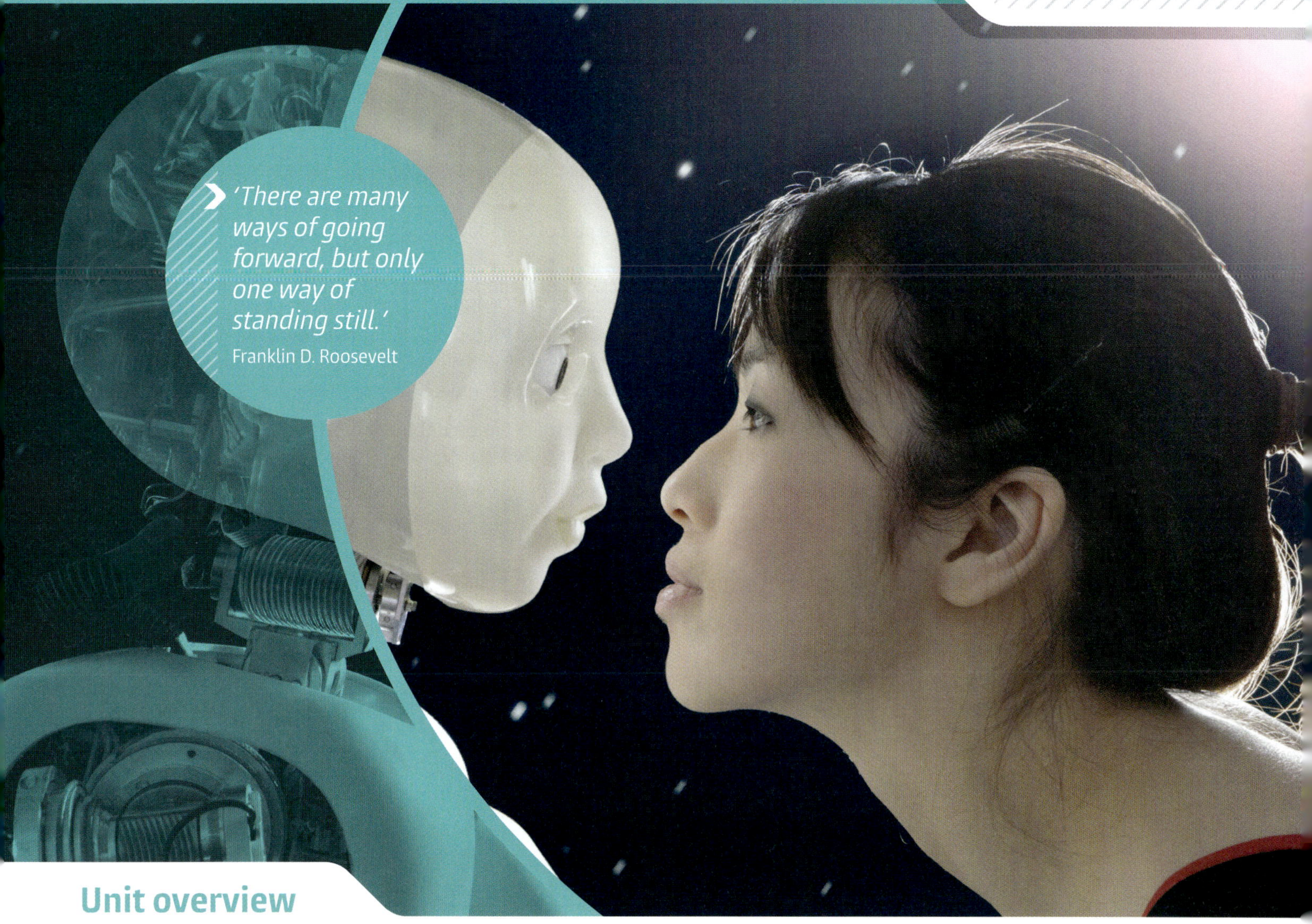

'There are many ways of going forward, but only one way of standing still.'
Franklin D. Roosevelt

Unit overview

7.1	**A nimble company** **Lesson outcome:** Learners can use vocabulary related to research and development.	**Video:** Developing a new product **Vocabulary:** Research and development **Project:** Planning product testing
7.2	**Innovation** **Lesson outcome:** Learners can use *(don't) have to, (don't) need to* and *can('t)* to talk about obligation, necessity and possibility.	**Reading:** Henn na Hotel **Grammar:** *can, have to, need to* **Speaking and writing:** Explanation of a process
7.3	**Communication skills:** Giving explanations **Lesson outcome:** Learners can give clear and effective explanations.	**Video:** Giving explanations **Functional language:** Explaining a procedure clearly and effectively **Task:** Explain how to use an app
7.4	**Business skills:** Dealing with technical problems **Lesson outcome:** Learners can use a range of expressions to signal or deal with technical problems during online meetings.	**Listening:** Problems and solutions in a webinar **Functional language:** Signalling and dealing with technical problems **Task:** Dealing with technical problems in an online meeting
7.5	**Writing:** Preparing slides **Lesson outcome:** Learners can prepare effective slides for a presentation.	**Model text:** Presentation slides **Functional language:** Language used in slides **Grammar:** *Wh-* questions **Task:** Slides for a presentation

Business workshop 7: p.100 | **Review 7:** p.110 | **Pronunciation:** 7.2 *can* and *can't* p.117, 7.3 Phrasing and pausing when giving instructions p.118 | **Grammar reference:** p.123

7.1 A nimble company

Lesson outcome Learners can use vocabulary related to research and development.

Lead-in

1 **Look at the picture. What everyday tasks will be difficult for this man?**

2 **What products do these people use to help them?**

1 people with visual impairment / people who are partially sighted (= can't see well)
2 elderly (= older) people
3 disabled (= not able to walk or use a part of their body) people

VIDEO

3 **Look at the pictures of a product called a Nimble. What do you think it is used for?**

4A 7.1.1 **Watch the first part of the video (00:00–01:26) about developing a new product. Answer the questions.**

1 What does the Nimble do? 2 Who uses the Nimble?

B **Look at the steps. What order do you think Simon did them in? Number the steps in order. Then watch the next part of the video (01:27–03:22) and check your answers.**

- ☐ **a** make the first version of the product
- ☐ **b** make more designs
- ☐ **c** make drawings
- ☐ **d** win a competition
- ☐ **e** test the product
- ☐ **f** choose a final design
- ☐ **g** sell the product
- ☐ **h** make final changes

C **Watch the final part of the video (03:23–03:41). What kind of product is Simon going to make next?**

5 **Work in pairs or groups. Discuss these questions.**

1 Do you know anyone who would use a Nimble?
2 Can you think of other possible uses for it not mentioned or shown in the video?

T Teacher's resources: extra activities

Vocabulary

Research and development

6 **Complete the steps in the R&D process using the words from the video.**

brief	challenges	feedback	improvements	launch	prototype	sketches	solutions

R&D: What design companies do

Receive or create a(n) 1 ___________ that says what a problem is and asks for a solution. →

Think about possible 2 ___________ to the problem. →

Make simple 3 ___________ – develop ideas with pen and paper. ↓

Develop a(n) 4 ___________ – the very first version of the product. ←

Deal with problems and design 5 ___________ – so the product works better. ↓

Make 6 ___________ to the design. ↑

Make final design for testing and 7 ___________ . ←

8 ___________ the product – make it available to buy.

7 **Who does what? Match the sentence halves.**

1 Designers
2 Product testers
3 Consumers

a **purchase** the **finished product**.
b **create** and **develop** new product ideas.
c give feedback on a product's **usefulness**, **design** and **function**.

8 **Complete the text using the words in the box. Some are not used.**

brief	challenge	create	designer	feedback	function	purchase	solution

I've worked as a [1]__________ for a medical products company for about ten years. I chose to work in this field because I wanted to [2]__________ things that help people. My company sometimes develops completely new products, but my main job is trying to improve the [3]__________ of products we already make. It's always exciting for me to get the [4]__________ for a new design. This document usually suggests improvements on a design we already have because of [5]__________ from both doctors and patients. I really enjoy the [6]__________ of improving a product that is already very good.

9 **Work in pairs. Discuss the questions.**

I don't have much experience in research and development.

1 What type of product would you like to be a product tester for? Why?
2 Think of a product you often use, for example your phone. What improvements would you suggest for its design or function?
3 What new products have been launched in the past year or two that you would like to own?

I have some experience in research and development.

1 What product or service did you test? Why did you test it?
2 Who did you work with and what process did you use?
3 Were the results generally positive or negative? Did any of the results surprise you? Why?

T Teacher's resources: extra activities

PROJECT: Planning product testing

10A **Work in pairs or small groups. Look at the three product ideas below. For each one, answer the questions.**

- A water bottle with a small container on the side that can hold a key and a little money.
- A device that reads written text, such as letters or books, and 'speaks' them out loud or stores them as computer files.
- A game based on finance where users have to manage their money well.

1 What problem does the product solve?
2 What type of consumer would use the product? Think about age, men or women, location, interests, and so on.
3 When developing the product, how could the company test it? What type of information do you think they should try to get?
4 Where do you think the company could find people to test it?

B **Choose one of the products above, or think of an idea of your own. Make a plan for developing, testing and launching the product. Explain:**

- what the product will be used for.
- who will use it.
- who will test it.
- where and how you will launch it – the type of stores that will sell it, and how you will advertise it.

C **Give a presentation to another group or the whole class. Explain how you will develop and launch your product.**

Self-assessment

- How successfully have you achieved the lesson outcome? Give yourself a score from 0 (I need more practice) to 5 (I know this well).
- Go to My Self-assessment in MyEnglishLab to reflect on what you have learnt.

7.2 Innovation

Lesson outcome

Learners can use *(don't) have to*, *(don't) need to* and *can('t)* to talk about obligation, necessity and possibility.

Lead-in

1 Work in pairs or small groups. Which of these things have you seen or used in the past year? Where?

Devices

a robot – a machine that can move and do some of the work of a person

an automated kiosk – a machine that provides information or services

Security systems

facial recognition – a security system that recognises users' faces

key card security – door systems that unlock with a plastic card rather than a traditional key

Reading

2 Read the article quickly and answer the questions.

1 What job do robots do in the Henn na Hotel?
2 Why are they good for business?

3 Read the article again and decide if these sentences are *true* (T) or *false* (F).

1 Henn na Hotel guests don't talk to anyone when they check in.
2 The robots communicate through written messages on a computer.
3 In some Henn na Hotels, guests don't need a room key because a camera recognises their face.
4 The hotel is cheaper than other hotels of the same size because it has fewer workers.
5 More hotels in Japan are starting to offer customers new services and experiences.
6 The writer of the article asks if some customers would prefer to have human contact.

Teacher's resources: extra activities

4 Would you enjoy staying at a hotel with robots? Why? / Why not? What are the potential advantages/ disadvantages of staying at a hotel with robots?

NIKKEI ASIAN REVIEW

At Tokyo's Henn na Hotel, robots run the show

A new hotel has opened in Tokyo's stylish Ginza district. The name – *Henn na* – means 'strange' in Japanese, and the hotel is indeed unique. It is run mostly by robots, and a few humans.

Here's how it works: [a]First, guests **have to** give their names to a human receptionist. After that, they're asked to go to an automated kiosk where the robots say hello to them and help them to check in. Impressively, these robots speak four languages – Japanese, English, Mandarin Chinese and Korean. [b]Guests **don't have to** say which language they speak. Cleverly, the robots decide which language to use from the guests' passports. [c]Next, guests **need to** follow the robot's instructions to complete their check-in. Then they get their room key card and a receipt from the kiosk. Finally, they use the key card to open their room door. [d]Guests at other Henn na Hotels **can** decide to use facial recognition. [e]This means they **don't need to** use a key during their stay because they can enter their rooms by simply looking into a camera by the door.

The 98-room hotel has just seven human staff members. [f]Most traditional hotels of the same size **can't** operate with fewer than about 30 workers. This allows the hotel to lower the price of the rooms, too.

In a competitive market, innovation is very important for attracting guests. 'Hotel operators are coming up with new types of facilities with unique characters and services to cater to the guests' lifestyle choices,' hotel industry expert Kiyoshi Tsuchiya said.

There is no doubt that some people will really like this new technology and it will certainly help in a country in which the number of older people is growing fast, but a question remains: Will anyone miss the human touch in what is, after all, the hospitality industry?

Grammar *can, have to, need to*

5 Look at the underlined sentences in the article. Which sentences explain:

1 what's possible. ____
2 what's not possible. ____
3 what's necessary. ____ , ____
4 what's not necessary. ____ , ____

page 123 See Grammar reference: *can, have to, need to*

6 Choose the correct option in italics to complete the sentences.

1 The hotel reception is open 24 hours, so we *can / have to* call them at any time.
2 There's a taxi here now, so we *can't / don't need to* call one.
3 I *need to / don't have to* book a hotel because I'm not staying tonight.
4 You *need to / can* check in before they tell you your room number.
5 They lock the front door at midnight, so you *don't need to / have to* use a key after that.
6 We *can't / don't have to* serve breakfast because the chef hasn't arrived.

Teacher's resources: extra activities

7 Complete the paragraphs about flight check-in using the words and phrases in the boxes.

can	can't	don't have to	need to

At the airport, you [1]__________ check in at the desk by speaking to an employee, you [2]__________ use the self-service check-in kiosk instead. At the kiosk, you [3]__________ type in your name and reservation number. If you don't know your reservation number, you [4]__________ use the kiosk.

can	can't	have to	don't need to

After typing in your reservation number, you [5]__________ put your ID into the machine. After checking your ID, the kiosk prints your boarding pass, and you [6]__________ go directly to the security check and then the departure gate. However, you [7]__________ go directly to the gate if you have a large suitcase. You need to take it to the baggage drop first. If you have plenty of time, you [8]__________ go to the departure gate immediately, you can do some shopping or stop for a cup of coffee.

page 117 See Pronunciation bank: *can* and *can't*

Speaking and writing

8A Work in pairs. Look at the picture of a vending machine and read the information. Use *can*, *have to* and *need to* to talk about what is possible, not possible, necessary and not necessary when using the vending machine.

Note: Right now, this machine takes only cash, not cards. If you only have a card, please go to the shop around the corner. It isn't necessary to have the exact money. The machine will give you change.

Instructions:
1 Put in your money *before* you choose your product.
2 Press the correct button to make your choice. It isn't necessary to hold the button, or to press it more than once.
3 Wait for the product to come out.
4 Press the 'Change' button for change. Otherwise, it won't come out.

B Work with another pair. Take turns explaining how to use the vending machine. Was their explanation the same as yours?

9 Think of another process you're familiar with, for example buying a train ticket at a self-service ticket machine. Write an explanation of how to do it in 75–100 words. Try to use all the words and phrases in the box at least once.

can	can't	have to	don't have to	need to	don't need to

Self-assessment

- How successfully have you achieved the lesson outcome? Give yourself a score from 0 (I need more practice) to 5 (I know this well).
- Go to My Self-assessment in MyEnglishLab to reflect on what you have learnt.

7.3 COMMUNICATION SKILLS
Giving explanations

Lesson outcome Learners can give clear and effective explanations.

Lead-in

1 Work in pairs. Discuss what makes a good presentation.

VIDEO

expenses claim (noun) – a list of the amounts of money an employee spends while doing their job (travel, hotels, etc.) which is paid back by the employer to the employee.

2 ▶ 7.3.1 Azra and Thiago are talking about a training session. Watch the video and answer the questions.

1 What does Thiago dislike about the current expenses system?
2 How does Thiago think the system could be improved?
3 How does Thiago feel about the training session?
4 What kind of training session do you think Thiago would like?

Video A ▶ 7.3.2

3A Watch Shaun explaining how to use *Expenses 220* and answer the questions.

1 What do we learn about *Expenses 220*?
2 What is the problem for Caroline?

B In pairs, discuss the questions.

1 How clear is Shaun's explanation? Why?
2 What is the effect on the audience?
3 How could Shaun improve the way he gives explanations?

Video B ▶ 7.3.3

4A Watch Orla explaining how to use *Expenses 220* and answer the questions.

1 Put the steps for using *Expenses 220* in the correct order (1–7).
   a Choose the currency. ☐
   b Take a photo of the receipt. ☐
   c Submit the report. ☐
   d Enter the date. ☐
   e Click 'Create an expense report'. [1]
   f Choose the type of expense. ☐
   g Enter the expense item. ☐
2 How is Thiago going to learn about the new expenses system?

B In pairs, discuss the questions.

1 How clear is Orla's explanation? Why?
2 What is the effect on the audience?

Tip

When you give explanations, you can help the listener by speaking clearly, using sequencing words to provide structure, checking the listener has understood, giving a reason and examples, and giving the listeners opportunities to ask questions.

C Read the tip. Watch Video B again and tick (✓) the techniques Orla uses.

1 Speaks clearly ☐
2 Uses sequencing words to provide structure ☐
3 Checks the listeners have understood ☐
4 Gives a context or reason ☐
5 Gives examples ☐
6 Gives the audience an opportunity to ask questions ☐

5 ▶ 7.3.4 Watch the Conclusions section of the video and note the four points the speaker makes about giving explanations.

Reflection

6 Think about how good you are at giving explanations. In pairs, discuss how you could improve your skills.

Functional language

Explaining a procedure clearly and effectively

7A **Look at these expressions from the video. Match the beginnings (1–7) with the endings (a–g).**

1 **You start by** clicking *b*
2 **Then, you**
3 **After that,**
4 **The next step is to**
5 **Once you've done**
6 **The last step is to**
7 **When you've completed all the steps,**

a enter the date.
b 'Create an expense report'.
c take a photo of your receipt.
d enter the expense item.
e press 'Submit'.
f choose the type of expense.
g that, choose your currency.

B **Put the expressions in bold from Exercise 7A in the correct place in the table.**

Starting	Ordering	Finishing
	Then, you ...	

C **Add these expressions to the correct section of the table.**

When you finish that, then ... The first thing you do is ... Next, ... Finally, ...
Once you've finished ... The last thing you do is ... To begin, (you should) ...

8A **Match the underlined expressions with their function (1–4).**

OK, so you start by clicking 'Create an expense report'. Do you see that? Then, you enter the expense item – like this: 'hotel bill'. After that, enter the date. Don't enter it manually, just select the 'calendar'; because it's the easiest thing to do ... Any questions so far?

1 Give an example
2 Give an opportunity to ask questions
3 Check the listener has understood
4 Give a reason

B **Look at the videoscript on page 146 and find one more example of each function.**

T Teacher's resources: extra activities

→ page 118 See Pronunciation bank: Phrasing and pausing when giving instructions

TASK

9 **Work in pairs. Take turns to explain a procedure to your partner. Use a procedure of your choice or choose one of the options below.**

Student A: Look at the app below and explain how to book a car.

Student B: Look at the app below and explain how to book a hotel.

When you have finished, discuss how well you managed to explain the procedure in English.

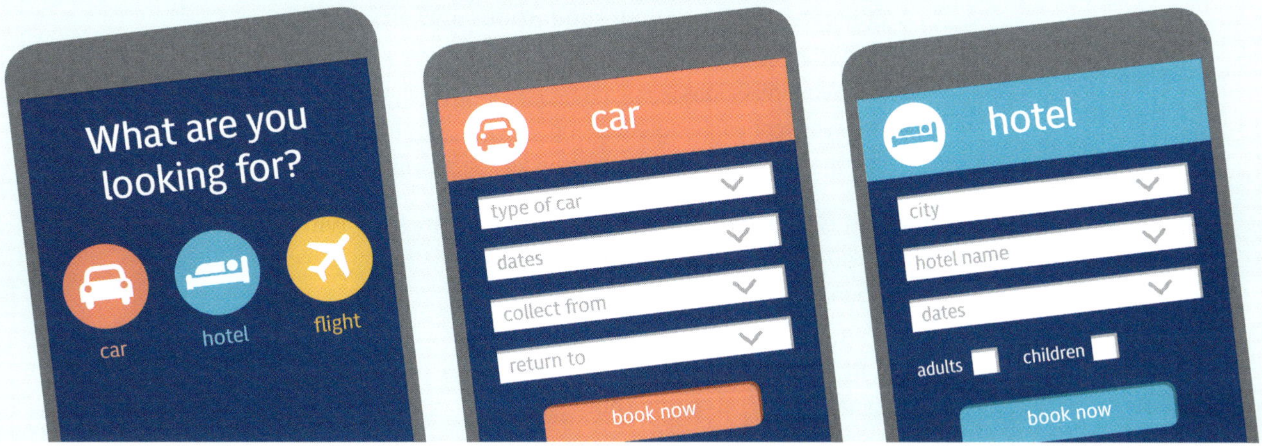

Self-assessment

- How successfully have you achieved the lesson outcome? Give yourself a score from 0 (I need more practice) to 5 (I know this well).
- Go to My Self-assessment in MyEnglishLab to reflect on what you have learnt.

7.4 BUSINESS SKILLS
Dealing with technical problems

Lesson outcome

Learners can use a range of expressions to signal or deal with technical problems during online meetings.

Lead-in

1A In pairs, look at the picture and discuss the questions.

1 Are ground rules necessary during meetings? Why? / Why not?
2 Who should make the ground rules? Why?
3 Do you use ground rules in your meetings or during your English class? Are they successful? Why? / Why not?

ground rules (noun) – basic rules for behaviour during a meeting that everyone agrees to at the start

B Write two or three ground rules for online meetings.

Speak clearly.

Listening

2A Label the pictures with the words in the box.

blank (screen)	cut out	echo	hang up	mute button	volume settings

1 ___________

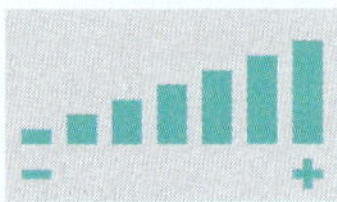

2 ___________

3 ___________

4 ___________

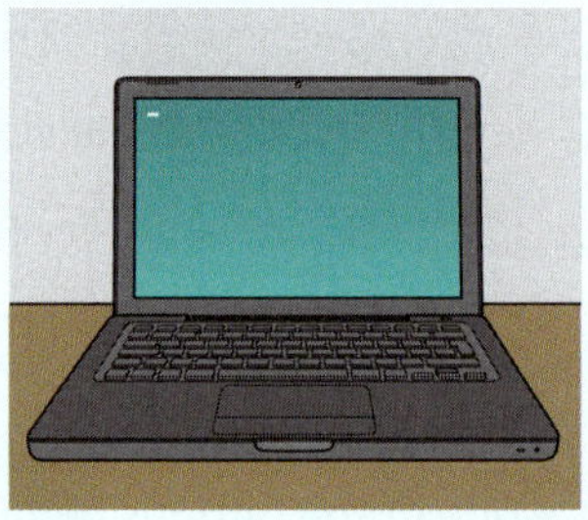

5 ___________

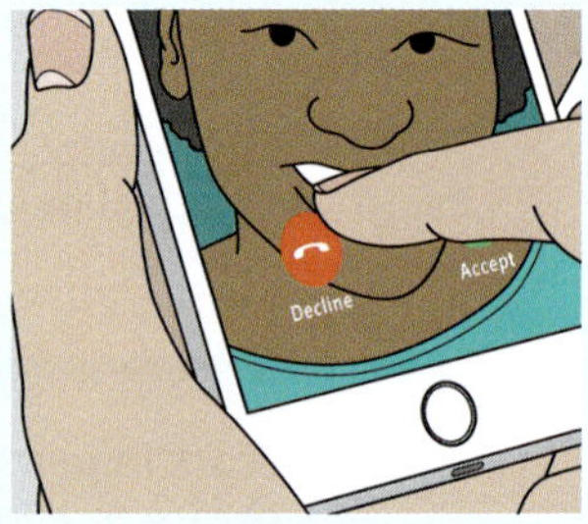

6 ___________

B 🔊 7.01 Sam's team are participating in a webinar. Before the Q&A (question and answer) session, Sam sets some ground rules. Listen and complete the rules. Compare them with your suggestions in Exercise 1B.

1 Give your ___________ and division ___________ you speak.
2 Keep your questions ___________, so everyone has the chance to ___________.
3 Help your colleagues by speaking ___________ and ___________.
4 Use the mute ___________ to stop any background ___________.

3A 🔊 7.02 Listen and match the participants (1–4) with the correct problem(s) (a–f). Use one of the problems twice.

1 Donna	a background noise
2 Paul	b bad internet connection
3 Karl	c blank screen
4 Lena	d cutting out
	e echo
	f low volume

B In pairs, note down the solution to each problem in Exercise 3A. Listen again and check.

T Teacher's resources: extra activities

Functional language

Signalling and dealing with technical problems

4A Put the words in the correct order to make sentences or expressions from the audio.

1 your / switched on / webcam / have you / ?
Have you switched on your webcam?

2 is / your / blank / screen

3 you / out / cutting / keep

4 is / bad / the / connection

5 call you back / would you mind / hanging up / and I'll / ?

6 we can't / I'm afraid / very well / hear you / either

7 to the microphone / could you / move closer / ?

8 please / if you can / your volume settings / just check / ?

9 an echo / bit of / there's a

10 away from / your computer / mobile phone / can you move / your / ?

11 can hear / background noise / I / a lot of

12 the mute button / using / would you mind / ?

B Write S (*signalling a problem*) or D (*dealing with a problem*) next to each sentence in Exercise 4A.

Have you switched on your webcam? D *Your screen is blank. S*

C In pairs, practise signalling and dealing with technical problems. Use the expressions in Exercise 4A. There may be more than one possible combination.

A: *I can hear a lot of background noise.*
B: *Can you move your mobile phone away from your computer?*

TASK

5A Work in small groups. You are going to hold an online meeting where you will have to deal with some technical problems. Choose a topic for your meeting from the list, or use your own ideas.

1 Organising the next office party.
2 Choosing a guest speaker for the next conference.
3 Ideas for your company's next team-building activity.

B Student A: Look at page 134; Student B: Look at page 130; Student C: Look at page 137. Read the information. Add any further information if necessary.

C Take a few minutes to prepare, then hold your meeting. During the meeting, choose a new problem from the cards on page 138 every 60 seconds. Use expressions from Exercise 4 to signal and deal with the technical problem on the card.

D Choose a different topic, change roles (A, B and C) and hold the meeting again.

E When you have finished, discuss how easy or difficult it was to manage technical problems during an online meeting in English. Share your experience with another group.

Self-assessment

- How successfully have you achieved the lesson outcome? Give yourself a score from 0 (I need more practice) to 5 (I know this well).
- Go to My Self-assessment in MyEnglishLab to reflect on what you have learnt.

Preparing slides

Lesson outcome Learners can prepare effective slides for a presentation.

Lead-in

1A 7.03 **Listen to the start of a presentation and number the slides in the correct order.**

A SCHEDULE ☐

Month 1
- decide on [1]__________
- choose material

Month 2
- start [2]__________
- send out press release

Month 3
- launch rebranded product [3]__________

B COLOUR ☐

- keeping [4]__________
- making it brighter
- adding 1 or 2 more [5]__________

C OVERVIEW ☐

- [6]__________?
  - negative customer feedback
  - falling sales
  - eco-friendly packaging
- [7]__________?
  - colour change
  - use of recycled materials
- [8]__________?
  - three months

B **Listen again and complete the slides. Use only one word in each gap.**

Functional language

2 **Look at the tips for preparing slides and find examples for 1–5 in the slides in Exercise 1.**

Tips	Details
Use similar grammar forms on each slide	• infinitives, e.g. [1]__________ • *-ing* form of the verb, e.g. [2]__________ • nouns, e.g. [3]__________ • other, e.g. Past Simple, comparatives
Drop articles	• definite (*the*), e.g. [4]__________ • indefinite (*a/an*), e.g. [5]__________
Check spelling	• use a dictionary where necessary • don't always trust your computer's spell checker
Use bullet points	• use (●) for main lists • use (–) for secondary lists
Use images	• consider using a graph, photo or diagram • keep people looking at you, not the slide

T Teacher's resources: extra activities

L The presentation contains examples of *Wh-* questions. Go to MyEnglishLab for optional grammar work.

→ page 124 See Grammar reference: *Wh-* questions

TASK

3A **Work in pairs. Look at the examples of three bad slides on page 140. Discuss ways in which you could improve them using the five tips above.**

B 7.04 **Listen to the presentation about the redesign of a best-selling product and read the audioscript on page 151. Prepare three slides to go with the presentation.**

C **Exchange slides with your partner. Which of the five things in the table above did your partner do? How well did your partner do them?**

Self-assessment

- How successfully have you achieved the lesson outcome? Give yourself a score from 0 (I need more practice) to 5 (I know this well).
- Go to My Self-assessment in MyEnglishLab to reflect on what you have learnt.

Green solutions

8

> 'The future will either be green or not at all.'
> Bob Brown, Australian ex-politician and environmentalist

Unit overview

8.1	**Green business** **Lesson outcome:** Learners can use vocabulary related to environmental issues.	**Video:** Tourism in Punta de Lobos **Vocabulary:** The environment **Project:** Protecting the environment
8.2	**Transport solutions** **Lesson outcome:** Learners can use *should, shouldn't* and *could* to give and ask for advice and suggestions.	**Listening:** An interview about public transport **Grammar:** *should* and *could* for advice and suggestions **Writing:** Email offering advice and suggestions
8.3	**Communication skills:** Giving and receiving feedback **Lesson outcome:** Learners can use a range of expressions to give and respond to feedback.	**Video:** Feedback in a review meeting **Functional language:** Giving and receiving feedback **Task:** Practise giving and receiving feedback
8.4	**Business skills:** Managing questions **Lesson outcome:** Learners can use a variety of expressions to manage the question and answer session of a presentation.	**Listening:** A Q&A session in a presentation **Functional language:** Managing a Q&A session **Task:** Roleplay a Q&A session
8.5	**Writing:** An intranet update **Lesson outcome:** Learners can organise information in a short intranet update giving details of work-related plans.	**Model text:** An intranet update **Functional language:** Language for giving an update **Grammar:** Future forms **Task:** Write an intranet update

Business workshop 8: p.102 | **Review 8:** p.111 | **Pronunciation:** 8.1 Vowel sounds: /ɜː/, /ʊ/, /uː/ and /əʊ/ 8.2 *should* and *could* p.118 | **Grammar reference:** p.124

8.1 Green business

Lesson outcome
Learners can use vocabulary related to environmental issues.

Lead-in

1 Discuss the questions.

1 What are some of the most beautiful natural places to visit in your country or region? Use the words in the box to help you.

beach	cave	cliffs	forest	lake	mountain
national park	river	ocean	volcano	waterfall	

2 Do these places get many visitors? What do people like to do at these places?

BBC VIDEO

2A 8.1.1 **Punta de Lobos is a popular tourist destination in Chile. Watch the first part of a travel programme (0:00–0:49) without the sound. Tick (✓) the things you see.**

☐ beach	☐ cliffs	☐ surfers
☐ buildings	☐ fence	☐ traffic
☐ cacti	☐ rocks	☐ waves

B Would you like to visit a place like this? What would you do there?

3 Watch the complete video and number the information in the order it is mentioned.

a The work of the Punta de Lobos Foundation
b Why Punta de Lobos is important for Chile
c The opinion of one hotel owner
d The number of visitors to Punta de Lobos
e Plans for construction projects

4 Watch the video again and decide if these sentences are *true* (T) or *false* (F).

1 Five thousand visitors go to Punta de Lobos every day in summer.
2 Construction plans include a small surf resort.
3 The Punta de Lobos Foundation wants to stop these plans.
4 It also wants to stop the public going to the cliffs.
5 One problem was there was no road to Punta de Lobos.
6 The Foundation built toilets and also a fence on the cliff.
7 The hotel at Punta de Lobos beach has 40 rooms.
8 Punta de Lobos is a good example for other projects in Chile.

Teacher's resources: alternative video and extra activities

5 Work in pairs or small groups. Discuss the questions.

1 What are some of the problems created by the popularity of Punta de Lobos?
2 In what ways is the hotel on the beach special?
3 What are the advantages and disadvantages of big building plans in popular tourist areas?

→ page 118 See Pronunciation bank: Vowel sounds: /ɜː/, /ʊ/, /uː/ and /əʊ/

Vocabulary

The environment

6 Look at these extracts from the video. What do the words in bold mean? Match them with the definitions (a–d).

1 They've put a fence along the cliff to **protect** it from visitors' feet.
2 Some local businesses see **conservation** as important, too.
3 (It was) … Designed to have as little **impact** as possible …
4 … it was built with local and **recycled** materials.

a created from previously used materials by a special process
b keep someone or something safe from harm, damage or illness
c a big change in someone or something caused by an event, situation, etc.
d keeping natural things such as animals or plants safe from harm

7 **Replace the underlined phrase in each sentence with a word in the box.**

damage destruction environment pollution reduction

1 The things that people do have negative effects on the land, air and water on Earth.
2 Traffic is responsible for air becoming dangerously dirty in many cities.
3 Plastic is causing serious negative effects to oceans and marine life.
4 A decrease in the amount of water we use is very important for the planet.
5 The cutting of trees in forests will cause the death of many types of animals and plants.

8 **Complete the table with the correct verb forms. Use a dictionary to help you if necessary.**

Noun	Verb
conservation	
damage	
destruction	
protection	
pollution	
recycling	
reduction	

T Teacher's resources: extra activities

9A **Choose the correct option to complete the questions.**

1 What things do you usually *impact* / *recycle*? Could you do more?
2 What are some of the causes of *impact* / *pollution* where you live?
3 What are some typical ways we can *reduce* / *destroy* water and energy use?
4 What are some of the best ways to *protect* / *damage* the environment?
5 Do you think we should *reduce* / *damage* traffic in cities? How?

B **Work in pairs or small groups. Discuss the questions in Exercise 9A.**

PROJECT: Protecting the environment

10A **Work in three groups. You are going to prepare a questionnaire about habits to find out who is protecting the environment. Add two or three more questions to your card.**

Group A:
Habits at home

- Do you switch off lights when you're not using them?
- Do you unplug TVs, computers, etc. when you're not using them?
- How do you conserve water?
- ______
- ______
- ______

Group B:
Habits where you work/study

- How do you usually get to where you work/study?
- Do you often use air conditioning and/or heating?
- Do you use recycled paper?
- ______
- ______
- ______

Group C:
Habits on holiday

- How many times a year do you take a plane?
- How much driving do you do on holiday?
- Do you use clean towels every day in your hotel?
- ______
- ______

B **Regroup and work in groups of three with one student from each group, A, B and C. Interview each other about your habits.**

C **Report back to your original group. Who is doing the most to protect the environment a) at home, b) where they work/study, c) on holiday? Give reasons for your answers.**

Self-assessment

- How successfully have you achieved the lesson outcome? Give yourself a score from 0 (I need more practice) to 5 (I know this well).
- Go to My Self-assessment in MyEnglishLab to reflect on what you have learnt.

8.2 Transport solutions

Lesson outcome Learners can use *should*, *shouldn't* and *could* to give and ask for advice and suggestions.

Lead-in

1A **Do you live in the countryside or a city or town? How happy are you with the local transport system?**

B **Check the meaning of the phrases in the box. Which of these do you have in the area where you live?**

car-sharing scheme congestion charge cycle lanes electric buses public bike hire scheme traffic jams underground/metro trains

Listening

2 8.01 **Listen to a radio interview with Kyra Sharma, an expert in public transport. Why has she written her book?**

1 to present technological solutions to transport problems
2 to suggest why cities need good public transport systems
3 to say that governments should spend more on road building

3 **Listen again and complete the information on the back cover of Kyra Sharma's book. Use one to three words in each gap.**

Kyra Sharma is a university lecturer and [1]___________ in public transport.

This book shows

- why the [2]___________ is the worst way to travel in cities and the least efficient use of [3]___________ .
- how congestion on [4]___________ causes serious air pollution and [5]___________ problems.

In *Travel Chaos*, Sharma studies the transport solutions that [6]___________ could give but says that these better ways to travel and power our vehicles are [7]___________ .

Dr Sharma wants governments to [8]___________ on public transport and gives examples from developed Asian countries such as Hong Kong, Korea and Singapore. The book also looks at ways European cities are using [9]___________ in public transport and promoting walking and cycling.

Dr Sharma believes our cities need solutions that offer a good [10]___________ to the people living and working in them.

Delacroix Press

TRAVEL CHAOS SHARMA

Delacroix Press

KYRA SHARMA

Teacher's resources: extra activities

4 **Work in pairs or small groups. Discuss these questions.**

1 What are some advantages and disadvantages of private cars and public transport? Complete the table.

	Advantages	Disadvantages
Private transport	*convenient*	
Public transport	*saves money on fuel and looking after the car*	

2 What arguments would you use to say that cars in cities are useful?

Grammar *should* and *could* for advice and suggestions

5A Match each extract (1–4) from the radio interview with the phrase (a–d) that has a similar meaning.

1 ... people shouldn't drive in cities.
2 ... other cities could use a similar method ...
3 ... they should simply spend more on public transport.
4 How should governments plan urban mobility?

a I think this is a really good idea.
b I think this is a really bad idea.
c I think this is a possible option.
d Please give me your ideas.

B Underline the words in extracts 1–4 in Exercise 5A which give the meanings a–d. What verb form comes after all these words?

→ page 124 See Grammar reference: *should* and *could* for advice and suggestions
→ page 118 See Pronunciation bank: *should* and *could*

6A Match the situations (1–5) with the advice and suggestions (a–e).

1 I don't know what I want to study at university.
2 I'd like to get a summer job.
3 It takes me a long time to get to work every day.
4 I'm very busy and don't get enough exercise these days.
5 I have an important job interview next week.

a You shouldn't arrive late for that.
b I think you should talk to your teachers.
c You should walk to work. It's not far.
d You could move closer to where you work.
e You could call some hotels and campsites.

B Complete the sentences using *should, shouldn't* and *could*. There may be more than one possible answer. Then match the sentences with the situations in Exercise 6A.

1 You / take your CV to shops and restaurants in town.
2 You / think about the job you want to do in the future.
3 You / lie when they ask you questions.
4 You / ask if you can work from home some days.
5 You / work so hard. It's bad for your health.

C What other advice or suggestions would you give the person in each situation in Exercise 6A? Write one reply for each situation using *should, shouldn't* or *could*.

D Work in small groups. Compare your answers to Exercise 6C. What are the best ideas?

7A Work in pairs. Write three questions using *should* to ask for advice or suggestions about work, studies or travel.

I feel very nervous when I give presentations. What should I do?

B Exchange your questions with another pair. Write answers to the questions using *should* and *could*.

C Read the replies. Which are the best suggestions?

T Teacher's resources: extra activities

Writing

8 You received this email from a work colleague in another country. Write your reply in 80–100 words giving advice and suggestions.

Hello,

I'll be in your country this spring for a two-day conference in the capital. After that I'd like to travel around the country for ten days with my family. What places do you think we should visit? Should we hire a car or take public transport? I'd appreciate any advice and suggestions you can offer me.

Best wishes,

Jenny

Self-assessment

- How successfully have you achieved the lesson outcome? Give yourself a score from 0 (I need more practice) to 5 (I know this well).
- Go to My Self-assessment in MyEnglishLab to reflect on what you have learnt.

8.3 COMMUNICATION SKILLS
Giving and receiving feedback

Lesson outcome Learners can use a range of expressions to give and respond to feedback.

Lead-in

feedback (noun) – information about how well you are doing your job, and advice about how you could do it better

1A Read the definition and think about the questions.

1 How often do you receive feedback from your supervisor / English teacher?
2 How do you usually feel when you receive feedback?
3 What is most difficult for you when you give feedback to others?

B Work in pairs. Look at the diagram and discuss the questions.

1 Begin with some positive feedback.
2 Praise the employee's strong points.
3 Compliment the employee where necessary.
4 Give the corrective feedback.
5 Remind the employee of their strong points.
6 Thank the employee, offer support for the areas for improvement and finish on a positive note.

1 What do you think 'corrective feedback' means?
2 Why are both types of feedback (positive and corrective) so important for a) employees and b) employers?
3 What do you think about this model for giving feedback?

VIDEO

2A 8.3.1 **Thiago is thinking about his six-month review meeting with Orla. Watch the video and answer the questions.**

1 Why does Thiago seem nervous about his review meeting?
2 Why was Thiago annoyed with Della?
3 What was Della's reason for her actions?

B In pairs, discuss what feedback Thiago might receive, based on the three flashback scenes.

Video A 8.3.2

3A Watch Video A and answer the questions.

1 What does Thiago think about his performance during the first six months?
2 Note down three positive things that Orla says about Thiago.
3 Thiago is usually good with people. What example of this does Orla give?

B In pairs, discuss the questions.

1 What type of feedback does Orla start with?
2 What does Orla do at the beginning of the meeting?
3 Which parts of the diagram in Exercise 1B does Orla use to give the feedback?

Video B 8.3.3

4A Watch Video B. Tick (✓) the points Orla wants Thiago to improve.

1 his admin skills ☐
2 his management skills ☐
3 his relationship with colleagues ☐
4 his report-writing skills ☐
5 his time-management skills ☐

B In pairs, discuss the questions.

1 After giving feedback about each point in Exercise 4A, what does Orla do?
2 After talking about Della, what does Orla ask Thiago to do?
3 Does Thiago respond positively or negatively to the corrective feedback?

5 8.3.4 **Watch the Conclusions section of the video and note the four points the speaker mentions about giving and receiving corrective feedback.**

Reflection

6 Think about how good you are at giving and receiving positive and corrective feedback. In pairs, discuss how you could improve your skills.

Functional language

Giving and receiving feedback

7 Complete the expressions for giving feedback using the words in the box.

could improve	for improvement	great with	have	~~pleased with~~	were

1 We're ___*pleased with*___ your progress.
2 You're ______________ technology.
3 You ______________ very supportive.
4 You ______________ an excellent sense of humour.
5 There are a couple of areas ______________ .
6 We think you ______________ your admin skills.

8A Match the expressions (1–4) with the correct heading (a–d).

1 Is that OK with you?
2 The reason we're concerned is ...
3 However, I have to point out some areas for development.
4 Would that be a fair assessment?

a Preparing someone for the feedback
b Asking for consent (agreement)
c Giving clarification
d Encouraging self-assessment

B Match the expressions in the box with the correct heading (a–d) in Exercise 8A.

A good example of that was ... How did you feel it went? We're worried because ...
Let me explain the process. Let me explain why we're concerned. How about that?
One example of this is ... What are your thoughts? What do you think about ... ?
We'll start with the positive feedback, then we'll move on to areas for improvement.

C Put the words in the correct order. Which expressions could you use to respond to positive feedback or corrective feedback or both? Write P (*positive*), C (*corrective*) or B (*both*) for each one.

1 appreciate / comments / I / thanks / your *I appreciate your comments, thanks. B*
2 mostly / assessment / agree with / I / your
3 but ... / interesting / an / that's / idea
4 to try / in the future / I'd like / and do that
5 for me / this is / I accept that / a problem / sometimes
6 glad / that / to hear / I'm /
7 helpful / very / your feedback / thank you / is
8 to / good / that's / know

T Teacher's resources: extra activities

TASK

9A Work in pairs. Student A: Look at page 141; Student B: Look at page 139. Read the information about your partner and prepare for their feedback meeting.

B When giving feedback, remember to follow these steps:

1 Prepare the listener for feedback.
2 Ask the listener for consent (agreement).
3 Give clarification.
4 Encourage the listener to carry out a self-assessment.

C How easy or difficult was it to give and receive feedback in English?

Self-assessment

- How successfully have you achieved the lesson outcome? Give yourself a score from 0 (I need more practice) to 5 (I know this well).
- Go to My Self-assessment in MyEnglishLab to reflect on what you have learnt.

8.4 BUSINESS SKILLS
Managing questions

Lesson outcome Learners can use a variety of expressions to manage the question and answer session of a presentation.

Lead-in

1 In small groups, discuss these pieces of advice for managing a Q&A session. Which ones do you think are the most useful? Why?

- Breathe deeply.
- Wait a few seconds before you answer a question.
- Ask a colleague/friend to attend the presentation to give you support.
- Prepare to answer possible questions before the meeting.
- Ask a colleague to ask a question you prepared before the meeting.
- Repeat the question to check you have understood and make sure the audience have heard it.

Listening

2A Work in small groups. Brainstorm two or three advantages of working in an open-plan office and a closed office.

Open-plan offices encourage colleagues to work together. / It's easier to concentrate in a closed office.

B 8.02 **Elena and Ted have just given a presentation to colleagues. The company they work for is moving to a new site. Listen to the first part of the Q&A session and match the names (1–3) with the topic(s) (a–d).**

1 Steve
2 Keira
3 Ben

a travel to other sites
b a place to hold meetings
c the timing of the move
d some staff moving to the temporary office

C Listen again and decide if the statements are *true* (T) or *false* (F). In pairs, correct the false statements.

1. Staff will no longer have their own office.
2. There will be one meeting room on every second floor at the new site.
3. Most of the staff will move to the new site in May.
4. Staff will have to take a thirty-minute bus trip to reach the temporary site.
5. Ben will not be moving to the temporary site.

3A 8.03 **Listen to the next part of the Q&A session and answer the questions.**

1. How does Jen feel about the move to the new site?
2. What is she worried about the most?
3. How does Elena manage Jen's question?
4. Why do staff members need storage space?
5. What does Jen want to do?

B In pairs, discuss the questions.

1. Which two strategies in Exercise 1 did Elena and Ted use to manage the Q&A session?
2. What other strategies do *you* think Elena used during the Q&A session?

Functional language

Managing a Q&A session

4A Complete the expressions from the Q&A session with the phrases in the box.

answer your question	have a question	is about	
good question	not sure	that right	you're asking

1. Does anyone ________ ________ ________?
2. So the question ________ ________ meeting rooms.
3. It's a(n) ________ ________, thanks.
4. Does that ________ ________ ________?
5. Sorry, ________ ________ how we allocate space. Is ________ ________?
6. I'm ________ ________ I can answer that.

B **Put the expressions from Exercise 4A into the correct section in the table.**

Inviting (more) questions	1 ______ Are there any (more) questions?
Repeating the question	2 ______ So, Ben asked who's moving to Oxford Road.
Thanking	3 ______ Thanks for your question.
Checking/Clarifying	4 ______ I'm sorry, I'm not sure what you mean.
Making sure the question is answered	5 ______ Does that help?
Saying you can't answer the question	6 ______ Sorry, I don't have the answer. Maybe I can email you.

5 **Work in pairs. Use one or two expressions from Exercise 4 to respond to each question.**

1 I don't understand why we have to move to new offices. Can you explain the reasons?
2 I'm worried about noise. What happens if I can't concentrate on my work?
3 Can you explain exactly how you've chosen our desks? What if I don't like where I'm sitting?

T Teacher's resources: extra activities

TASK

6A **Work in groups of three. You are going to take part in a Q&A session following a presentation. Read the scenario and decide who will be the Presenter, Questioner 1 and Questioner 2.**

Scenario

Your team is moving to a new building where they will have to work in an open-plan office. An informal presentation to explain the move has taken place and now it is time for the Q&A session. Not everyone agrees with the idea.

Here are the benefits of an open-plan office for the company. You may also think of some of your own.

improved communication and opportunities to work together, savings on equipment costs, reduced heating bills, better work processes, more creativity

Here are ideas the company have thought about. You may also think of some of your own.

closed meeting rooms, allowing staff to work from home when necessary, a system to reserve meeting rooms online, a plan for everyone to change desks once a year, a relaxation area with a TV, table tennis competitions and similar activities to encourage team-building

B **Presenters: Look at page 136 and read your information. Work as a group to think about what questions Questioners 1 and 2 might ask, and prepare possible answers. Questioners 1 and 2: Look at page 137 and read the information for Q&A session 1. Work as a group to prepare some questions.**

C **Perform the Q&A session as a Presenter and the Questioners. Then change roles and repeat the activity with Q&A sessions 2 (page 141) and 3 (page 139). Make sure that a different person leads each session.**

D **When you have finished, discuss how easy or difficult it was to manage the Q&A session in English. Share your experience with another group.**

Self-assessment

- How successfully have you achieved the lesson outcome? Give yourself a score from 0 (I need more practice) to 5 (I know this well).
- Go to My Self-assessment in MyEnglishLab to reflect on what you have learnt.

WRITING
An intranet update

Lesson outcome

Learners can organise information in a short intranet update giving details of work-related plans.

Lead-in

1 Read the intranet update. Choose the correct option in italics. Then compare in pairs.

Proposal for going green

As you [1]*know / see*, we are trying to make the company [2]*more / much* green. We asked all our staff for [3]*suggestions / offers* and had meetings to discuss the ideas. We are now ready to [4]*propose / intend* a number of changes as a [5]*reason / result* of our research.

[6]*Firstly / Originally*, we are going to change all our vehicles and buy electric vehicles over the next two years. This will reduce pollution from petrol. Secondly, we are going to [7]*introduce / make* a new manufacturing process because this will mean there is less waste and pollution from the factory. We also plan to use less plastic in our offices and try to use greener materials.

We are therefore [8]*holding / attending* a meeting next week to explain how we are going to [9]*make / put* these proposals into action. We will answer any [10]*problems / questions* then.

Functional language

2 Complete the table below with the words and phrases in the box.

also plan   are going to   as you know   can explain   finally   has decided   is arranging   is planning to   ready   therefore   this will reduce   will answer

Purpose of update (Paragraph 1)	1 ________ , we are trying to ... We are now 2 ________ to ... The company 3 ________ to make some changes.
Further details (Paragraph 2)	Firstly, we 4 ________ change ... 5 ________ the amount of ... We 6 ________ to use less plastic ... The Team Director 7 ________ increase the number of teams. 8 ________ , we will move our office to ...
Next steps (Paragraph 3)	We are 9 ________ holding a meeting next week to ... Consequently, the company 10 ________ more training. We 11 ________ any questions ... We 12 ________ everything to you then.

T Teacher's resources: extra activities

L The intranet update contains examples of future forms. Go to MyEnglishLab for optional grammar work.

page 125 See Grammar reference: Future forms

TASK

3A Work in pairs. Look at the informal intranet update on page 140 and find seven language mistakes. Think about grammar, spelling, missing words and unnecessary words.

B Look at the notes on page 140. Write an intranet update in 120–140 words and include a suitable title.

C Exchange proposals with your partner. Did your partner organise the intranet update into three paragraphs? Did your partner use phrases from the functional language and think of a suitable title?

Self-assessment

- How successfully have you achieved the lesson outcome? Give yourself a score from 0 (I need more practice) to 5 (I know this well).
- Go to My Self-assessment in MyEnglishLab to reflect on what you have learnt.

Business Workshops

BUSINESS WORKSHOP 1 A business trip

Lesson outcome Learners can discuss the purpose of a business trip, can agree on, make and amend travel plans, and can deal with travel problems.

Background

1 Read the background and answer the questions with a partner.

1 Which industry does JK Talent Spot work in?
2 Which country does Junko Kimura want to do business in?
3 Would JK's performers be popular in your country? Why? / Why not?

BACKGROUND

JK Talent Spot is a small talent management agency based in Osaka, Japan. The company's owner, Junko Kimura, manages six Japanese artists – four bands and two singer-songwriters. All six of the acts are popular in the Osaka area. However, instead of touring Japan to make her acts more popular, Junko wants to take them to Australia to discover audiences and create new fans there. Junko and her assistant, Itsuki Shibata, are researching the music market in Australia and looking for contacts there who can help them introduce their artists to the market. So far, they've discovered that J-pop – popular Japanese music – is well-known in Australia. They've also learnt that there are talent agencies and record companies in several Australian cities looking for new acts. Their next step is to choose someone to contact.

Making contacts

2A Read the website. Match each paragraph (1–6) with an OzMusicNow service (a–f).

a Organising concerts, travel and hotels for bands ____
b Getting people to talk to their friends about new music ____
c Organising business trips to Australia ____
d Introducing bands from abroad to Australians ____
e Helping singers and bands become good businesspeople ____
f Recording concerts ____

T Teacher's resources: extra activities

B Is OzMusicNow a good contact for Junko at JK Talent Spot? Why? / Why not?

OZMUSICNOW PROMOTIONS

Got talent? We'll help you show the world!

[1]OzMusicNow Promotions specialises in helping new international artists find audiences in Australia. We offer:

[2]The best tour promotion and management in the country
We work with the best live music venues in Australia's biggest cities. We can get your acts on stage in front of thousands of fans and take care of every detail of tour planning. We promote every event with advertisements online, on the radio and on posters and billboards.

[3]The highest quality live video production
Live tours are only the beginning. Our team of video producers create high-quality tour videos that you can upload to your online video channel to find even more fans. Today, Australia. Tomorrow, the world!

[4]The most active social media management
Advertising is useful, but the best way to spread the word about new music is online. Our social media accounts are followed by industry experts who are specifically interested in new music – including top music journalists. And when they find something they like, people share it.

[5]The most complete career guidance available
Creating great music and getting more fans is only the beginning. A big hit can be amazing. But what happens after that? Artists need to manage their time, money and image to develop and grow a career. We can help.

[6]Don't wait! Come and see us and we'll build an Australian future together in music!
Musicians and managers – contact us now and we'll help you plan a visit Down Under* to get to know us better!

** ***Oz** and **Down Under** are both nicknames for Australia.

A business trip

3A BW 1.01 **Junko is now planning a visit to Australia. Listen to her phone call with Sam from OzMusicNow. Complete Sam's notes for the phone call.**

1 Arrival date? ______________
2 How many hotel rooms? ______________
3 After Sydney, visit Brisbane or Melbourne? ______________
4 Hotel choice in second city? ______________
5 Departure date? ______________

T Teacher's resources: extra activities

B Read Sam's email to Junko. Correct the mistakes. Then listen again and check your answers.

Dear Junko,

Thanks for the call yesterday. I'm writing to confirm your travel arrangements for your Australia visit next month. Here's the itinerary:

June 1 Osaka–Sydney flight
Hotel: Sydney Downtown (2 nights, 2 rooms)

June 2 Morning: Meet OzMusicNow in Sydney offices
Afternoon–evening: Visit Sydney music venues

June 3 Morning: Sydney–Brisbane flight
Afternoon–evening: Visit Brisbane music venues
Hotel: Brisbane town centre hotel

June 4 Brisbane–Sydney–Osaka flight

Let me know if you have any questions or comments. We can help you arrange the bookings, if necessary.

Best regards,

Sam

4 BW 1.02 **As she flies to Australia, Junko is connected to the wi-fi on the plane, so she can send voice messages. Listen to her exchange with Sam and answer the questions.**

1 What is the problem?
2 What caused it?
3 What is Sam going to do?

TASK
Rearrange plans

5A Work in pairs. Read the following information. Make a new travel plan for Junko.

JK Talent Spot is paying for the trip. The company isn't rich, and Junko tries to save money when she can. On the other hand, this is a business trip, so she wants to use her time well in Australia. Remember that her original plan was to have a meeting with Sam the morning of 3rd June. For each item (1–3) compare the two options, then choose one.

***A:** The airport bus is cheaper than a taxi.*
***B:** Yes, but taking a taxi is easier and a lot faster.*

1 Travel to Canberra accommodation
  a Number 11 bus – waiting time up to 20 minutes, journey time 20 minutes – $4.90
  b Taxi – waiting time about 2 minutes, journey time 12 minutes – $30
2 Hotel in Canberra
  a Canberra Lodge Hotel – near city centre, very quiet – $150
  b Canberra Luxury Suites – in city centre, near live music venues – $220
3 Morning travel from Canberra to Sydney
  a Train (first class) – departs Canberra 7.00 a.m., arrives Sydney 11.10 a.m. – $80
  b Coach – departs Canberra 10.00 a.m., arrives Sydney 1.30 p.m. – $45

B With your partner, write an email to Junko explaining the new travel plan.

Remember to:

- use the choices you made in Exercise 5A.
- use the email in Exercise 3B as a model.
- apologise for the situation, tell her not to worry, and explain what you're sending.
- list the details of the new itinerary, with dates (today is 2nd June).
- tell her you'll meet her at the coach or train station in Sydney.
- ask if she has any questions or needs more help.

Self-assessment

- How successfully have you achieved the lesson outcome? Give yourself a score from 0 (I need more practice) to 5 (I know this well).
- Go to My Self-assessment in MyEnglishLab to reflect on what you have learnt.

A new location

Lesson outcome

Learners can identify the main points in short presentations about business locations and participate in a short meeting to choose a new location.

Background

1 Read the background and answer the questions with a partner.

1. Why do EM Animations need to leave London?
2. Why is Berlin a good place for the company to go?
3. What situation(s) would make you want to move to another country to live and work?

BACKGROUND

Ewa Kowalska and Mark Anderson started EM Animation Studios four years ago. They began their animation partnership at university, where Ewa studied business and Mark studied animation. After finishing university, they moved to London, where they have a small team of staff. They work on many animation projects including advertisements, software apps and video games. The company now needs more space but rents for bigger offices in the capital are too expensive for them.

Ewa, now CEO, is thinking about moving the company to Berlin. With a population of 3.5 million, Berlin is an exciting, international city in the heart of Europe which offers excellent value. EM Animation Studios will still be able to hire great people from all over the world. Also, with the money they save on rent and other costs, they can attract staff with better salaries and invest more in their business.

Offices for rent

2A BW 2.01 **Listen to Ewa presenting three possible locations for the new office in Berlin. Put her slides in the correct order.**

SLIDE A OFFICE LOCATIONS

SLIDE B OFFICE LOCATIONS: KREUZBERG

- Co-working space in an old [1]__________ in the south of the city.
- [2]__________ m² in total with workstations for [3]__________ people and meeting rooms.
- Includes high-speed internet, use of [4]__________, shared kitchen.
- Rent €[5]__________ per workstation/month. No deposit required. Min. rent period [6]__________. One-month cancellation.

SLIDE C OFFICE LOCATIONS

SLIDE D OFFICE LOCATIONS: MITTE

- Office room in modern building in the [1]__________ of Berlin.
- [2]__________ m² large room and [3]__________ m² small office for meetings.
- Includes furniture, high-speed internet, [4]__________ service, shared kitchen.
- Rent €[5]__________/month plus one-month deposit. Min. rent period [6]__________. One-month cancellation.

SLIDE E OFFICE LOCATIONS

SLIDE F OFFICE LOCATIONS: PRENZLAUER BERG

- Has no [1]__________. Office in old building in [2]__________ Berlin.
- [3]__________ m² including two [4]__________.
- Includes kitchen, two toilets.
- Rent €[5]__________/month plus [6]__________ deposit. Min. rent period six months. Three-month cancellation.

T Teacher's resources: extra activities

B Listen again and complete Ewa's presentation slides. Use one to two words in each gap.

3 Discuss the good and bad points of each location. Which would you choose for the company? Why?

A trip to Berlin

4A BW 2.02 **Listen to Ewa and Mark discussing the three offices after their visit. Complete the notes.**

MITTE OFFICE	PRENZLAUER BERG OFFICE	KREUZBERG OFFICE
Pros ______	Pros ______	Pros ______
Cons ______	Cons ______	Cons ______

B What do you think they should do?

5 Ewa reads this report in a magazine on the flight back to London. What are the possible advantages/disadvantages of Estonia?

World's best places to locate your business

Estonia is a small country with a population of just 1.3 million. This country in northern Europe, which is becoming well-known for advances in technology, was the first in the world to introduce an e-residency scheme with a digital ID card. It allows an e-resident to access digital services without living in Estonia.

In business-friendly Estonia, most people speak more than one language and younger people in particular have a high level of English. About one in four residents come from countries close by, including Russia and Finland, as well as professionals from other EU countries and the USA. The capital, Tallinn, famous for its medieval old town, has one of the highest number of start-ups per person in the EU.

T Teacher's resources: extra activities

TASK
Choose a location

6A Work in groups of three or four. You're going to decide on the new location for EM Animation Studios. Decide who is going to be Ewa and who Mark. The other students choose from the roles as other employees. Look at your information and prepare for the discussion.

Ewa: Look at page 138.

Mark: Look at page 131.

Paul: Look at page 133.

Yelena: Look at page 139.

B Hold a meeting and agree on the new location. Consider these points in your discussion.

- The size and type of the space
- The cost and conditions of rent
- The pros and cons of each location
- Your personal preferences

Self-assessment

- How successfully have you achieved the lesson outcome? Give yourself a score from 0 (I need more practice) to 5 (I know this well).
- Go to My Self-assessment in MyEnglishLab to reflect on what you have learnt.

BUSINESS WORKSHOP 3 Pop-up stores

Lesson outcome

Learners can exchange information about texts they have read and can make and respond to suggestions for their own alternative retail store.

Background

1 Read the background and answer the questions with a partner.

1. What type of area was Yaletown, Vancouver, in the past? What type of area is it now?
2. What is a pop-up store?
3. Who could benefit from opening a pop-up store?
4. What do you think are some good things about having a pop-up store?

BACKGROUND

Yaletown in the Downtown South area of Vancouver, Canada, was an old industrial part of the city. For many years the factories and warehouses were not used and empty. Today this popular area of the city has many new high-rise office buildings and apartments, and some older buildings from the industrial days still remain.

The owners of one redbrick factory building on Hamilton Street plan to change the ground floor into pop-up stores. This type of temporary store can open for a day or stay for several months.

Pop-up stores are a good option for people starting a new business, existing small businesses and online businesses looking for a cheap option to open a store. The most successful stores often become permanent. Today many large retailers are also opening pop-up stores to create more interest in their products.

Pop-up stories

2A Read the article about one famous retailer. How is the company experimenting with its stores? Why?

B Do you think pop-up stores are a good option for large retailers? Why? / Why not?

FT

Ikea moves focus to city centre stores

Ikea Group is focusing on the city centre. The popularity of its out-of-town warehouses is falling and the world's largest furniture retailer is trying to meet the needs of urban and online shoppers.

Jesper Brodin, Ikea's new Chief Executive, told the *Financial Times* that the retailer will try different types of stores in the centre of cities such as Copenhagen in Denmark. Mr Brodin said, 'We are testing new formats. We have penetrated parts of the city centre but we are mostly outside so the opportunities are there.'

The Netherlands-based retailer is experimenting with different types of stores from its traditional large warehouses based on the edge of cities. It has opened city-centre pop-up stores and collection points, as well as smaller stores in some areas.

Mr Brodin said, 'We are basically creating structures in a way that we can test many aspects in many places. They are test laboratories to figure out the new world of Ikea.'

3A Work in groups of three. Find out about some other pop-up stores.

Student A: Read the article and answer the questions below. **Student B:** Read the article on page 137 and answer the questions below. **Student C:** Read the article on page 132 and answer the questions below.

1 What does the article say about the person who has the pop-up store?
2 What does the pop-up store sell?
3 What advantages and opportunities does he/she talk about for his/her pop-up store?

Richard's Pop-up Chocolates

Richard Murphy left his office job to start his chocolate business three years ago. He makes his artisan chocolates at home and also sells online. 'A pop-up shop gives me the opportunity to sell my product in a retail store without paying all the costs of a permanent location.'

He says he can also plan his pop-up shops around major 'chocolate' holidays, such as the winter holidays and Mother's Day.

'In the past I tried to sell my products in farmers' markets, but it wasn't the right place for expensive handmade chocolates and sales weren't good. I learnt that location is very important when you want to open any shop.'

He says a pop-up shop gives him face-to-face time with customers. 'It's my opportunity to chat to people, and offer them samples to taste. If they like it, they'll buy and they'll become repeat customers. You can't have that relationship online.'

B Tell the other students in your group <u>in your own words</u> about the pop-up store you read about.

Teacher's resources: extra activities

C Who would be possible customers for each store? Do you think Yaletown will be a good place for any of these pop-up stores?

What people want

4 BW 3.01 Listen to three extracts from market research interviews with people in Yaletown. Find five more differences between these notes and the interviews.

Teacher's resources: extra activities

One young person I interviewed said ~~all~~ *some of* the places to go in the evening were expensive. He said he and his co-workers liked to have dinner together after work.

One office worker I spoke to said she likes to buy natural health care products. The price of the products was more important to her than the quality.

Another shopper I interviewed told me she likes to go to shopping malls. She always wears the clothes and colours that are popular.

TASK
Design your own pop-up store

5A Work in small groups. You want to open a pop-up store in the building on Hamilton Street in Yaletown. Discuss and decide what type of business it will be.

Remember to:

- choose from one of the pop-up stores you read about or think of an idea of your own.
- think of a (new) name for your business.
- decide what you are going to sell, e.g. different products for different times of the year.
- design your shop so it attracts customers.
- discuss where you will advertise the business – newspapers, flyers, social media, etc.
- decide what your opening hours will be.
- agree what job each of you will have in the business.
- think of a special offer that will attract customers to your new pop-up store.

B Work in pairs with someone from another group. Present your ideas. Do you like the other group's special offer? Would it make you visit their pop-up?

C Work with your group again. What did other students think about your special offer? Do you need to change or improve it?

D Design a flyer, newspaper advertisement or online advertisement for your pop-up. Remember to include information about your products and the special offer.

Self-assessment

- How successfully have you achieved the lesson outcome? Give yourself a score from 0 (I need more practice) to 5 (I know this well).
- Go to My Self-assessment in MyEnglishLab to reflect on what you have learnt.

BUSINESS WORKSHOP 4 The Holsted way

Lesson outcome

Learners can identify the main points in short audio recordings about work patterns and hold a simple negotiation to change work patterns.

Background

1 Read the background and answer the questions with a partner.

1 What is special about the location of Holsted's head office?
2 What does the company do?
3 Why is the Vice President in Madrid?
4 In what ways can cultural differences affect working life?

BACKGROUND

Holsted Pharmaceuticals is a Danish multinational company with headquarters near Copenhagen in Medicon Valley. This area of eastern Denmark and southern Sweden has a large number of pharmaceutical and biotechnology companies and research institutions.

The company manufactures and markets pharmaceutical products and services. It has factories in seven countries, offices in over 70 countries and sells its products in 180 countries. It employs more than 30,000 people globally.

Holsted recently bought a Spanish pharmaceutical laboratory based in Madrid, Spain. Clara Olsen, the Vice President for Europe, has gone to Madrid to manage the company operations there. As part of her work, she plans to investigate the work culture in the Madrid laboratory to decide what changes she needs to make. She wants to introduce managers to *the Holsted way*.

The Holsted way

2A BW 4.01 Listen to Clara Olsen giving a presentation to the senior managers in Madrid about the company culture at Holsted. Find one difference between each point below and the presentation.

The Holsted company culture

- Employees work ~~40~~ *37* hours a week from Monday to Friday.
- They are often expected to work long hours.
- The working hours are fixed for most employees.
- The work culture is very strict but effective.
- Managers are responsible for how employees organise their time and projects.
- Senior staff in the company can tell us their ideas and opinions.
- It's important to arrive on time for work; it shows you are professional.

T Teacher's resources: extra activities

B Would you like to work for a company with this work culture? What would you like most/least?

Investigating work patterns

3A BW 4.02 Listen to part of a meeting between Clara Olsen, Vice President; Marina Beltran, Human Resources Manager; and Álvaro Martínez, Finance Manager; in Madrid. Look at Clara's list of questions. Which questions are they discussing?

MEETING ABOUT WORK PATTERNS

1 What types of contracts are there? (full-time, part-time?)
2 How much holiday do employees get?
3 What are the working hours – start time, finish time?
4 Does the company let employees work flexible hours?
5 How long is the lunch break?
6 Can employees work from home?

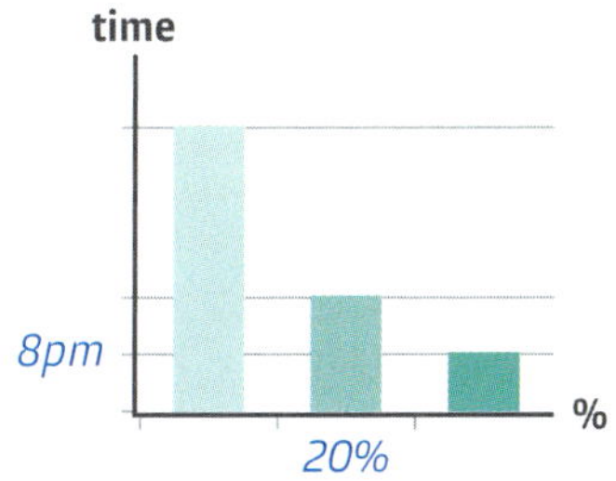

B **Listen again and complete this extract from the meeting (0:00–0:36). Then complete the bar chart with the correct percentages and times.**

As you can see from this bar graph, the working day is very long here in the Madrid office. On an average day only [1]__________ of our employees leave work by [2]__________ o'clock. At [3]__________ o'clock, [4]__________ percent of the staff are still here in the office and [5]__________ percent are still at their desks at [6]__________ in the evening.

C **Work in pairs. What is a suitable title for the graph?**

D **Listen to the rest of the meeting again (0:37–2:24) and answer the questions.**

1. What does Álvaro say about the lunch break?
2. What do Marina and Álvaro disagree about?
3. What does Marina say about staff working long days?
4. What risks does she say are possible?

E **What do you think Clara and her team should do about the two issues they discuss? Use the phrases in the box to help you and your own ideas.**

stop staff using work email at home see how long staff are working
reduce the number of hours that staff can use the building
make the lunch break shorter switch off office lights after a certain time
stop people being able to use the computer at certain times

T Teacher's resources: extra activities

4A **You are going to negotiate new work patterns for the company. In groups of three, take the roles of:**

Clara Olsen (meeting leader), Vice President for Europe of Holsted Pharmaceuticals

Marina Beltran, Human Resources Manager of Holsted Pharmaceuticals in Spain

Álvaro Martínez, Finance Manager of Holsted Pharmaceuticals in Spain

B **Look at your information and the agenda for the meeting and prepare for the discussion.**

Vice President: Look at page 135.

Human Resources Manager: Look at page 141.

Finance Manager: Look at page 134.

Points to negotiate:
- The working hours
- A schedule with flexible hours
- The lunch break
- Working from home

C **Roleplay your meeting. The Vice President leads the meeting. Discuss the points on the agenda. Try to reach agreement on all four areas.**

D **Work in pairs with someone from another group. Compare the result of your negotiations. Were your decisions similar or different?**

Writing

5 **You are the Vice President. Read this email from another manager. Write a reply of 120–150 words.**

Hello Clara,

Sorry I could not attend the meeting. As you know, I was away on urgent business. What decisions did the team make about the working hours?

Best regards,

Carlos

Remember to:
- say why you're writing.
- list all the decisions you made.
- tell your colleague not to tell anyone about this until the changes are official.

Self-assessment

- How successfully have you achieved the lesson outcome? Give yourself a score from 0 (I need more practice) to 5 (I know this well).
- Go to My Self-assessment in MyEnglishLab to reflect on what you have learnt.

BUSINESS WORKSHOP 5 Local economy boost

Lesson outcome

Learners can understand some common alternatives to traditional money and can evaluate different options for community projects.

Background

1 Read the background and answer the questions with a partner.

1 People in the town want to make two things better. What are they?
2 What two opposite ideas are mentioned about cash?
3 Where are people looking for ideas?

BACKGROUND

Members of a community of about 8,000 people want to improve the local economy, and at the same time improve the quality of life for the people who live there. People are already discussing possible ideas. Many agree that just bringing more money to the area isn't enough. They want to make it easier for people to use local businesses, and encourage new ones. Some people also believe that cash-only businesses should be encouraged. However, others suggest trading goods and services and not using money is better in some situations. Some people are doing research into solutions that other towns and cities around the world have used. As a next step, the town council is planning an open meeting to share ideas and hear suggestions from local people.

Suggestions

2A BW 5.01 **Read the town councillor's notes for the meeting. Then listen and complete them.**

Topic: Practical ideas and real solutions

1 Advertise to attract ________________
2 Create a local ________________
3 Set up a ________________ bank
4 Start an online goods ________________ – on social media?
5 Start a Saturday ________________ in the town centre

B Match the ideas (a–e) with the descriptions (1–5) in Exercise 2A. Listen again and check your answers.

a Develop a type of money that's only for our town
b Make it easy for people to trade things they don't need for things they need
c Arrange a place in town for local people to sell things
d Invite people from other places to visit our town – and spend money
e Get people to share their skills by trading hours of work

3 BW 5.02 **Now listen to the end of the meeting. Which ideas does the town vote to consider more seriously?**

Looking more closely at options

4A **Read the information from the town council on page 97. Each project has three advantages and one disadvantage. What are they? Use one of the advantages twice.**

Advantages encourages people to make their own local products
allows people to sell things they make all people's skills are the same value
gives unemployed people a work opportunity helps small, cash-only businesses
increases the exchange of goods and services keeps money in the local economy
encourages people to get to know each other

Disadvantages some businesses might not like the idea
might require expensive insurance some people may think it isn't fair

Local currency

Local currencies increase economic activity. If people have a local currency, they often use it for goods and services that they wouldn't pay for with 'real' cash. Also, if small businesses accept credit cards, they have to pay a fee to the bank. If more people pay with a local currency, it's possible to run a cash-only business. This increases local economic activity. Local currency also keeps money in the local area, because it has no value in other places. However, sometimes, local businesses don't like the idea of a local currency. If businesses don't accept it, it won't work.

Time bank

If people share their time instead of paying someone, everyone's time has the same value. An hour is an hour. This gives more value to people with fewer skills. In addition, local people get to know other local people. And spending time together can lead to more friendships, and also to people understanding those who are different from themselves. Another benefit is that people who are unemployed will have the opportunity to work, and also the opportunity to receive services from others in the community. However, it may be difficult to get people who have valuable skills to trade them with those who are less skilled.

Saturday market

People who make food such as cakes and pies or who make clothes will have the chance to sell them, creating new economic activity in the community. And shoppers will have more opportunity to buy local products. If people see others selling local products, they'll get ideas of their own for things to make and sell. In addition, people going to the market will get to know the sellers and also the other shoppers better. However, the town would need to buy insurance for the market. This could be expensive – people who sell things would have to pay, and some sellers may not want to do this.

B **Work in pairs and compare your notes. Did you identify the same advantages and disadvantages?**

5A BW 5.03 **Listen to local residents Ellen and David discussing the projects. Which project does Ellen like the best? Which one does David like the best?**

B **Listen again. Who expressed each opinion? Write E (*Ellen*), D (*David*) or N (*neither*).**

1 Local currency

- **a** It's interesting – good for business. ____
- **b** It's weird – lots of people think this. ____
- **c** It's old-fashioned – we don't need it. ____

2 Saturday market

- **a** It would help to create jobs – people will make things to sell. ____
- **b** It's easy to understand – people will go to see other people. ____
- **c** It's not interesting – you can sell stuff online. ____

3 Time bank

- **a** I'm too busy to use it. ____
- **b** I'd rather just pay people. ____
- **c** It's a good way to meet people. ____

T Teacher's resources: extra activities

TASK
Choose a project

6A **Work in groups of four. You are going to discuss the three projects and vote on the one you prefer. Look at your information.**

Student A (meeting leader): Look at page 140. **Student B:** Look at page 128. **Student C:** Look at page 137. **Student D:** Look at page 141.

B **Discuss the three projects together and try to convince the others of your arguments.**

C **Tell the class which project your group voted for. Say why.**

Writing

7 **Write an announcement for the town council website of 80–100 words explaining the decision made and the reasons for it. End the email on a positive note; explain you might also try one of the other projects in future.**

Self-assessment

- How successfully have you achieved the lesson outcome? Give yourself a score from 0 (I need more practice) to 5 (I know this well).
- Go to My Self-assessment in MyEnglishLab to reflect on what you have learnt.

BUSINESS WORKSHOP 6 The Amazing Chair Company

Lesson outcome

Learners can discuss members of a team and identify how best to make use of people's natural skills, abilities and preferences.

Background

1 Read the background and answer the questions with a partner.

1 Why did Natalya start The Amazing Chair Company?
2 What are the three jobs on the team?
3 Why do you think the team might be unhappy?

BACKGROUND

The Amazing Chair Company was started in New York City three years ago by Natalya Ivanova. Her interest in furniture began as a hobby – she took a furniture-making class and made a chair for her apartment. However, when her friends saw her work, they asked where they could buy one, and soon a successful business was born. Natalya hired furniture designer, Leila Mostafa, to help with new ideas. As the business grew, she realised that she needed to hire a part-time accountant and bookkeeper – João Sousa – to deal with the financial side of the business. The company is just successful enough to pay Natalya as Director, and her two employees, but not yet big enough to hire more staff. But can this team make the business a success?

Team roles

2A BW 6.01 **Listen to João talking about his job.**

1 What did he study at university? 2 How does he feel about his job?

B Listen again. Tick (✓) the boxes to show how João feels about each area of work.

	Likes	Isn't very interested in
numbers		
solving problems		
being creative		
accounting		

3A BW 6.02 **Listen to Leila talking about her job. What did she like about her last job?**

B Listen again. Complete the notes using the words and phrases in the box. Two are not used.

bothers concentrate leave work on time listens to share ideas talks to

Communication
Good = no one ¹__________ me
Bad = no one ²__________ me

Creativity
Good = it's easy to ³__________
Bad = can't ⁴__________

4A BW 6.03 **Listen to Natalya talking about her job. Is she happy in her work?**

B Listen again. Choose the correct option to complete the sentences.

1 Natalya thinks it's quite *easy* / *difficult* to run a small company.
2 She thinks João and Leila *want to leave the company* / *are not really happy*.
3 She most enjoys *making a great product* / *managing the business*.

T Teacher's resources: extra activities

Natalya's email inbox

5A Read the email to Natalya. What good news does it contain?

Dear Natalya,

Thanks for meeting with us yesterday. As discussed, we'd like to order twenty chairs immediately for our hotel in Chelsea, and over the next year, another 200 for our other hotels. Get in touch when you can and we'll discuss the details.

Alessandra

B BW 6.04 **Listen to Natalya talking about her good news. What does she plan to do now?**

C Read two more emails to Natalya. Answer the questions.

Hello Natalya,

Can we possibly get together tomorrow? I know you're busy, but I'm having a few problems with the new designs, and I really need someone to talk to. Let me know when you're free!

Leila

Hi Natalya,

When you have time, we need to have a conversation. My other part-time job has ended, and I really need more work. I may need to leave The Amazing Chair Company and look for something full-time. Give me a call when you have a minute.

João

Teacher's resources: extra activities

1 What's difficult for Leila right now?
2 How does she want Natalya to help?
3 What has changed in João's life?
4 What does João plan to do?

6A Work in small groups. Think about everything you've learnt about Natalya, Leila and João. Read the descriptions and tick (✓) the correct box for each.

	Natalya	Leila	João
1 Works part time, but wants a full-time job			
2 Would prefer to work more in a team			
3 Wants a job with more problem-solving and that is more creative			
4 Wants to hire a part-time worker to deal with daily business problems			
5 Wants to concentrate more on selling chairs			
6 Is good with numbers			
7 Needs to talk to other people more			
8 Doesn't enjoy full-time business management			

B Look at Natalya's list opposite. Use the information in Exercise 6A to decide who in the company (Natalya, Leila or João) should do each job.

C What do you recommend for The Amazing Chair Company? Consider:

- João, who wants to be more creative and do more problem-solving in a full-time job.
- Leila, who needs someone to talk to.
- Natalya, who needs help managing the business.

ROLES AND RESPONSIBILITIES

1 *Listen to Leila to help her with her work*
2 *Go out and sell more chairs*
3 *Organise and manage the schedule for making 220 chairs this year*
4 *Deal with problems with suppliers*
5 *Create new chair designs*

D Read the information below about The Amazing Chair Company. Can you make any other suggestions for making teamwork better?

- Natalya, Leila and João each have a small, private office.
- In the office space, there is no area for eating or other shared social space.
- Natalya, Leila and João often don't feel they have time for informal conversation at work.

Self-assessment

- How successfully have you achieved the lesson outcome? Give yourself a score from 0 (I need more practice) to 5 (I know this well).
- Go to My Self-assessment in MyEnglishLab to reflect on what you have learnt.

BUSINESS WORKSHOP 7

Zapatos Trujillo S.A.

Lesson outcome

Learners can understand and discuss simple production processes and choose one to put in place.

Background

1 Read the background and answer the questions with a partner.

1 What is Zapatos Trujillo S.A.'s main business?
2 Who are their customers?
3 What new business would they like to enter?
4 What is Due Scarpe's main business?
5 What are Sofia, Oscar and Mario deciding together?

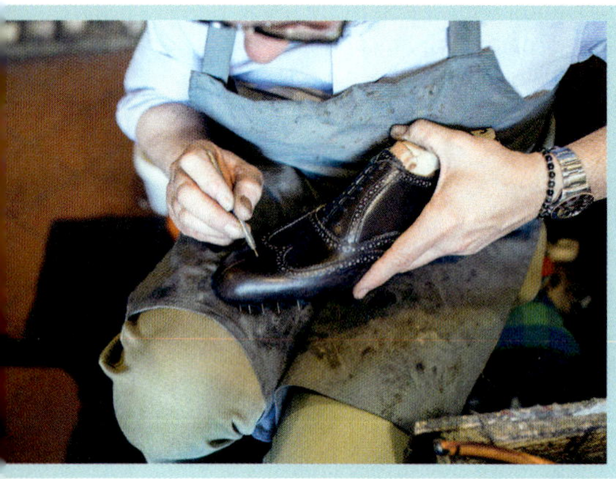

BACKGROUND

Zapatos Trujillo S.A. is a shoe factory located in León, Mexico. For the past forty years, the company has successfully produced footwear for well-known global companies. However, CEO Oscar García believes that with the right designs, the company could be successful producing its own line of shoes for both the Mexican and international markets. To help plan the new product line, the company has hired an international shoe manufacturing consultancy – Due Scarpe. Sofia Rossi, Due Scarpe's Italy-based Consultant, is now in Mexico working with Oscar García and his new Head of Design, Mario Pardo. Together they are deciding on what type of footwear to produce, and the best production processes to use. Sofia writes reports every few days for her boss, shoe expert John McDermott.

Discussing processes and products

2A BW 7.01 **Listen to Sofia and Oscar's conversation after a factory tour. Tick (✓) the topics they discuss.**

☐ How long it takes to complete a shoe order
☐ How many employees the company has
☐ Making costs lower
☐ Improving quality

B Listen again and complete Sofia's notes.

- *Current production =* 1 ________ *pairs of shoes in* 2 ________ *weeks.*
- *Automation could speed up production by* 3 ________ *or* 4 ________ *percent.*
- *Oscar really values his workers'* 5 ________ .

3A BW 7.02 **Listen to Sofia, Oscar and Mario's conversation about shoe designs. Choose two ideas from 1-6 that demonstrate each person's opinion (S, M, O).**

Sofia, Consultant
Mario, Head of Design
Oscar, CEO

1 increase automation
2 don't improve the factory
3 our designs are good quality and completed by hand
4 hire more workers
5 create high-quality shoes that we can take to fashion shows
6 produce more shoes quickly

B Listen again. What's going to happen next?

They're going to:

a buy some machines to make a cheaper shoe.
b find a way to produce high-quality shoes.
c go to a trade show in Paris or Berlin to get ideas.

T Teacher's resources: extra activities

Considering options

4A Read the report. Who do you think wrote it? Who did he/she write it for?

Progress report

Zapatos Trujillo S.A. has a production staff of fifty and can produce approximately 3,000 pairs of high-quality shoes in twelve weeks – that's 12,000 a year. The factory uses basic machines but has a highly skilled workforce. They would like to produce a shoe that should sell wholesale for about $100 a pair with a recommended retail price of $189. At that price, they'd need to produce 20,000 pairs per year for the business to make a profit, and that's possible only with automation. At the current rate of production, the wholesale price would need to be $130 a pair to make a profit, and I think that's too expensive. So, they need to cut down production time or possibly use cheaper materials. The other possibility would be to produce a shoe that's actually worth $130 a pair. That's possible, but probably the most difficult option and I don't recommend it.

B Read the report again. Which of these is not an option for Zapatos Trujillo S.A.?

1 to produce more shoes by adding automation
2 to produce 12,000 pairs per year and sell them wholesale for $100
3 to produce shoes using cheaper materials
4 to produce a very high-quality shoe that they can sell wholesale for $130

T Teacher's resources: extra activities

5 BW 7.03 **Listen to the conversation between Sofia and her boss, John. What's worrying her the most about Zapatos Trujillo S.A.? What advice does he give her?**

TASK Manage production

6A Work in pairs or small groups. Read the three options for the design and production of Zapatos Trujillo S.A.'s new shoe. Discuss the questions.

Option 1
- Use Mario's design
- Produce 12,000 per year
- Don't hire any new workers
- Sell shoes wholesale for $130 as handmade
- Profit $525,000

Option 2
- Use a simpler design with cheaper materials
- Produce 15,000 per year
- Hire 10 new workers at a total cost of $50,000 per year
- Sell shoes wholesale for $105 as handmade
- Profit $535,000

Option 3
- Use a simpler design with cheaper materials
- Produce 20,000 per year
- Lay off 10 workers to save $50,000 per year
- Add automation
- Pay $100,000 for new machines
- Sell shoes wholesale for $90
- Profit $610,000

1 Which option definitely produces a high-quality shoe?
2 Which option is the least acceptable for CEO Oscar Garcia?
3 Which shoe would the company probably feel the most proud of?

B Work in groups of three to six. Imagine you are members of the board of Zapatos Trujillo S.A. Decide on roles A–C.

Role A: Decide why Option 1 is the best choice. Then think of two or three reasons why the other options aren't good.
Role B: Decide why Option 2 is the best choice. Then think of two or three reasons why the other options aren't good.
Role C: Decide why Option 3 is the best choice. Then think of two or three reasons why the other options aren't good.

C Discuss the three options with your group. Take turns trying to convince the group that your option is the best. At the end, vote to choose one option.

Writing

7 Write an email of 75–100 words to Mario Pardo, Head of Design. Explain the board's decision.

Remember to:
- say why you're writing.
- say which option was chosen.
- give the reasons.
- say you hope that the new line of shoes will be a big success.

Self-assessment
- How successfully have you achieved the lesson outcome? Give yourself a score from 0 (I need more practice) to 5 (I know this well).
- Go to My Self-assessment in MyEnglishLab to reflect on what you have learnt.

BUSINESS WORKSHOP 8 Walsh Ryan's green office

Lesson outcome

Learners can understand information in a simple report about green offices and discuss what actions to take.

Background

1 Read the background and answer the questions with a partner.

1 What type of company is Walsh Ryan?
2 How is the new head office described?
3 What does the Facilities Department do?
4 What is the G.O project for?

BACKGROUND

Walsh Ryan employs over 400 staff in its head office in Dublin, Ireland. The company offers many different products, for example car, home, business, farm, travel and life insurance. Walsh Ryan has spent €35 million on its new office six kilometres from the city centre. The building has four floors and is designed to save energy. It has solar panels, LED lights and smart temperature controls.

The Facilities Department will be responsible for the day-to-day operations in the building, such as energy use, security, cleaning and maintenance. It is always trying to reduce costs. Senior management want the Facilities Department to lead a green office project called G.O. The project will reduce costs and help protect the environment. Walsh Ryan's new green offices will be good for business, good for the planet and good for the company's reputation.

The green office report

2A Read part of a report by the Facilities Manager. Put these headings into the correct section of the report. Three are not used.

Energy use	Paper use	Pollution	Transport	Waste	Water use

MEASURING ENERGY USE AND WASTE IN WALSH RYAN

The Facilities Department's objective for the G.O project is to reduce costs by three to six percent. This reduction will be possible by moving into the new offices and by introducing low-cost changes there.

This report presents data on the energy use and waste production in our old building so that we can find opportunities for savings.

1 ____________________

Walsh Ryan currently spends nearly 29 percent of its day-to-day operations budget for the building on utilities. Most of this spending is on electricity and natural gas bills. Energy costs in our old office are over €60,000 per year.

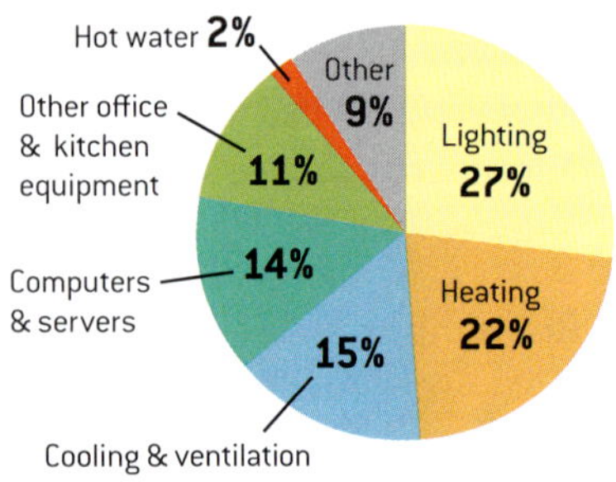

This pie chart shows the different energy costs in our offices.

Lighting, heating, cooling and ventilation* represent almost two-thirds of energy costs. The move to the new office building with its solar panels, smart temperature controls and energy-efficient LED lights will help us to make savings in these areas. We can also make other low-cost savings.

2 ____________________

The company currently uses 10,000 sheets of copy paper per person every year. That's four boxes of paper per staff member at a cost of €10 per box. According to the Waste and Resource Action Programme (WRAP), a good office can use as few as 3,500 sheets per person per year. At Walsh Ryan we are using three times that amount of paper. Also, approximately 60 percent of this paper is waste.

3 ____________________

The company creates two kilos of waste per staff member per day. This includes paper, plastic cups, food waste in the canteen and general office waste. WRAP's figures show that a good office produces less than half that amount of waste per person.

Dublin City Council is planning to raise the cost of waste disposal, and companies that produce more waste will pay more. So, if we can reduce waste, it will cut disposal costs as well. WRAP reports that by introducing a more efficient recycling scheme many offices can recycle between 60 and 70 percent of the waste.

B What do you think the Facilities Department can do to improve in each of the three areas?

Use real cups and glasses not plastic cups.
Don't sell bottled water in vending machines.

T Teacher's resources: extra activities

*ventilation: air that is moved through a building

The Facilities Department meeting

3A BW 8.01 **Listen to Patricia, the Facilities Manager, and her team discussing ideas for the G.O project. Put the things in the order they are mentioned.**

B **What three options do they want to find out more about?**

C **Listen again and complete the notes. Use one to three words in each gap.**

REDUCING ENERGY COSTS

- *LED lights in new building:*
  - *motion sensors switch the [1]__________ on and off in [2]__________, corridors, storerooms, the stairs and in the [3]__________*
- *Costs from computer servers:*
  - *electricity to run the [4]__________*
  - *cooling and ventilation to keep the server room at the [5]__________*

  Possible solution: Use a cloud computing service

REDUCING WASTE

- *Employees are using too much paper – the current printers are old and the [6]__________ is terrible. They also use a lot of toner.*

  Possible solution: New multifunctional printers.
- *Waste levels currently two kilos per person per day.*

  Possible solution: More recycling

Reducing waste is important for company's [7]__________ and [8]__________.

T Teacher's resources: extra activities

TASK
Present ideas on waste and energy reduction

4A **You are the staff in the Facilities Department at Walsh Ryan. Work in groups of six. Read about your option and prepare to present it to your colleagues.**

Pair A: Look at page 130: Multifunctional printers.

Pair B: Look at page 134: Cloud computing.

Pair C: Look at page 128: Waste reduction and recycling.

B **Give a presentation to your colleagues in the Facilities Department about your option. You can use presentation slides if you want.**

Remember to:

- introduce the present situation and the need for change.
- explain what this option is about.
- give the main numbers for costs and savings.
- say how this option helps the company's green office reputation.

C **Discuss the three options. Which ones will you choose and why? Work in your group of six.**

Self-assessment

- How successfully have you achieved the lesson outcome? Give yourself a score from 0 (I need more practice) to 5 (I know this well).
- Go to My Self-assessment in MyEnglishLab to reflect on what you have learnt.

1.1 Transport, accommodation and travel

1 Complete the missing words.

1 I have made a r __ s __ __ __ a __ __ __ n for you for two nights at the Orion Hotel.
2 The p __ __ __ i __ t __ __ __ s __ __ r __ __ t __ __ n in the city is very quick and cheap.
3 Inés always travels business class when she takes l __ __ __ g - __ au __ flights.
4 They enjoyed their s __ __ y in Mexico and want to go back next year.
5 How often do you have to go a __ __ __ o __ d on business trips?
6 Do you ever use a r __ d __ s __ __ __ r __ __ __ g app to travel around the city?
7 We need to buy a new v __ __ __ __ le for deliveries.
8 The flight to Brunei was d __ __ __ __ y __ d yesterday, so we arrived at the meeting late.

1.2 Comparatives and superlatives

2 Complete the sentences using the phrases in the box.

happier than	less important than
more difficult than	the best
the least expensive	the worst

1 Managing large teams is hard. In fact, it's ___________ managing small teams.
2 The staff are ___________ they were in the old offices.
3 ___________ day to have company meetings is Friday because everyone is tired.
4 The CEO stayed in ___________ hotel in town, of course!
5 This restaurant is ___________ one in town, but the food is great.
6 This report is ___________ the interviews for new staff so could you do those first, please?

Functional language

1.3 Making small talk

3 Complete the dialogue using the words and phrases in the box.

about six hours	yes, a little	do you know
do you live	visiting	how long was	that's right
what are you	you come from	

A: Hi, I was introduced to you earlier. You work in sales.
B: [1]___________. I remember you. I'm Grigor.
A: Hi, Grigor. I'm Dina. Where do [2]___________?
B: Russia, but I work in Dubai.
A: Really? That's interesting. [3]___________ your flight from there to Rome?
B: [4]___________. It wasn't too bad. And you? Where [5]___________?
A: In London.
B: Very nice! [6]___________ Rome?
A: [7]___________. I came here on a business trip last year. I hope to do some more sightseeing when I'm not at this conference. [8]___________ doing here?
B: I'm [9]___________ some clients and watching them give talks.

1.4 Explaining and solving IT problems

4 Complete the dialogue. Use only one word in each gap.

A: I'm [1]___________ trouble logging on to the system. I don't know [2]___________ to connect to the intranet.
B: You [3]___________ to use the login details I gave you.
A: I [4]___________ find my login details. Can you give them to me again?
B: [5]___________ 'expert123'. [6]___________ you try logging on again now?
A: OK ... No, I still can't log on.
B: Right. Can you try setting up a new account name?
A: [7]___________ do I do that?
B: Don't worry, I'll [8]___________ it for you.

1.5 Email – Asking for information

5 Choose the correct option in italics to complete the email.

[1]*Hello / Dear* Sir or Madam,

I am writing to [2]*ask / enquire* for information about your conference facilities. We are [3]*asking / looking* for a venue which can accommodate 150 people. We [4]*would / can* also like to book all your bedrooms for the period of the conference. Would that be possible? We [5]*need / hear* each room to have a desk and wi-fi. The conference is four days, 3–6 November next year, and we are planning to have breakfast and lunch at your hotel each day. Please can you [6]*inform / confirm* your best price for this?

I [7]*look / hope* forward to hearing from you.

[8]*All / Kind* regards,

2.1 Location

1 Complete the text using the words in the box.

close	convenient	lab	leisure
links	port	studios	warehouse

Our new HQ will include three more design ¹__________ and a new innovation ²__________. In the building you will also find sports and ³__________ facilities, which we believe our employees will really enjoy using. The new location is also ⁴__________ to the airport and other transport ⁵__________. As you know, our central ⁶__________ is already near the motorway which goes straight to the main ⁷__________. This is very ⁸__________ because we ship most of our products from there.

2.2 *enough* and *too*

2 Complete the text with the words in brackets and *(not) enough*, *too*, *too many* and *too much*.

Unfortunately, the factory we looked at is small and really is ¹__________ (big) for us to consider. We would need to make ²__________ (changes) for it to be suitable for our company. It was also ³__________ (money) for its size. Additionally, the car park was ⁴__________ (small) and the location was ⁵__________ (far) from the motorway. We need ⁶__________ (space) for three separate production lines and several offices, and there must be ⁷__________ (parking spaces) for everyone.

Functional language

2.3 Checking and clarifying

3 Complete the missing words.

A: So, we need to talk about the second interviews.

B: Can I just ¹c _ _ _ _, we've now got full details for all the candidates we interviewed?

A: ²C _ _ _ _ _ _ _ _, and there are four for the second interviews.

B: Oh ... only four. Is that ³r _ _ _ _? I thought we said six.

A: ⁴E _ _ _ _ _ _ _. We did, but the others don't have everything we're looking for.

B: Could you be more ⁵s _ _ _ _ _ _ _ c? Why are the others not suitable?

A: Well, what I ⁶m _ _ _ is, only four have both the qualifications and personality.

B: OK ... So what you're ⁷s _ _ _ _ _ is that personality is more important than experience?

A: No, but it is very important. We need all three – qualifications, experience and personality.

2.4 Opening a meeting, referring to the agenda and stating purpose

4 Complete the conversation using the words in the box. Some are <u>not</u> used.

add	agenda	busy	catch	copy	item	minutes
reason	see	start	time-keeper	volunteer		

A: Morning! Nice to ¹__________ everyone. Does everyone have a(n) ²__________ of the ³__________? Good. Right, now I know Marta isn't here yet, but I'd like to ⁴__________ on time. As you know, one ⁵__________ for the meeting is to introduce you all to the new member of our team, Holly.

B: Hello, everyone.

C: Welcome to the team, Holly.

A: Now, could I have a(n) ⁶__________ to take the ⁷__________?

D: Sure. I'll do it.

A: Thanks, Govinder. And Ali, can I ask you to be ⁸__________? Make sure we finish at 10.30.

C: Of course.

A: Does anyone want to ⁹__________ anything to the agenda? No? Then let's look at ¹⁰__________ one – Matters Arising.

2.5 Short communications

5 Write the abbreviations in full.

1 WFH ____________________
2 BTW ____________________
3 ASAP ____________________
4 TBC ____________________
5 ETA ____________________

6 Cross out the words you can leave out to make the sentences shorter.

1 I am very sorry I can't come to the meeting.
2 I will be with you in 15 minutes.
3 We know other suppliers are interested.
4 John sent a message to the boss yesterday.
5 I'm reading the document now.

3.1 Shops and the shopping experience

1 Choose the correct option in italics.

1 Please go to the *bakery / pharmacy / butcher's* and get me some medicine for my cold.
2 I couldn't pay the *euros / profit / bill* because I didn't have enough money.
3 There's a *branch / chain / centre* of the store in the next town.
4 What? The hotel *costs / pays / charges* customers €3 per day for the wi-fi?
5 You can pay *by / in / for* credit card if you like.
6 How much time do you *make / serve / spend* shopping online every day?
7 I never visit department *centres / chains / stores*. I prefer small shops.
8 We *ordered / made / served* our meal at 7 p.m., but it didn't arrive until 8 p.m.

3.2 Past Simple

2 Complete the text with the Past Simple form of the verbs in brackets.

Yesterday my colleague and I [1]__________ (decide) to visit the new shopping centre in town to find some furniture for our new office. We [2]__________ (not want) to drive to town, so we [3]__________ (catch) a bus. We [4]__________ (arrive) at 8.30 and [5]__________ (go) to a coffee shop. Suddenly my phone [6]__________ (ring). It was my assistant. She [7]__________ (not have) all the information she needed to prepare a contract. I [8]__________ (tell) her to wait for me to get back.

3.2 Past Continuous

3 Complete the dialogue with the Past Continuous form of the verbs in brackets.

A: What [1]__________ (you / do) at 10.30 yesterday morning?
B: I [2]__________ (have) a meeting with my team.
A: What [3]__________ (you / talk) about?
B: We [4]__________ (discuss) the new project. [5]__________ (you / visit) the new factory at that time?
A: No, I [6]__________ (not / be). I was with my colleague, and we [7]__________ (sit) in a traffic jam!

Functional language

3.3 Solving problems

4 Complete the dialogue using the words and phrases in the box.

about	having	help	how are
just	looking	moment	with

A: Ah, [1]__________ the person I was [2]__________ for! Have you got a(n) [3]__________ ?
B: Yes, of course. What is it?
A: [4]__________ you doing with that sales report I asked you to prepare?
B: Well, I'm not great [5]__________ numbers, so I'm having problems. It's the graphs mainly.
A: How [6]__________ asking Juan to help you? He's really good at those things.
B: [7]__________ Juan with me would really [8]__________ .

3.4 Signposting a presentation

5 Read the extracts from a presentation. Correct the incorrect word in each one.

1 Good morning. Second of all, I'd like to start by looking at the global sales figures.
2 So, let's be started and jump right in.
3 Now, let's start on to look at sales in the USA.
4 I'll give you over to Julia to explain the results here.
5 So, to hand on the main points discussed so far, ...
6 That's great. Let's sum it up there and break for lunch.

3.5 An online review form

6 Complete the review using the words and phrases in the box.

always excellent	was visiting	highly
unfortunately	once a week	last

How often do you stay here?
I usually stay at the hotel [1]__________ .

When did you stay here?
I [2]__________ stayed there yesterday.

What was the purpose of your last visit?
I [3]__________ our company head office.

What do/did you like about the hotel?
The room service is [4]__________ .

Is/Was there anything you aren't/weren't happy with?
[5]__________ , I couldn't check into my room before 12.

Would you recommend us?
I would [6]__________ recommend the hotel.

4.1 Describing jobs and contracts

1 Complete the missing words. The first and last letters are given.

1 Karim is still a student, but he's working for a global company as an i__________n to get some experience.
2 We always need t__________y workers in the summer because it's our busiest time.
3 Virginia can't find a job and is u__________d at the moment.
4 My father is r__________d now. He worked as a doctor for thirty years and stopped work last month.
5 Franz works for several different companies because he is s__________f-e__________d.
6 We can work f__________e hours if we want. On some days, I work for six hours, on other days, I might work for eight.

4.2 Present Perfect Simple

2 Complete the sentences with the Present Perfect Simple form of the verbs in the box.

be	go	learn	spend	teach	visit	win	work

1 I __________ a lot of time in South America.
2 __________ you __________ in India? Or just been there on holiday?
3 This experience __________ me to plan my work more carefully.
4 The boss isn't here, he __________ to the USA for a board meeting.
5 I __________ never __________ to the Australian factory.
6 The CEO __________ our offices here, but not recently.
7 The company __________ a prize for innovation.
8 They __________ a lot of useful skills on this project.

Functional language

4.3 Facilitating a decision-making meeting

3 Choose the correct option in italics.

1 What does everybody *think* / *add* about the suggestion?
2 Gerhardt, I'd like to get your *point* / *input* on this idea.
3 Does anyone have anything they'd like to *add* / *view* before we move on?
4 You may have a *thought* / *point* there.
5 Can we *go* / *move* away and think about it?
6 Natalya, we haven't *known* / *heard* much from you so far.
7 Let's not rush *about* / *into* anything.
8 What are your *decisions* / *thoughts* on the proposal?

4.4 Rescheduling appointments on the phone

4 Complete the dialogue using the words and phrases in the box.

better for	bring it	calling about	check	for being free	if we fix	out for me	postpone	set for	suit

A: Hi, Marga! I'm [1]__________ our meeting on the 20th. Do you mind [2]__________ another time to meet?
B: Not at all. Do you want to [3]__________ it?
A: No. In fact, can we [4]__________ forward?
B: Let me just [5]__________ my schedule. I'm [6]__________ on the morning of Friday 16th. How does that [7]__________ you?
A: Friday's [8]__________, I'm afraid. I'm busy all day. How about Thursday 15th? Is that convenient for you?
B: Yes, that'd be fine. Which is [9]__________ you: morning or afternoon?
A: Let's say 10 in the morning. Thanks [10]__________ so flexible.
B: So, just to confirm. We're all [11]__________ 10 a.m. on Thursday 15th.
A: Yes, see you then.

4.5 Confirming arrangements

5 Complete the two emails using the phrases in the box.

am delighted	contact me	our meeting	to confirm	to seeing	unable to

This is [1]__________ our meeting next Monday to discuss the new schedule. The meeting is at 10.00 a.m. in our New York offices. I also invite you to stay for lunch when we finish. Please [2]__________ if you have any questions before the meeting.

I very much look forward [3]__________ you next week.

Thanks for your email. I [4]__________ to confirm that I am able to attend the meeting on Monday. Unfortunately, I am [5]__________ have lunch with you as I am flying to Europe that afternoon.

I look forward to [6]__________ .

5 REVIEW

5.1 Money

1 Choose the correct option in italics.

1 People don't use paper money in a *cashless / financial* economy.
2 The country's *mobile / financial* system helps young people to buy their own houses.
3 He's got a *mobile / cashless* wallet. He uses a phone app to pay for things.
4 The *financial system / currency* of the USA is the United States dollar.
5 Governments need tax *economies / revenues* so that they can pay for public services.
6 How did you make your *payment / penny*? Was it by credit card?

5.1 Collocations

2 Complete the sentences using the words in the box.

dispensers delivery hand petty short withdraw

1 We pay some temporary workers cash in ___________ because they don't have bank accounts.
2 I'm ___________ of cash this week, so I can't go out with you tonight.
3 There are lots of cash ___________ inside the shopping centre if you want to take money out.
4 We usually pay cash on ___________ for our supplies.
5 We always keep about €100 in ___________ cash so we can buy small items for the office.
6 We had to ___________ some money from the bank to pay for the goods in cash.

5.2 First conditional

3 Complete the sentences with the correct form of the verbs in brackets.

1 We ___________ (not have) to drive to work if the company ___________ (provide) transport for us.
2 If you ___________ (not pay) your credit card bill this month, you ___________ (need) to pay back a lot more next month.
3 If you ___________ (walk) to work every day, you ___________ (save) a lot of money.
4 My salary ___________ (increase) if I ___________ (get) the new job.
5 If I ___________ (eat) lunch now, I ___________ (not feel) hungry in the meeting.
6 Consumers ___________ (stop) buying from us if the price ___________ (go) up.

Functional language

5.3 Agreeing on team roles in meetings

4 Complete the conversation using only one word in each gap.

A: I'd like Zeynep to be the lead presenter. Is that OK [1]___________ everyone? Zeynep?
B: I don't [2]___________, but I'd [3]___________ not to do it. I'm not very good [4]___________ presenting. Marek's much better than me.
A: So, [5]___________ would you like to be the lead presenter then, Marek?
C: Sorry, but I'd [6]___________ not be the lead presenter on my own. I was thinking Zeynep and I could do it together.
A: How would you [7]___________ about that, Zeynep?
B: No problem.
A: Great! If you're both happy, then that's fine [8]___________ me.

5.4 Quoting figures in presentations

5 Complete the presentation using the words in the box. Some are <u>not</u> used.

context look quarter see shows thing third

I'd like you to have a(n) [1]___________ at this chart which [2]___________ the results of our customer survey. As you can [3]___________, more than half of our customers (59 percent) are very happy with our products. However just over a(n) [4]___________ of them (26 percent) are dissatisfied with our products. To put that in [5]___________ that's almost one million people who are not happy with us. About a(n) [6]___________ of all our customers (32 percent) mentioned that our prices are not as cheap as our main competitors. Therefore, the most surprising [7]___________ is only 10 percent of our customers are thinking about moving to cheaper suppliers.

5.5 Letter about a price increase

6 Choose the correct option in italics.

Dear [1]*Sir / Sirs* or Madam,

As you [2]*aware / know*, we have not [3]*raised / dropped* our prices for some time. [4]*Fortunately / Unfortunately*, because of rising costs, we need to increase them from January.

We are, however, [5]*keeping / remaining* the rise small so our prices remain competitive.

[6]*We enclose / Enclosed* our new price [7]*list / letter*.

We [8]*appreciate / thank* your business and look forward to [9]*understanding / supplying* you in the future.

Yours [10]*faithfully / sincerely*,

6 REVIEW

6.1 Teamwork

1 Complete the sentences using the words in the box. Change the form if necessary. One is not used.

agree	argument	communication	cooperate
deal	experienced	management	reliable	respect

1 The team wasn't a big success, only two or three members really ____________ .
2 People who are not ____________ are often late for work and don't do their job properly.
3 It's important to show ____________ for other team members.
4 When we have different ideas about something, we sometimes have ____________ .
5 ____________ team members are happy to help younger members.
6 He is ____________ with that problem now. Don't worry.
7 If team members don't ____________ with each other, there will be problems.
8 They often ____________ with the boss, but he doesn't want people to question his ideas.

6.2 Pronouns with *some-* and *every-*

2 Choose the correct option in italics to complete the conversation.

A: Good morning, [1]*someone / everyone*. Thank you all for coming. Has [2]*somebody / everybody* got [3]*everything / something* they need for the meeting? The plans, the schedule, the design sheets? Have you lost [4]*everything / something*, Jannie?

B: Yes, sorry. I think I've left my plans [5]*everywhere / somewhere*. I've looked [6]*everywhere / somewhere* for them, and they're definitely not in my folder.

C: I've just remembered [7]*everything / something*. [8]*Someone / Everyone* put two sets of plans in my folder. Has [9]*someone / everyone* got two sets or is it just me? Maybe this one is yours, Jannie?

Functional language

6.3 Encouraging and motivating

3 Put the words in B's responses in the correct order.

A: I didn't get that job I applied for.
B: [1]disappointed / be / so / you / must

A: I wanted to do the presentation this time, but she wouldn't let me.
B: [2]how / it / I / you / know / important / was / to

A: I failed my Level 4 professional exam.
B: [3]again / try / always / can / you

A: I didn't get that job I applied for.
B: [4]it / out / didn't / sorry / for / I'm / you / work

6.4 Supporting, building on and questioning ideas

4 Complete the missing words.

A: Any thoughts on how we can stop so many graduates leaving after a year?

B: Well, how about letting them work from home three days a week?

A: I [1]r _ _ _ _ _ like that idea. We've got the technology to do it.

C: Yes, but I'm just [2]w _ _ _ _ _ _ _ _ _ about team spirit. Won't we lose that if people are working from home?

B: Maybe we could have video meetings each morning?

D: Well, while we're on the [3]s _ _ _ _ _ _ _ of the daily meetings, [4]w _ _ d _ _ ' _ we just stop having them? Many employees think that meetings should only happen when they're necessary.

B: You know, that [5]m _ _ _ _ not be [6]s _ _ _ _ a bad idea!

A: And [7]d _ _ _ _ that means we [8]c _ _ _ _ have more time to concentrate on what really matters.

6.5 Making requests

5 Complete the email using the phrases in the box.

can you	could you let	do you think
if possible, I'd like	please	would you mind

Our new store opens in two weeks' time, so I'm writing to let you know the next steps for the opening.

[1]____________ Erik to check the products we need will arrive in our warehouse at least one week before the opening. If necessary, [2]____________ order products from other suppliers.

Unfortunately, we're having problems hiring staff for the new store. Andrea, [3]____________ speaking to the new Store Manager to try and find out why we're having these problems? Then [4]____________ Michelle know your findings. After that, Michelle, [5]____________ think of ways to find more staff? [6]____________ I could have a list of candidates on my desk within two or three days?

7.1 Research and development

1 Complete the missing words.

1 She has a fantastic job trying out the latest ideas for chocolate bars. She's a p _ _ _ _ _ _ t t _ s _ _ _ for a chocolate company!
2 We always ask our customers for f _ _ _ _ _ a _ _ _ so we can see if we need to change anything.
3 We l _ _ _ n _ _ _ _ _ the new product last month and it's sold very well since then.
4 One thing we ask people to tell us about is the u _ _ _ f _ _ l _ _ _ _ s of the product. It's got to be something they need.
5 We had to deal with some difficult design c _ _ _ _ _ _ e _ _ _ _ s before the product finally entered the market.
6 One customer p _ _ _ _ _ _ a _ _ _ d 5,000 units in the first month.

7.2 *can, have to, need to*

2 Complete the dialogue with *can, can't, (don't) have to* and *(don't) need to*. There may be more than one possible answer.

A: I [1] ___________ work late tonight on these new designs.
B: Do you [2] ___________ do that today? You've got a lot of time.
A: No, I haven't. I'm going on holiday next week, and unfortunately, I [3] ___________ finish everything before I go – it's impossible. There isn't enough time!
B: Don't worry, I'm not too busy this week so I [4] ___________ help you. But first I [5] ___________ finish my reports.
A: When do you [6] ___________ finish them by?
B: Tomorrow evening. After that I [7] ___________ help you because I don't have anything urgent in my diary for Thursday!

Functional language

7.3 Explaining a procedure clearly and effectively

3 Complete the dialogue using the words and phrases in the box.

any questions	because	do you see	like this
next step	once you've	start by	you've completed

A: I'll show you how to prepare an invoice. You [1] ___________ going to 'Create' on your screen and choosing 'Invoice'. Click on the 'Client' box and choose from the list.
B: What happens if it's a new client?
A: That's easy. You just click on the plus sign, and the [2] ___________ is to type the name of the new client in the box. [3] ___________ that?
B: Yes, thanks. That plus sign is very small though!
A: Now click on 'Item' to choose what the invoice is for. You can add new items using the plus symbol and typing in the box [4] ___________ : 'services July'. [5] ___________ so far?
B: No, I think that's all clear, thanks.
A: [6] ___________ done that, choose 'Amount' and add in the numbers. When [7] ___________ all the steps, send a copy to Accounts as well [8] ___________ they need the information to process payment.

7.4 Signalling and dealing with technical problems

4 Choose the correct option in italics.

1 I can hear a lot of *background / echo* noise.
2 Use the *settings / mute* button to stop any background noise.
3 The *computer / connection* is bad. I can't hear you very well.
4 Would you mind *cutting out / hanging up* and I'll call you back?
5 There's a bit of a(n) *echo / volume*.
6 Have you *switched on / muted* your webcam? We can't see you.
7 We can't hear you at all. If you can check your *noise / volume* settings?
8 You keep *switching on / cutting out* and we lose you a lot of the time.

7.5 Preparing slides

5 Choose the best option in italics to improve the text on the slide.

Slide 1

Research and development plans
- [1]*reporting / report* on progress so far
- design product features
- recommend future steps

Slide 2

Progress report
- opened [2]*a new / new* R&D department
- [3]*recruited / recruit* two more engineers
- prototype for product completed

Slide 3

New design features
As you can see it's:
- [4]*very lightweight / very small and easy to carry*
- [5]*easy-to-use / you can use it easily*
- comfortable

8 REVIEW

8.1 The environment

1 Choose the correct option in italics.

1 Plastic seriously *pollutes / protects* our oceans and harms animal life.

2 It's important to use *recycled / conserved* materials in our products.

3 Tourists to the island have had a huge *impact / damage* on the environment

4 The *destruction / protection* of the rainforest has left many animals without homes.

5 Bees are used in some parts of Africa to *reduce / protect* farms from elephants.

6 Modern farming causes a lot of *recycling / damage* to large areas of land.

8.2 *should* and *could* for advice and suggestions

2 Complete the mini dialogues using *should*, *shouldn't* or *could*.

A: What do you think I [1]__________ do? Drive to work or take a taxi?

B: You [2]__________ use your own car. A taxi is quicker, and you don't have to find somewhere to park!

C: Our company needs to save some money. Any ideas?

D: You [3]__________ try to become a paperless office. Or another possibility is you [4]__________ use those lights that are only on when someone's in the office.

E: How can we reduce the amount of plastic we use in the world?

F: Firstly, supermarkets [5]__________ use so much packaging; it's terrible. And people [6]__________ take their own bags for the food, to reduce plastic bag use.

Functional language

8.3 Giving and receiving feedback

3 Match the sentence halves.

1 We're very pleased with
2 I'm glad to
3 Is that
4 We think you
5 Would that be a
6 Let me explain why
7 I accept that this is
8 We'll start with the

a OK with you?
b we're concerned.
c positive feedback.
d could improve your technical skills.
e your progress.
f fair assessment?
g hear that.
h a problem for me sometimes.

8.4 Managing a Q&A session

4 Complete the dialogue.

A: Does [1]__________ __________ a question? Yes, Harben.

B: Thanks. I have a question about the plan to have a paperless office. Is that really going to be possible?

A: That's a [2]__________ __________, thanks Harben. So, [3]__________ __________ how realistic this plan is? Is that right?

B: Yes. I mean, what happens if we can't get online? I often have to use our paper records.

A: Well, with the new system we can check information offline, but we have to be online to make changes. [4]__________ __________ help?

B: A bit. But at the moment it can take a long time to get back online.

A: So, the [5]__________ was __________ what happens if we can't get back online quickly.

B: Yes.

A: Sorry, I don't have [6]__________ __________, but I will try to find out.

8.5 An intranet update

5 Complete the sentences from an intranet update using the phrases in the box.

also plan to	are holding	are going to	
now ready	therefore	will reduce	you know

1 As __________, we have decided to set up an environmental charity.

2 We are __________ to tell you what the charity will focus on in the coming year.

3 Firstly, we __________ focus on how we can make the town centre more eco-friendly.

4 Better public transport will encourage people to leave their cars at home. This __________ pollution.

5 We __________ ask local schoolchildren to plant a special garden in the park.

6 We are __________ inviting you all to spend some time each month helping.

7 We __________ a meeting next Friday for all those interested in taking part.

Pronunciation bank

Introduction

Pronunciation is important. You can use the right words and the right grammar, but other people won't understand you if your pronunciation isn't clear. Learning about the important features of pronunciation will also help you to understand spoken English better.

Syllables, stress and intonation

Different words have different numbers of syllables:

1 syllable	*grow, growth*	4 syllables	*in•ter•view•er, co•or•di•nate*
2 syllables	*prod•uct, re•port*	5 syllables	*char•ac•ter•is•tic*
3 syllables	*in•ter•view, pro•duc•tion*	6 syllables	*re•spon•si•bil•i•ty*

In words with more than one syllable, one of the syllables is stressed, i.e. clearer, louder and longer than the other syllables, and it carries the main intonation, i.e. the movement of the voice up or down:

PRODuct	INterview	INterviewer
rePORT	proDUCtion	coORdinate

In longer words and compound nouns there is often a second, less important stress, i.e. a less strong stress earlier in the word:

characteRIStic   responsiBILity   mobile PHONE

Stress is important in making words easy to recognise. Stress and intonation are used to highlight important information:

A: Are you still using that same old comPUter? **B:** No, I've got a NEW one.

A: Did you get it as a PREsent? **B:** No, I BOUGHT it.

The sounds of English

These are the sounds of standard British English and American English pronunciation. See also the section 'Varieties of English' on the following page.

Consonants	
Symbol	**Keyword**
p	pen
b	back
t	tea
ţ (*AmE*)	city
d	day
k	key
g	get
tʃ	church
dʒ	job
f	fact
v	view
θ	thing
ð	this
s	soon
z	zero
ʃ	ship
ʒ	pleasure
h	hot
m	more
n	nice
ŋ	ring
l	light
r	right
j	yet
w	wet

Vowels		
Symbol	**Symbol**	**Keyword**
BrE	AmE	
ɪ	ɪ	kit
e	e	dress
æ	æ	bad
ʌ	ʌ	but
ʊ	ʊ	foot
ɒ	ä	odd
ə	ə	about
i	i	happy
u	u	situation
iː	i	feel
ɑː	ɑ	father
ɔː	ɔ	north
uː	u	choose
ɜː	ɚ	stir
eɪ	eɪ	face
aɪ	aɪ	price
ɔɪ	ɔɪ	boy
əʊ	oʊ	no
aʊ	aʊ	mouth
ɪə	ɪr	near
eə	er	hair
ʊə	ʊr	sure

/ţ/ means that many American speakers use a voiced sound like a quick /d/ for the /t/ in words like *city, party, little*.

: shows a long vowel

Sounds and spelling

In English, the relationship between spoken and written language is particularly complicated.

The same sound can be spelt in different ways, e.g.

- /əʊ/ *sl**ow*** *g**o*** *l**oa**n* *t**oe*** *alth**ough*** *kn**ow***
- /s/ ***s**ell* ***sc**ien**ce*** ***c**ent*

The same letter can be pronounced in different ways, e.g.

- the letter *u* can be pronounced /ʌ/ as in *c**u**t*, /ʊ/ as in *f**u**ll*, /ɔː/ as in *s**u**re* in British English or /ɪ/ as in *b**u**sy*;
- the letter *s* can be pronounced /s/ as in ***s**ell*, /z/ as in *ea**s**y*, /ʃ/ as in *ten**s**ion* or /ʒ/ as in *deci**s**ion*.

Using a dictionary

Try to learn the phonetic symbols in the table in The sounds of English section. When you recognise these you will be able to use a dictionary to find the pronunciation of any word. As well as the sounds in a word, dictionaries also show word stress. Look at this dictionary entry for *controversial*:

> **con·tro·ver·sial** /ˌkɒntrəˈvɜːʃəl/ *adj* causing a lot of disagreement, because many people have strong opinions about the subject being discussed

- The ˈ sign shows you that the syllable immediately after it is stressed.
- The ˌ sign shows you that the syllable immediately after it has secondary stress.
- The **ː** sign shows you that the vowel is long.

Simplifications

In normal everyday speech, however, words often do not have the same pronunciation as shown in dictionaries. This is important for listening. Vowels in stressed syllables are usually pronounced clearly, but sometimes speakers make various simplifications:

- Some sounds are missed out, e.g. *facts* can sound like 'facs', *compete* can sound like 'cmpete', *characteristic* can sound like 'charrtristic'.
- Some sounds are merged together, e.g. *on Monday* can sound like 'om Monday', *ten groups* can sound like 'teng groups', *this show* can sound like 'thishow'.

Varieties of English

English is spoken by some people as a first language, but it is also spoken by more people who learn it as an additional language and use it as a lingua franca for international communication.

There is a large amount of variation in how English is pronounced:

- Variation among traditional 'native' accents such as British, American and Australian. There are also big differences between the accents of different regions of the United Kingdom.
- Variation among accents of English as a lingua franca. Many of these differences are caused by the influence of speakers' first languages, e.g. Japanese speakers often do not distinguish between /l/ and /r/, and Spanish speakers often add an /e/ at the front of words beginning with /sp/, /sk/ and /st/.

Consonant sounds are generally similar in different varieties of English, but there is much more variation in vowel sounds. The number of vowel sounds speakers use and the exact quality of the sounds can be different.

In the course audio and video recordings – and in your everyday life and work – you will hear speakers from various English-speaking and non-English-speaking backgrounds communicating successfully with each other despite their differences in pronunciation. For example, many speakers do not use the /θ/ sound of '**th**ink' and the /ð/ sound of '**th**en', but this does not generally affect their ability to make themselves understood. Particularly important things to concentrate on include:

- word stress,
- stress and intonation in phrases and sentences, for highlighting important information,
- consonant sounds,
- groups of consonants at the beginning of words – e.g. ***str**ong*,
- the difference between long and short vowels.

Good pronunciation does not necessarily mean speaking like a 'native' speaker; it means being understood by others when communicating in English. Understanding pronunciation features and practising them will help you improve both your speaking and your listening comprehension.

Lesson 1.2

The letter 'r'

Many speakers (e.g. most speakers of American, Irish and Scottish English) always pronounce the letter 'r'. Others (e.g. many speakers of British English) only pronounce 'r' before a vowel sound.
Listen and compare American English with British English:
P1.01 *Planning a party for 200 people is harder than planning a party for 20.*

1 Underline all the letter 'r's in the sentences.

1. A party for 50 is cheaper than a party for 500.
2. The better option is a big tent in the park.
3. Some people think this is the worst hotel in town.
4. The barbecue is bigger than the restaurant.
5. A circus theme is more fun than just having a meal.
6. Are some venues better than others?

2A P1.02 Listen to two speakers saying the sentences in Exercise 1. Circle the letters 'r' that are pronounced.

B Which sentences in Exercise 2 were said by a British English speaker and which by an American English speaker?

3 Work in pairs. Take turns to say the sentences in Exercise 1. Try pronouncing all the 'r's and then pronouncing only the 'r's before vowel sounds. Which type of pronunciation is easier for you?

Lesson 1.3

Showing interest in small talk

When you ask *wh-* questions to make small talk, show interest in the person you are talking to by using a strong downward movement starting from the main stress.
Listen and compare a less interested version with a more interested version of this question:

P1.03 *Where are you <u>from</u>?*

1 P1.04 Listen to two versions of each question. Which version sounds more interested – a or b?

1. Where do you work?
2. What are you doing in Dublin?
3. How long was your trip?
4. What do you think about the food here?
5. What do you know about Dublin?

2 P1.05 Listen to the more interested versions again and repeat.

3 Work in pairs. Make small talk using the questions in Exercise 1. Use the AAA model from Exercise 8B on page 13.

Lesson 2.1

Syllables and stress

In a word with more than one syllable, one of the syllables is stressed more strongly (the main stress). For example:
P2.01 *WAREhouse loCATE MOtorway*

1 Work in pairs. Underline the syllable with the main stress in each word.

1 access	3 facilities	5 studio
2 convenient	4 hotel	6 transport

2 P2.02 Listen and check. Then listen again and repeat.

3 P2.03 Work in pairs. Take turns to say the sentences. Listen and check.

1. How are the transport links in your town?
2. The train station's very convenient.
3. What leisure facilities are there close to your home?
4. They want to locate their next hotel in the city centre.
5. It's a technology design studio.
6. It's important for the factory to have good access to motorways.

Lesson 2.2

Stress in noun phrases

Compound nouns usually – but not always – have the main stress on the first word. For example:
P2.04 *THEME park LUXury resort city CENtre*

1 P2.05 Listen to the compound nouns. Which one has the main stress on the *second* word?

1 ski resort	4 wildlife park
2 bird park	5 shopping experience
3 city zoo	

2 Listen again and underline the main stressed word. If the stressed word has more than one syllable, underline the stressed syllable.

3 Listen again and repeat.

4 Work in pairs. Take turns to say *one* word of a compound noun in Exercise 1. Your partner says the complete compound.

A: *Park …*
B: *BIRD park. City …*
A: *City ZOO. Ski …*

Lesson 3.2
Past Simple

The vowel sounds /aɪ/, /eɪ/, /iː/, /ɜː/ and /ɔː/ used in Past Simple forms are often spelt in different ways in different verbs.
For example, the vowel sound /aɪ/ can be spelt 'i' (e.g. 'liked') or 'ie' (e.g. 'tried'). Some words are pronounced differently from what the spelling suggests. For example, 'said' is pronounced /sed/.
P3.01 *liked tried said*

1 P3.02 Do the verbs have the same vowel sound or different vowel sounds? Listen and check.

1 chose – taught — *same / different*
2 paid – said — *same / different*
3 heard – served — *same / different*
4 chose – could — *same / different*
5 saw – thought — *same / different*
6 agreed – received — *same / different*
7 came – played — *same / different*
8 could – thought — *same / different*
9 arrived – cried — *same / different*
10 paid – tried — *same / different*

2 Look at the pairs of words with the same vowel sounds in Exercise 1. What different spellings can you see?

3 Work in pairs. Take turns to say one of the verbs in Exercise 1; your partner says the infinitive of the verb.

Lesson 3.3
Stress in short sentences

Contrasting stressed and unstressed words is essential for natural spoken English and for expressing what you want to say. Short sentences often have two or three main stresses, usually on the 'content' words – these are the words that carry most meaning. Without stress, it is difficult to hear the important words in speech.
Listen and compare two versions of these sentences:
P3.03 *Sorry to bother you.*
Just the person I was looking for!

1A Which two words do you think are stressed in these sentences?

1 How's it going?
2 You look a bit worried.
3 I'm sure he'll understand.
4 I'm still having problems.

B Which three words do you think are stressed in these sentences?

5 I'm going as fast as I can.
6 How about asking someone to help?
7 I'll see if I can get you some support.
8 How are you doing with that report?

2 P3.04 Listen and check.

3 Work in pairs. Take turns to say one of the sentences in Exercise 1 and clap your hands on the two or three main stresses. Then repeat the sentence and both clap together.

Lesson 4.1
Vowel sounds: British English and American English

Some vowels are pronounced differently in British English and American English. Listen and compare British English with American English:
P4.01 *job clock app taxi*

1 P4.02 You will hear each word twice. The first version is British. Is the second version *British* (B) or *American* (A)?

1 job
2 clock
3 project
4 possible
5 app
6 taxi
7 pattern
8 aspect

2 P4.03 You will hear each word twice. Which version is British and which is American? Write B–A (*British* → *American*) or A–B (*American* → *British*).

1 job
2 clock
3 project
4 possible
5 holiday
6 economy
7 app
8 taxi
9 pattern
10 aspect
11 management

3 P4.04 Now you will hear each word once. Is it *British* (B) or *American* (A)?

1 job
2 clock
3 project
4 possible
5 holiday
6 economy
7 app
8 taxi
9 pattern
10 aspect
11 management

4 Work in pairs. Practise saying the words in Exercises 1–3. Does your partner sound British or American?

Lesson 4.2

Present Perfect Simple

In the Present Perfect Simple, *have* and *has* are usually pronounced as weak forms. For example:
P4.05 *It was the worst job I'<u>ve</u> /v/ ever had.*
This job'<u>s</u> /z/ helped me a lot.

We usually use /həv/ **and** /həz/ **in questions, and** /hæv/, /hævnt/, /hæz/ **and** /hæznt/ **in short answers. For example:**
P4.06 ***A:*** *Have /həv/ you finished?*
B: *Yes, I have /hæv/. or: No, I haven't /hævnt/.*

We also use /hæz/ **and** /hæv/ **for stress. For example:**
P4.07 ***A:*** *He hasn't /hæznt/ sent the contract.*
B: *He has /hæz/ sent it – look, it's here!*

1 P4.08 **Listen and complete the sentences. Use *'ve, have, 's* or *has*.**

1 __________ never bought any good business books. But __________ read a few.
2 __________ read a few, too. I read some when I was a student.
3 __________ heard of Daniel Kahneman. I think __________ won a Nobel Prize.
4 Yes, __________ . __________ written a lot about how we make decisions.
5 __________ read this book? I started it once or twice, but __________ never finished it.
6 __________ just finished it. I liked it.

2 **Work in pairs and practise saying the sentences in Exercise 1.**

Lesson 5.2

Intonation in conditionals

When the *if* clause comes first in a conditional sentence, we often use a fall-rise in the *if* clause and a fall in the main clause. These intonation patterns start on the main stressed word in the clause. For example:

P5.01 *If I buy a <u>car</u>, I'll buy a second-<u>hand</u> one.*

If interest rates <u>increase</u>, borrowing will go <u>down</u>.

1 P5.02 **Listen and underline the main stressed word in each clause.**

1 If I want to earn more money, I'll need to improve my English.
2 If you cycle to work, you'll save thousands.
3 If she has more money in the future, she'll move to a bigger flat.
4 If I sell my car, I'll buy a bicycle.
5 If the weather's fine, I'll walk to work tomorrow.
6 If you take your lunch to work, you'll save hundreds a year.
7 If they don't spend so much on transport, they'll save money.
8 If he doesn't start saving for a deposit, he'll never buy a house.

2 **Work in pairs and practise saying the sentences in Exercise 1.**

Lesson 5.4

Numbers and figures

It is important to know how to say numbers and figures when we are presenting or discussing them with colleagues.

'%' is pronounced /pəˈsent/.
P5.03 *10% 65% 100%*

'–' is usually pronounced /tə/.
P5.04 *aged 17–20 the years 1955–1987 50–55%*

'.' in numbers is pronounced /pɔɪnt/.
P5.05 *3.5 27.2 85.5%*

Years are usually pronounced in two parts: 1814 'eighteen fourteen', 1945 'nineteen forty-five', 2019 'twenty nineteen'. But 2000 is 'two thousand' and 2001–2009 are 'two thousand <u>and</u> one', etc.
P5.06 *1814 1945 2019 BUT: 2000 2001*

The number '0' is usually 'oh' in room numbers, years and telephone numbers, 'oh', 'nought' or 'zero' in decimal numbers, 'oh' in 24-clock times and 'zero' for a temperature of 0°.
P5.07 *room 305 the year 1802*
305 063 (= phone number) 0.05 13.05 (= time)
just above 0°

1 **Look at the numbers and decide how they will be pronounced.**

1 room 101
2 46.092
3 the years 1605–1615
4 0.5%
5 072 460 705 (= phone number)
6 10–12-year-olds
7 18.07%
8 below 0°
9 12.45–14.05 (= times)
10 rooms 405–409
11 0371 050 368 280
12 the years 2006–2018

2 P5.08 **Listen and check.**

3 **Work in pairs and practise saying the numbers and figures in Exercise 1.**

Lesson 6.1

Vowel sounds: /ɪ/, /iː/, /aɪ/ and /ɪə/

Listen to the examples of words with these four vowel sounds:
P6.01 /ɪ/ *give* /iː/ *feel* /aɪ/ *price* /ɪə/ *near*

1 **Work in pairs. Put the words in the box in the correct column according to the pronunciation of the letters in bold.**

believe busy city clearly climbing complete experienced high hiker issue metres people reliable realise simple zero

/ɪ/ give	/iː/ feel	/aɪ/ price	/ɪə/ near

2 P6.02 **Listen and check. Then listen again and repeat.**

3 P6.03 **Work in pairs. Listen and practise saying the sentences.**

1 I feel really tired after that meeting.
2 I don't think my manager realises how experienced I am.
3 We're going to issue a new price list next week.
4 The simple fact is that the company needs more reliable people.
5 I can't believe how busy we've been this month.

Lesson 6.2

Linking between words

When one word ends with a consonant sound (e.g. 's' in 'companies') and the next word begins with a vowel sound (e.g. 'e' in 'encourage'), the consonant is usually linked with the vowel. For example:
P6.04 *companies_encourage*
their_employees
get fit_and
know_each_other

Compare a linked and an unlinked sentence.
P6.05 *Many companies_encourage their_employees to get fit_and to get to know_each_other.*

1 P6.06 **Listen and repeat these phrases.**

1 you're_all
2 have_everything
3 looked_everywhere for_it
4 just_ask_if
5 report_and_a pen_or pencil
6 print_out_an_extra

2 **Work in pairs. Complete the sentences and questions with the phrases in Exercise 1.**

1 Do you ________________ you need?
2 ________________ copy.
3 I've ________________ .
4 A copy of the ________________ .
5 I'm glad ________________ here.
6 ________________ you need help.

3 P6.07 **Listen and check. Then listen again and repeat.**

4 **Take turns to say the sentences and questions in Exercise 2. Listen and check that your partner includes the consonant-vowel links.**

Lesson 7.2

can and *can't*

Can **is pronounced /kən/ (weak form) when unstressed (e.g. in positive sentences and questions), and /kæn/ (strong form) when stressed, e.g. in question tags and short answers.**
Can't **is pronounced /kɑːnt/, but often without a clear /t/ at the end.**
P7.01 *You can /kən/ check in any time.*
We can't /kɑːnt/ leave our suitcases here, can /kæn/ we?
A: *Can /kən/ you check in after midnight?*
B: *Yes, you can /kæn/.*
I can't /kɑːnt/ find my reservation number.

1 P7.02 **Listen and complete the sentences with *can* or *can't*.**

1 I __________ open my door with my key card.
2 You __________ use the check-in kiosk.
3 You __________ go directly to the gate.
4 __________ I check in without my ID?
5 This robot __________ talk, __________ it?
6 Yes, it __________!

2 P7.03 **Listen again to the sentences in Exercise 1 with *can*. Decide if you hear the *weak form* (W) or the *strong form* (S).**

3 **Work in pairs. Take turns to say the sentences in Exercise 1. Tell your partner if you hear 'weak *can*', 'strong *can*' or '*can't*'.**

Lesson 7.3

Phrasing and pausing when giving instructions

To give clear instructions, it is important not to speak too fast and to pause between phrases. For example:
P7.04 First of all – you need to click on 'Register' – you can find it – at the bottom of the screen – then enter your surname – name – and email address.

1 P7.05 **Listen to this set of instructions and mark the pauses.**

The first step/is to sign in to your account./To do this you'll need to enter your name and ID number. When you've done this, go to the drop-down menu in the top right-hand corner of the screen, and select 'Create new report'. Then you can type your report or paste it in.

2 **Work in pairs. Take turns to practise the instructions in Exercise 1, and give feedback: Does your partner use enough pauses?**

Lesson 8.1

Vowel sounds: /ɜː/, /ʊ/, /uː/ and /əʊ/

Listen to the examples of words with these four vowel sounds:
P8.01 /ɜː/ *bird* /ʊ/ *foot* /uː/ *group* /əʊ/ *no*

1 P8.02 **Listen and underline the example of each sound in the sentences.**

1 /ɜː/ (b**ir**d) It's a popular surf and tourist destination.
2 /ʊ/ (f**oo**t) The foundation is looking for solutions.
3 /uː/ (gr**ou**p) The traffic has already improved a lot.
4 /əʊ/ (n**o**) They want to stop construction on the coast.

2 **Listen again and repeat.**

3 **Work in pairs. Say one of the key words in Exercise 1, e.g. 'bird'. Your partner says the sentence that has that sound.**

Lesson 8.2

should and *could*

Should **and** ***could*** **are pronounced** /ʃəd/ **and** /kəd/ **(weak forms) when unstressed e.g. in positive sentences.**
Should **and** ***could*** **are pronounced** / ʃʊd/ **and** /kʊd/ **(strong forms) when stressed, e.g. in question tags and short answers, and for emphasis.**
Shouldn't **is pronounced** /ʃʊdnt/**, but often without a clear** /t/ **at the end.**
P8.03
A: *You should /ʃəd/ do more exercise.*
B: *Yes, I think I should /ʃʊd/.*

You shouldn't /ʃʊdnt/ eat so much.

A: *We could /kəd/ meet in the hotel reception.*
B: *We could /kʊd/, but it's so noisy there.*

1 P8.04 **Listen and complete the sentences with** ***should, shouldn't*** **or** ***could*****.**

1 We ___________ catch a bus or get a taxi.
2 We ___________ wait here any longer.
3 Do you think I ___________ walk more?
4 Yes, and you ___________ , easily.
5 They ___________ spend more on public transport.
6 Yes, they definitely ___________ .

2 P8.05 **Listen again to the sentences in Exercise 1 with** ***should*** **and** ***could*****. Decide if you hear the** ***weak form*** **(W) or the** ***strong form*** **(S).**

3 **Work in pairs. Take turns to say the sentences in Exercise 1 with** ***should*** **or** ***could*****. Tell you partner if you hear strong or weak forms.**

1.2 Comparatives and superlatives

Comparatives

We use **comparatives** to say **how two things are different**.

Planning a business lunch is ***easier than*** *planning a wedding.*

An outdoor event is always ***more difficult than*** *an indoor event, because of the weather.*

For this event, the schedule is ***less important than*** *the budget.*

One syllable: add *-er*	hard → hard**er** cheap → cheap**er**
Two syllables ending in -*y*: change *y* to *i* and add *-er*	easy → eas**ier** happy → happ**ier**
Two or more syllables: use *more*	expensive → **more** expensive
Irregular	good → better bad → worse fun → more fun
Adjectives ending consonant + vowel + consonant: double the final consonant and add *-er*	big → big**ger**

Note: We can use *less* with all adjectives, both short and long.

Superlatives

We use **superlatives** to say that **one thing has more or less of a quality than any other thing** in the same group.

The Green Room is ***the biggest*** *dining room in the hotel.*

This is ***the most expensive*** *restaurant in town.*

Small events are ***the least difficult****.*

One syllable: add *-est*	hard → hard**est** cheap → cheap**est**
Two syllables ending in -*y*: change *y* to *i* and add *-est*	easy → eas**iest** happy → happ**iest**
Two or more syllables: use *most*	expensive → **most** expensive
Irregular	good → best bad → worst fun → most fun
Adjectives ending consonant + vowel + consonant: double the final consonant and add *-est*	big → big**gest**

Note: We can use *least* with all adjectives, both short and long.

1.5 *can* and *could* to ask for information

We use ***can*** and ***could*** to **ask people to do things**.

- ***Can you ... ?*** is generally a little less formal than ***Could you ... ?*** but both are often used in semi-formal writing.
  Can you *confirm that you have rooms available?*
  Could you *tell me what your best price is?*
- We often use ***please*** with *can* and *could*. *Please* can go in three places in the question.
  Please *can you confirm how long it takes to walk to the centre?*
  Can you ***please*** *confirm how long it takes to walk to the centre?*
  Can you confirm how long it takes to walk to the centre, ***please****?*

2.2 *enough* and *too*

enough

We use ***enough***:

- in **positive sentences** to say that **the size, number, etc. of something is what is needed or wanted**.
  The hotel rooms are ***large enough*** *for three guests.*
  There is ***enough time*** *to see the city.*
- in **negative sentences** to say that **the size, number, etc. of something is less than is needed or wanted**.
  He ***isn't tall enough*** *to go on the ride.*
  There ***isn't enough money*** *for a taxi.*
- in **questions** to ask if **the size, number, etc. of something is what is needed or wanted**.
  Is it ***close enough*** *to walk?*
  Are there ***enough places*** *to eat?*

1 adjective + (*not*) *enough*

Positive and negative				
subject	***be***	**adjective**	***enough***	
He	isn't	tall	enough	to go on the ride.
The hotel rooms	are	large	enough	for three guests.

Questions				
be	**subject**	**adjective**	***enough***	**?**
Is	the car	big	enough	for five people?
Are	the shops	close	enough	to walk to?

2 *There* + *be* + (*not*) *enough* + noun

Positive and negative				
There	***be***	***(not) enough***	**noun / noun phrase**	
There	is	enough	time	to visit the zoo.
There	are	enough	attractions	to spend a day at the park.
There	isn't	enough	money	for a holiday this year.
There	aren't	enough	places	to eat.

Questions				
be	***there***	***enough***	**noun / noun phrase**	**?**
Is	there	enough	time	to go shopping?
Are	there	enough	places	to eat?

too

We use ***too***:

- in **positive sentences** to say that **something is more or less than is right, good or needed**.
  The Bird Park is ***too small*** *for all the species.*
  There were ***too many people*** *at the theme park.*
  It is ***too much money*** *to spend on a holiday.*

1 *too* + adjective

subject	verb	*too*	adjective	
He	is	too	short	to go on the ride.
These prices	are	too	expensive	for me.
The hotel	was	too	far	from the centre of town.
They	were	too	tired	to concentrate.

2 *too many* + countable noun

subject	verb	*too many*	countable noun	
There	are	too many	tall buildings	on the coast.
There	were	too many	people	at the theme park.
		Too many	holidaymakers	go there in summer.

3 *too much* + uncountable noun

subject	verb	*too much*	uncountable noun	
It	is	too much	money	to spend on a holiday.
There	was	too much	noise	in the hotel.
		Too much	queuing	is not popular with visitors.

2.5 Present Continuous

We use the **Present Continuous**:

- to talk about **what is happening now**.

  *I'm **waiting** outside Duke St offices.*

  *I'm **phoning** the office now.*

  *He's **waiting** outside Duke St offices.*

  *He **isn't waiting** at Chester St offices.*

Positive		
I	am/'m	working.
You/We/They	are/'re	
He/She/It	is/'s	

Negative		
I	am not/'m not	working.
You/We/They	are not/aren't	
He/She/It	is not/isn't	

Yes/No questions		
Am	I	working?
Are	you/we/they	
Is	he/she/it	

Short answers					
Yes,	I	am.	No,	I	'm not.
	you/we/they	are.		you/we/they	aren't.
	he/she/it	is.		he/she/it	isn't.

Open questions			
When	am	I	working?
	are	you/we/they	
	is	he/she/it	

Spelling	
Most verbs: add *-ing* to the infinitive	wait → wait**ing** work → work**ing** go → go**ing**
Verbs ending in *-e*: replace *-e* with *-ing*	phone → phon**ing** make → mak**ing** take → tak**ing**
Verbs ending consonant + vowel + consonant: double the final consonant and add *-ing*	plan → plan**ning** get → get**ting** stop → stop**ping**
***Note*: Do not double the final consonant:** • if the verb has two syllables and the stress is on the first syllable.	happen → happen**ing** enter → enter**ing**
• if the verb ends in *-w*, *-x* or *-y*.	show → show**ing** fix → fix**ing** enjoy → enjoy**ing**

3.2 Past Simple and Past Continuous

Past Simple

We use the **Past Simple** to talk about:

- **completed actions and events in the past**.

  *She **had** a conference in Istanbul last week.*

  *I **went** to the new shopping mall yesterday.*

- **completed events and actions that happen one after another**.

  *We **spent** the day visiting the city. Then we **had** dinner in the hotel.*

  *The carpet seller **served** us tea and then we **negotiated** the price.*

We can use ***when*** to **connect two clauses in the past**.

***When** we sat down, the carpet seller served us tea.*

*The carpet seller served us tea **when** we sat down.*

Positive	
I/You/He/She/It/We/They	worked.

Negative		
I/You/He/She/It/We/They	didn't	work.

Yes/No questions		
Did	I/you/he/she/it/we/they	work?

Short answers		
Yes,	I/you/he/she/it/we/they	did.
No,	I/you/he/she/it/we/they	didn't.

Open questions			
When	did	I/you/he/she/it/we/they	work?

Note: ***be*** *and* ***can***

We form the negative and question forms of *be* in the Past Simple without the auxiliary *did*.

*He **wasn't** in the shop this morning.*

A: ***Were*** *you in Istanbul at the weekend?*

B: *Yes, I **was**.*

A: *Where **was** your hotel?*

B: *In the city centre.*

We form the negative of *can* in the Past Simple without the auxiliary *did*.

*She **couldn't** decide what to buy.*

Spelling	
Most verbs: add *-ed* to the infinitive	decide → decid**ed** walk → walk**ed** want → want**ed**
Verbs ending in *-e*: add *-d*	dance → dance**d** like → like**d** smile → smile**d**
Verbs ending consonant + *-y*: change *y* to *i* and add *-ed*	carr**y** → carr**ied** stud**y** → stud**ied** tr**y** on → tr**ied** on
Verbs ending consonant + vowel + consonant: double the final consonant and add *-ed*	plan → plan**ned** prefer → prefer**red** stop → stop**ped**
***Note:* Do <u>not</u> double the final consonant:** • if the verb has two syllables and the stress is on the first syllable.	<u>hap</u>pen → happen**ed** <u>en</u>ter → enter**ed**
• if the verb ends in *-w*, *-x* or *-y*.	show → show**ed** fix → fix**ed** enjoy → enjoy**ed**

Note: Many frequently used verbs are irregular.

be → was/were (negatives *wasn't/weren't*), *can → could* (negative *couldn't*), *come → came, get → got, go → went, have → had, make → made, say → said, see → saw, take → took*

See page 126 for a list of common irregular verbs.

Past Continuous

We use the **Past Continuous**:

- to talk about **actions and situations happening at a specific moment in the past.**

  A: *What **were** you **doing** at 10 o'clock this morning?*

  B: *I **was waiting** at the airport for the visitors to arrive.*

- to give **'background' details**, e.g. the weather, the location or extra details about someone's life at the time.

  *It **was raining** for hours last night.*

  *Shanghai **was holding** several conferences that week.*

  *She **was living** in Madrid at the time.*

We can use ***when*** to **connect a clause in the Past Simple with a clause in the Past Continuous**.

We were browsing in the bazaar (= situation) ***when*** *we saw a beautiful lamp* (= main action).

She was living in Madrid at the time (= situation). *One day she was shopping in the market* (= situation) ***when*** *she met an old school friend* (= main action).

Shanghai was holding several conferences that week (= situation). ***When*** *I arrived at the hotel* (= main action), *hundreds of guests were waiting in the reception* (= situation).

Positive		
I/He/She/It	was	working.
You/We/They	were	

Negative		
I/He/She/It	was not/wasn't	working.
You/We/They	were not / weren't	

***Yes/No* questions**		
Was	I/he/she/it	working?
Were	you/we/they	

Short answers		
Yes,	I/he/she/it	was.
	you/we/they	were.
No,	I/he/she/it	wasn't.
	you/we/they	weren't.

Open questions			
When	was	I/he/she/it	working?
	were	you/we/they	

Note: The spelling rules for *-ing* forms in the Past Continuous are the same as for the Present Continuous. See page 120 for full details.

Note: Verbs which describe states or feelings do not take the continuous form.

*I **was liking** the book.* ✗

*I **liked** the book.* ✓

*He **wasn't agreeing** with my opinion.* ✗

*He **didn't agree** with my opinion.* ✓

Some verbs can be both a state or an action verb.

*I **thought** the book was interesting.* ✓ (= opinion)

*I **was thinking** about writing a book.* ✓ (= action)

3.5 Types of adverbs

Type of adverb	**Example**
manner (how we do something)	They served the food very **slowly**. The food didn't come very **quickly**.
frequency (how often we do something)	We **often** bring our clients to the Orchid. The staff are **always** friendly and helpful.
time (when we do something)	We'll go to the Orchid Restaurant again **soon**. We last ate there **yesterday**.
place (where we do something)	We eat **here** every week. I had coffee **there** last night.
direction (which way something goes)	Turn **left** just past the Orchid Restaurant. Go **straight on** and you'll see the café.

Note: Adverbs can be one word like *yesterday*, *today*, *tomorrow* and *soon* or a phrase like *on Fridays*, *in the summer* and *at home*.

*We ate in the Orchid **last Friday**.*

*We visited you **in the summer**.*

*I had dinner **at home** last night.*

4.2 Present Perfect Simple

We use the **Present Perfect Simple** to talk about our **experiences when we do not say a specific time in the past**.

*I**'ve been** to Poland.*

*She**'s worked** in several countries.*

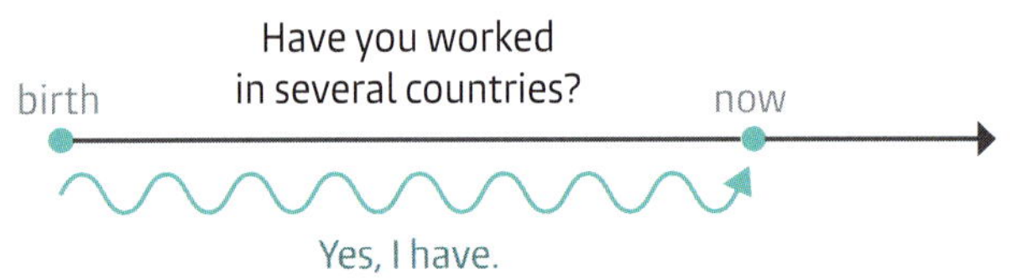

Positive		
I/You/We/They	have	worked.
He/She/It	has	

Negative		
I/You/We/They	have not / haven't	worked.
He/She/It	has not / hasn't	

***Yes/No* questions**		
Have	I/you/we/they	worked?
Has	he/she/it	

Short answers		
Yes,	I/you/we/they	have.
	he/she/it	has.
No,	I/you/we/they	haven't.
	he/she/it	hasn't.

Open questions			
When	have	I/you/we/they	worked?
	has	he/she/it	

Note: The spelling rules for *-ed* forms in the Present Perfect Simple are the same as for the Past Simple. See page 121 for full details.

Many frequently used verbs are irregular.

eat → *eaten*

have → *had*

meet → *met*

read /ri:d/ → *read* /red/

see → *seen*

teach → *taught*

See page 126 for a list of common irregular verbs.

been* and *gone

- We use ***been*** to say **we have visited a place at some time in our lives**.

  *She's **been** to New York.*

- We use ***gone*** to say that **a person is in that place now**.

  *She's **gone** to New York. She's not in the office this week.*

ever* and *never

- We use ***ever*** in questions to ask about **experiences that we may have had 'at any time'**.

  *Have you **ever** worked in Poland?*

- We use ***never*** in positive sentences to say **this is not an experience we have had**.

  *He's **never** worked abroad.*

Time expressions

We can use expressions of frequency with the Present Perfect Simple.

*I've been to Poland **once** / **twice** / **three times**, etc.*

Note: When we give details about the exact time of a past experience, we use the Past Simple.

***A:** Have you ever been to Poland?*

***B:** Yes, I have. I **went** there last spring.*

4.5 Prepositions of time

Preposition	Example
Use *on*: • with dates. • with days. • if the day name is before the part of the day.	*This is to confirm our meeting **on** 12th April.* *I am able to attend the meeting **on** Friday.* *I'll see you **on** Wednesday morning.*
Use *at*: • with times. • with words like *lunchtime*, *breakfast* and *the weekend*. • with *night*.	*The meeting is on Friday 12th April **at** 9 a.m.* *What did you do **at** the weekend?* *Some staff do not like working **at** night.*
Use *in*: • with parts of the day (except *night*). • with months. • with years. • with expressions like *in three days* and *in a year*.	*I am flying to Germany **in** the afternoon.* *I look forward to seeing you **in** March.* *We first met **in** 2012.* *I very much look forward to meeting you **in two weeks**. (= two weeks after today)*
Use *from ... to*: • to show the beginning and the end of something.	*The meetings last **from** 10 **to** 11.30 a.m.*
Use *until*: • to show when something stops or changes.	*The meeting will last **until** 12.30.*
Use **no preposition** with *this*, *next*, *last* and *every*.	*I look forward to meeting you **next** week.*

5.2 First conditional

We use **first conditional** sentences to talk about **conditions with possible results in the future**.

If you cycle to work, you'll save hundreds.

If banks raise the interest rate on savings, savers will earn more.

If can go in two places in the sentence.

condition (*If* + Present Simple)	result (*will* + infinitive)
If *interest rates* ***increase****,*	*borrowing* ***will go*** *down.*

result (*will* + infinitive)	condition (*if* + Present Simple)
Borrowing ***will go*** *down*	***If*** *interest rates* ***increase****.*

The condition never uses the word *will*.

condition	result
If I ~~will~~ ***sell*** *my car,*	*I* ***will save*** *a lot of money.*
result	**condition**
I ***will be*** *healthier*	*if I ~~will~~* ***cycle*** *to work.*

Both parts of a conditional sentence need to have a subject.

If ***you*** *make your lunch at home,* ***you*** *will save money.*

He*'ll save more money if* ***he*** *moves to a smaller flat.*

If you begin a conditional sentence with *if*, put a comma in the middle. You do not need a comma if you start with the result.

If interest rates go up, savers will be happy.

Savers will be happy if interest rates go up.

5.5 *because, so, so that*

We use ***because*** to introduce the **reason for something.** It joins two sentences together.

We need to increase our prices ***because*** *raw material costs are higher.*

We use ***because of*** with a **noun phrase** but not with a verb.

We need to increase our prices ***because of*** *rising costs.*

We can also put ***because*** at the beginning of the sentence. If we begin a sentence with ***because***, we put a comma after the ***because*** clause.

Because *raw material costs are higher****,*** *we need to increase our prices.*

Because of *rising costs****,*** *we need to increase our prices.*

We use ***so*** to introduce a **result**. It joins two sentences together. The result clause with ***so*** always comes after the main clause.

Raw material costs have increased ***so*** *we need to raise our prices.*

Note: If we want to put the result clause first, we must use ***because***.

We need to raise our prices ***because*** *raw material costs are higher.*

We use ***so that*** to introduce the **purpose of the action**.

We are keeping the rise small ***so that*** *our prices still remain competitive.*

We can also use ***to* + infinitive** to introduce the **purpose of the action**.

We increased prices ***to*** *cover costs.*

Note: We can only use ***to* + infinitive** if the subjects are the same in both parts of the sentence.

We *increased prices to cover costs. (=* ***We*** *increased prices so that* ***we*** *could cover costs.)*

We use ***so that*** when the subject is different in the two parts of the sentence.

We *increased our prices so that* ***they*** *covered* ***our*** *costs. (****they*** *= the prices)*

6.2 Pronouns with *some-* and *every-*

We use **pronouns with *some-*** to talk about '**a thing**', '**a person**' and '**in a place**'.

Have you lost ***something****?*

Someone/Somebody *phoned while you were out.*

I've left my keys ***somewhere****.*

We use **pronouns with *every-*** to talk about '**all things**', '**all people**' and '**in all places**'.

Do you have ***everything*** *you need for your trip?*

Everyone/Everybody *should do a little sport if they can.*

I've looked ***everywhere****, but I can't find my wallet.*

	-thing	*-one/-body*	*-where*
some-	something	someone somebody	somewhere
every-	everything	everyone everybody	everywhere

6.5 Linking words for sequence

We use ***First***, ***Then/Next***, ***After that*** and ***Finally*** to introduce **instructions in order**.

First, *I'd like Ana to meet him immediately.*

Then/Next, *if we like it, we'll book it.*

After that, *we can inform the catering company of the final numbers.*

Finally, *we'll need a press release.*

We use ***First***, ***Then***, ***After that*** and ***In the end*** to introduce **past events in order**.

First, *we had a meeting and made our decision.*

Then *we informed all our staff.*

After that, *we invited staff to another meeting.*

In the end, *everything was agreed.*

7.2 *can, have to, need to*

We use ***can*** to talk about what is **possible**.

You ***can*** *leave your suitcases here.*

We use ***can't*** to talk about what is **not possible**.

We ***can't*** *check in to the hotel because the computer isn't working.*

We use ***have to*** and ***need to*** to talk about what is **necessary**.

You ***have to*** *fill out this form.*

You ***need to*** *sign it at the bottom.*

We use ***don't have to*** and ***don't need to*** to talk about what is **not necessary**.

*I **don't have to** take my passport because I'm not going abroad.*

*We **don't need to** make a reservation because we already have one.*

Note: ***don't have to*** and ***don't need to*** talk about things that are not necessary but that **we can do if we want**.

*You **don't have to** talk to a robot, there is a human receptionist, too.*

*You **don't need to** tell the robot which language you speak because it knows from your passport.*

can

Positive		
I/You/He/She/It/We/They	can	finish it.

Negative		
I/You/He/She/It/We/They	can't	finish it.

***Yes/No* questions**		
Can	I/you/he/she/it/we/they	finish it?

Short answers		
Yes,	I/you/he/she/it/we/they	can.
No,	I/you/he/she/it/we/they	can't.

Open questions			
When	can	I/you/he/she/it/we/they	finish it?

have to / need to

Positive		
I/You/We/They	have to need to	finish it.
He/She/It	has to needs to	

Negative			
I/You/We/They	don't	have to need to	finish it.
He/She/It	doesn't		

***Yes/No* questions**			
Do	I/you/we/they	have to need to	finish it?
Does	he/she/it		

Short answers		
Yes,	I/you/we/they	do.
	he/she/it	does.
No,	I/you/we/they	don't.
	he/she/it	doesn't.

Open questions				
When	do	I/you/we/they	have to need to	finish it?
	does	he/she/it		

7.5 *Wh-* questions

The most common question words in English are ***Where? When? Which? How many? How? Why? Who? Whose? What?***

***When** is this happening?*

***Why** did we decide to make changes?*

***What** is the schedule for this?*

***Which** colour should we choose?*

Wh-	*be* or auxiliary verb
Wh- + noun	

We often use **negative questions** to:

- **make suggestions**.
  *Why **don't** we use recycled materials for the packaging?*
- **ask for more information**.
  A: *I don't like that colour.*
  B: *Which colour **don't** you like?*
  A: *We can't keep the same packaging.*
  B: *Why **can't** we keep the same packaging?*
  A: *I don't understand.*
  B: *What **don't** you understand?*

8.2 *should* and *could* for advice and suggestions

We use ***should*** to offer advice. It shows that the speaker thinks something is **a very good idea**.

*I think we **should** take the bus.*

We use ***shouldn't*** to offer advice. It shows that the speaker thinks something is **a very bad idea**.

*We **shouldn't** buy a diesel car.*

We use ***should*** in questions to **ask for advice**.

***Should** we hire a car on holiday?*

*What **should** we do about the problem?*

We use ***could*** to make suggestions. It shows that the speaker thinks something is **a possible option**.

A: *You **could** take the bus or the train to the airport.*

B: *Or you **could** take a taxi. It's quicker.*

C: *Thanks – I think a taxi is best!*

Note: We use ***could*** to give possible ideas, suggestions and solutions. We use ***should*** to give a stronger opinion. Sometimes both ***could*** and ***should*** are possible, depending on what we want to say.

should

Positive		
I/You/He/She/It/We/They	should	finish it.

Negative		
I/You/He/She/It/We/They	shouldn't	finish it.

***Yes/No* questions**		
Should	I/you/he/she/it/we/they	finish it?

Short answers		
Yes,	I/you/he/she/it/we/they	should.
No,	I/you/he/she/it/we/they	shouldn't.

Open questions			
When	should	I/you/he/she/it/we/they	finish it?

could

Positive		
I/You/He/She/It/We/They	could	finish it.

Note: We do not use the negative form *couldn't* to make suggestions or *could* to ask for advice.

8.5 Future forms

going to

We use ***going to*** to talk about our **future intentions or predictions**.

*We are **going to move** to a new location.*

*They are **going to introduce** a new manufacturing process.*

Positive			
I	am/'m	going to	finish.
You/We/They	are/'re		
He/She/It	is/'s		

Negative			
I	am not / 'm not	going to	finish.
You/We/They	are not / aren't		
He/She/It	is not / isn't		

Yes/No **questions**			
Am	I	going to	finish?
Are	you/we/they		
Is	he/she/it		

Short answers		
Yes,	I	am.
	you/we/they	are.
	he/she/it	is.
No,	I	'm not.
	you/we/they	aren't.
	he/she/it	isn't.

Open questions				
When	am	I	going to	finish?
	are	you/we/they		
	is	he/she/it		

Note: We often use time expressions like *this evening, tonight, tomorrow, on Sunday, next week* and *next month* with *going to*.

Present Continuous

We use the **Present Continuous** to talk about **future arrangements**.

*The company **is moving** offices on Friday.*

*We **are holding** a meeting next week.*

Note: See page 120 for the rules for forming the Present Continuous and the spelling rules for *-ing* forms.

will

We use ***will*** for **decisions, promises and facts about the future**.

*Using electric vehicles **will cut down** pollution from petrol.*

*We **will answer** any questions then.*

Positive		
I/You/He/She/It/We/They	will	finish it.

Negative		
I/You/He/She/It/We/They	won't	finish it.

Yes/No **questions**		
Will	I/you/he/she/it/we/they	finish it?

Short answers		
Yes,	I/you/he/she/it/we/they	will.
No,	I/you/he/she/it/we/they	won't.

Open questions			
When	will	I/you/he/she/it/we/they	finish it?

	INFINITIVE	PAST SIMPLE	PAST PARTICIPLE
P9.01	be [bɪː]	was/were [wɒz/wɜː]	been [bɪːn]
P9.02	become [bɪ'kʌm]	became [bɪ'keɪm]	become [bɪ'kʌm]
P9.03	begin [bɪ'gɪn]	began [bɪ'gæn]	begun [bɪ'gʌn]
P9.04	break [breɪk]	broke [brəʊk]	broken ['brəʊkən]
P9.05	bring [brɪŋ]	brought [brɔːt]	brought [brɔːt]
P9.06	build [bɪld]	built [bɪlt]	built [bɪlt]
P9.07	burn [bɜːn]	burned [bɜːnd]/ burnt [bɜːnt]	burned [bɜːnd]/ burnt [bɜːnt]
P9.08	buy [baɪ]	bought [bɔːt]	bought [bɔːt]
P9.09	can [kæn]	could [kʊd]	been able to [bɪːn 'eɪbl tə]
P9.10	catch [kætʃ]	caught [kɔːt]	caught [kɔːt]
P9.11	choose [tʃʊːz]	chose [tʃəʊz]	chosen [tʃəʊzn]
P9.12	come [kʌm]	came [keɪm]	come [kʌm]
P9.13	cost [kɒst]	cost [kɒst]	cost [kɒst]
P9.14	cut [kʌt]	cut [kʌt]	cut [kʌt]
P9.15	do [dʊː]	did [dɪd]	done [dʌn]
P9.16	draw [drɔː]	drew [drʊː]	drawn [drɔːn]
P9.17	drink [drɪnk]	drank [drænk]	drunk [drʌnk]
P9.18	drive [draɪv]	drove [drəʊv]	driven [drɪvn]
P9.19	eat [ɪːt]	ate [et/eɪt]	eaten [ɪːtn]
P9.20	fall [fɔːl]	fell [fel]	fallen [fɔːln]
P9.21	feel [fɪːl]	felt [felt]	felt [felt]
P9.22	fight [faɪt]	fought [fɔːt]	fought [fɔːt]
P9.23	find [faɪnd]	found [faʊnd]	found [faʊnd]
P9.24	fly [flaɪ]	flew [flʊː]	flown [fləʊn]
P9.25	forget [fə'get]	forgot [fə'gɒt]	forgotten [fə'gɒtn]
P9.26	get [get]	got [gɒt]	got [gɒt]
P9.27	give [gɪv]	gave [geɪv]	given [gɪvn]
P9.28	go [gəʊ]	went [went]	gone [gɒn]
P9.29	grow [grəʊ]	grew [gruː]	grown [grəʊn]
P9.30	have [hæv]	had [hæd]	had [hæd]
P9.31	hear [hɪə]	heard [hɜːd]	heard [hɜːd]
P9.32	hit [hɪt]	hit [hɪt]	hit [hɪt]
P9.33	hold [həʊld]	held [held]	held [held]
P9.34	hurt [hɜːt]	hurt [hɜːt]	hurt [hɜːt]
P9.35	keep [kiːp]	kept [kept]	kept [kept]
P9.36	know [nəʊ]	knew [njʊː]	known [nəʊn]

	INFINITIVE	PAST SIMPLE	PAST PARTICIPLE
P9.37	learn [lɜːn]	learned [lɜːnd]/ learnt [lɜːnt]	learned [lɜːnd]/ learnt [lɜːnt]
P9.38	leave [lɪːv]	left [left]	left [left]
P9.39	lend [lend]	lent [lent]	lent [lent]
P9.40	let [let]	let [let]	let [let]
P9.41	lose [lʊːz]	lost [lɒst]	lost [lɒst]
P9.42	make [meɪk]	made [meɪd]	made [meɪd]
P9.43	meet [miːt]	met [met]	met [met]
P9.44	pay [peɪ]	paid [peɪd]	paid [peɪd]
P9.45	put [pʊt]	put [pʊt]	put [pʊt]
P9.46	read [riːd]	read [red]	read [red]
P9.47	ride [raɪd]	rode [rəʊd]	ridden [rɪdn]
P9.48	ring [rɪŋ]	rang [ræŋ]	rung [rʌŋ]
P9.49	run [rʌn]	ran [ræn]	run [rʌn]
P9.50	say [seɪ]	said [sed]	said [sed]
P9.51	see [siː]	saw [sɔː]	seen [siːn]
P9.52	sell [sel]	sold [səʊld]	sold [səʊld]
P9.53	send [send]	sent [sent]	sent [sent]
P9.54	set [set]	set [set]	set [set]
P9.55	show [ʃəʊ]	showed [ʃəʊd]	shown [ʃəʊn]
P9.56	sit [sɪt]	sat [sæt]	sat [sæt]
P9.57	sleep [sliːp]	slept [slept]	slept [slept]
P9.58	speak [spiːk]	spoke [spəʊk]	spoken ['spəʊkən]
P9.59	spell [spend]	spelt [spelt]/ spelled [speld]	spelt [spelt]/ spelled [speld]
P9.60	spend [spend]	spent [spent]	spent [spent]
P9.61	stand [stænd]	stood [stʊd]	stood [stʊd]
P9.62	steal [stiːl]	stole [stəʊl]	stolen ['stəʊlən]
P9.63	swim [swɪm]	swam [swæm]	swum [swʌm]
P9.64	take [teɪk]	took [tʊk]	taken ['teɪkən]
P9.65	teach [tiːtʃ]	taught [tɔːt]	taught [tɔːt]
P9.66	tell [tel]	told [təʊld]	told [təʊld]
P9.67	think [θɪnk]	thought [θɔːt]	thought [θɔːt]
P9.68	understand [ˌʌndə'stænd]	understood [ˌʌndə'stʊd]	understood [ˌʌndə'stʊd]
P9.69	wake [weɪk]	woke [wəʊk]	woken ['wəʊkən]
P9.70	wear [weə]	wore [wɔː]	worn [wɔːn]
P9.71	win [wɪn]	won [wʌn]	won [wʌn]
P9.72	write [raɪt]	wrote [rəʊt]	written [rɪtn]

Lesson 1.4 6A

Student B

You work on the company IT help desk. Student A will call you to ask for help with an IT problem. Listen to his/her problems and choose solutions from the list which solve the problem (or think of your own IT solutions). Try to be polite and friendly during the process.

restart the computer
log on with a new user ID
offer to come and help in person
use the online manual
follow the link in an email you will send
get a new password

Lesson 2.5 3A

Good morning, Suki.

How are you today?

Good news! Basixlife are going to rent the offices. Can you email them a copy of the contract by close of business?

By the way, thanks for the report. It's very helpful but I also need the sales figures by the end of the day.

John Welles promises to send payment, but to be confirmed when. He apologises for the delay. He had a problem with his bank.

Lesson 2.5 3B

Text your colleague:

- greet him/her.
- confirm the meeting today at 2.30 in your office.
- ask him/her to prepare a short presentation on the new office location and explain why the company has decided to move there.
- remind him/her of an appointment tomorrow morning with the owner of the building. Say you are still waiting to confirm the time.
- invite him/her to contact you if he/she needs any more information before the meeting.

Email the building owner:

- greet him/her.
- confirm the appointment tomorrow morning and ask him/her to confirm the time.
- tell him/her that you are out of the office, so if he/she needs to speak to you, to call you on your mobile.
- ask him/her to send the contract details before close of business today.
- end the email by saying you expect to sign the contract tomorrow.

Lesson 1.5 3A

Information about a conference centre

1 How big are your main conference rooms?
2 Which hotels do you recommend?
3 Do you offer other facilities?
4 Are you near the city centre?
5 How many parking spaces are available?

Lesson 3.4 7A

Presentation B

Presenter 1

Introduction and overview

1 Introduce yourself and Presenter 2.
2 Introduce the subject of your talk: 'A comparison of customer visits to our e-commerce website before and after technical improvements made in Q2.'
3 Say who will talk about Parts 1, 2, 3 and 4.

Part 1: No. of visits we were getting in Q1

Industry average: 35,000/day
Our target figure: 40,000/day
Actual figure: 23,000/day (why so low?)

Part 2: Technical problems with site

1 Slow access speed (customers getting bored and leaving site without a purchase)
2 Not user-friendly (too complicated?)
3 Website down in Feb (lost business!)

Close and hand over to Presenter 2.

Presenter 2

Thank Presenter 1 and move on.

Part 3: Technical improvements in Q2

1 Moved website to a new host (faster, more reliable)
2 Redesigned site (easier to use)
3 Installed a better website optimisation tool (made us easier to find online)

Part 4: No. of visits we got in Q3–4

Q3: 39,000/day (the good news)
Q4: 45,500/day (even better news!)

Summary and conclusion

1 Customer visits doubled from Q1 to Q4!
2 We beat our Q1 target by 13%
3 We're now ahead of all our main competitors in this market!

Close and thank audience.

Lesson 2.3 9A

Group A

Scenario 1: Eco-clean

Eco-clean is a well-established company in Cardiff in the UK. It produces eco-friendly cleaning products.

You have asked TGC to hire an Accountant for a year. You would prefer someone with experience of small and medium-sized companies and some basic knowledge of the Welsh language.

The contract is for 12 months from 10 November. No travel is required. Benefits are free tea/coffee and lunch vouchers.

You only have time to interview 3–5 candidates and are available in the week beginning 19 October. You are worried about interviewing candidates for this role because you have very little knowledge of accountancy. Explain what you need to the person from TGC (Student B).

Scenario 2: Bike-co

Candidate Profile Form	TGC THE GALLAGHER CONSULTANCY	
Contract type	1 *replacement / maternity / new post / temp*	(circle)
Company name	Bike-co	
Job title	Marketing Consultant	
Location	2 ________________	
Contract length	3 10 months ????	(check)
Main responsibility	4 ________________	
Experience	5 ________________	
Language(s) spoken	6 ________________ and ________________	
Language level	7 *basic knowledge / working knowledge / fluent*	(circle)
Package offered	8 ________________ / ________________	
Business travel	9 *Yes / No / Negotiate with candidate*	(circle)
Number of candidates for interview	10 ________________	

BUSINESS WORKSHOP 8 4A

Pair C

Waste reduction and recycling

Current situation:

- We produce too much waste and need to reduce disposal costs.
- We sometimes put e-waste (e.g. batteries, computers, printers, mobile phones) into normal waste bins and this is illegal.

Cost:

- With the new council prices, waste disposal will cost approximately €8,000 per year.

Savings:

- If we can reduce waste by 50 percent, we can save at least €4,000 per year.

A waste reduction and recycling scheme means:

- no bins by staff desks.
- four recycling bins in every department on every floor for paper and cardboard (blue container), glass (green), plastic and cans (yellow) and food waste (brown).
- e-waste and toner cartridges go to the Facilities Department for disposal.
- staff get information every month about how much waste is being produced, recycling and how to throw away e-waste correctly.

A waste reduction and recycling scheme has these advantages for Walsh Ryan:

- It reduces waste disposal costs by €4,000 a year.
- Less waste and more recycling is good for the company's reputation.
- We avoid possible council fines* for incorrect disposal of e-waste in future.

****fine:** money that you have to pay as a punishment when you do something wrong*

BUSINESS WORKSHOP 5 6A

Student B

You are a local shopkeeper. You support the **local currency** project for the following reasons:

- It will encourage people to shop locally.
- It will make people feel proud of your town.
- It has been successful in many other towns.

You don't like the other projects for these reasons:

- Time bank: You're too busy to share your time.
- Saturday market: It will compete with your business.

Lesson 4.5 3A

To: John Bankes, JBankes Supplies
From: Marco Contini, Production Director
Subject: Meeting

Hi John,

The meeting is 11 a.m. next Wednesday at our factory in Milan. It finishes at 12.30. Would you like to have lunch after? Call me if you have any questions.

See you Wednesday!

Best wishes,

Marco

Lesson 6.3 1A

Score

1, 3 and 5: Yes = 2 points
It depends = 1 point
No = 0 points

2 and 4: Yes = 0 points
It depends = 1 point
No = 2 points

Results

0–5 You sometimes find it difficult to understand how other people are feeling and are not very comfortable sharing their problems with them. This can sometimes be a good thing in a crisis – when everybody else is stressed, you stay calm. But most jobs these days involve working with other people in situations which are occasionally stressful, so perhaps you need to develop your people skills a bit more.

6–10 You can usually understand the feelings of others and will offer support if you think they really need it. Sometimes people just want to be left alone to manage their own problems and you respect this, but perhaps you could make sure they don't need any help or advice first.

11–15 You find it easy to understand the feelings of others and usually do your best to support them. You are a good friend and colleague and a useful person to have in a team – especially in high-stress situations. But be careful you don't share other people's problems too much and make yourself unhappy as well!

Lesson 6.5 3B

Urgent instructions for the conference team

- **Speakers** – International trade speaker cancelled. Find another urgently. Any ideas?
- **Budget** – Need to find savings somewhere – Luis? Already spent too much!
- **Delegates** – Only 60 percent replied. Need to know who's coming by Friday – Claire?
- **Accommodation** – Blossom Hotel closed. Need fifty rooms somewhere – David?
- **Technical equipment** – Give venue details of what is needed. David should know.

Lesson 6.4 7A

Student D

Share as many ideas as you can in the meeting and remember to comment on other people's ideas, too. Here are a few suggestions to get you started:

- Send specially designed 50th anniversary 'thank you' cards to our clients.
- Create a special e-magazine about the agency.
- Interviews with our clients and/or staff and post the interviews on our YouTube channel.

Lesson 3.1 9A

1 ___________ ?
(You can choose more than one option.)
a small shops
b High Street chains
c department stores
d online shops
Why? ___________

2 ___________ ?
(Not including food shopping.)
a I never shop.
b I shop only when I really need to.
c I shop when I feel like it.
d I shop all the time. It's one of my favourite hobbies.

3 ___________ ?
a 0–30%
b 31–65%
c 66–100%

4 ___________ ?
(You can choose more than one option.)
a I like to see products in stores and then go online to find the best price.
b I usually go to the same shops every time.
c I often change the shops I use.
d I like to go to different shops to find the best price.
e I go to shops that are near me.

Lesson 3.3 9

Situation 2, Student 1 (S1)

You're a little worried about meeting S2 because:

1. several sales units have still not sent you their sales figures and you can't complete the performance charts S2 needs until you have these.
2. the company internet wasn't working for 24 hours this week, which has put you another day behind schedule.
3. the software you're using to produce the charts keeps crashing.

In your meeting with S2 make sure you:

1. apologise for being behind schedule.
2. explain the problems you're having, but don't make excuses.
3. try to suggest some possible solutions.

Here are a few ideas for suggestions you could make.

1. While you're waiting for some of the sales units to send you their figures, you could start adding the figures you have to S2's report.
2. You urgently need some IT support or new chart-making software.
3. If you can have a three-day extension as well, you're sure you can finish the job.

S2 will start the conversation.

BUSINESS WORKSHOP 8 > 4A

Pair A

Multifunctional printers (MFPs)

Current situation: Employees are using too much paper because the current printers are old, frequently break down and do not print very well.

MFPs:

- can scan, copy and print in a single machine.
- will reduce the amount of printing by being more efficient than the current printers.
- have lower maintenance costs than the current printers.
- allow each person to have a code to use them; this:
  - is good for security.
  - allows the Facilities Department to measure copies per person.
  - reduces unnecessary copying as people think before they print.

Cost:

- €10,800 per year to lease six machines including repair and maintenance service.

Savings:

- reducing printing by 50 percent means savings of more than €11,000 a year in electricity bills, toner and paper.

Exceptions:

- Not everyone can share printers.
  - Senior managers will want their own printers.
  - The Legal and Human Resources departments have documents that other people should not see, so they will need their own printers.

Lesson 1.5 > 3B

Your company has booked the Garden Hotel for three nights for you while you attend a conference in the AXCentre. You need some information from the hotel.

- double room needed
- large desk required
- meals included in price?
- distance from AXCentre
- any parking?
- swimming pool and gym

Lesson 6.3 > 10A

Helper

You are going to listen to the Speaker describing a disappointment to you. As he/she describes it, make sure you:

1. say how sorry you are.
2. show him/her that you understand how he/she feels.
3. encourage him/her to see the positive side.
4. encourage him/her to try again.
5. share a personal disappointment with him/her.
6. advise him/her to think of the future and learn from his/her experience.

Take a few minutes to look again at the expressions in Exercises 7 and 8. When the Speaker is ready, have your conversation.

Lesson 7.4 > 5B

Student B

You are leading the meeting. You hope it will be quick, as you have another meeting immediately afterwards. You know it's important to set some ground rules (you choose the rules) to make the meeting run smoothly. The technical equipment worked well when you checked it yesterday.

Lesson 3.5 > 3A

Review form – Flamingo Palace Hotel We value your feedback. Please leave your comments about the hotel here.

How often do you stay here?	The rooms are a little small and sometimes they are not cleaned very well, so we think it is a little bit too expensive.
When did you last stay here?	Our clients are usually happy with the Flamingo. The location of the hotel is very convenient for our company. The food is always good in the restaurant and the price is reasonable.
What was the purpose of your last visit?	We recommend the Flamingo Palace for low-cost business trips in the area, but unfortunately, we cannot recommend it to everyone.
What do/did you like about the hotel?	Our company sometimes has conferences at the Flamingo Palace and has visitors staying there almost every week.
Is/Was there anything you aren't/weren't happy with?	They were visiting our new factory and attending meetings in our offices.
Would you recommend us?	Two of our clients stayed there a few days ago.

Lesson 3.3 > 9

Situation 2, Student 2 (S2)

You're getting a little nervous about the report you have to write because:

1 it was late last sales quarter and the directors were not happy – that's why you brought in S1 to help you this time.
2 with only six days to complete the report for this sales quarter, it could be late again!
3 the sales unit performance charts are perhaps the most important part of the report.

In your meeting with S1 make sure you:

1 find out why he/she's having problems, but try not to blame him/her.
2 ask him/her to suggest some solutions.
3 suggest some solutions of your own.

Here are a few ideas for suggestions you could make.

1 You know the sales units are sometimes slow to send their sales figures through. If S1 is still waiting for them, offer to contact the units directly.
2 You're happy to give S1 any technical assistance he/she needs, e.g. IT support, an assistant for a couple of days.
3 You could also give S1 a one-day extension to finish the charts if you have to, but not more – when you have the charts, you need at least four days to complete the report.

You start: *Ah, there you are! Have you got a moment? How are you doing with those performance charts?*

BUSINESS WORKSHOP 2 > 6A

Mark

You understand the business needs to move, but you're not sure that moving to Berlin is the best idea.

- All your family and friends are in the UK.
- You don't speak any German or other languages.
- The e-residency is a good option that allows them to look for cheaper places to rent in the UK.

Lesson 6.4 > 7A

Student C

Share as many ideas as you can in the meeting and remember to comment on other people's ideas, too. Here are a few suggestions to get you started:

- Organise a quiz about the history of the company for staff and/or clients. Give prizes.
- Create a 30-minute reality TV show about a day in the life of the agency.
- Put an interactive timeline on the company website showing the company's history.

Lesson 4.4 > 7A

Student B

You can't go to the strategy meeting with your partner on the 10th because the HR Director has just told you he's visiting on that day. This could be good news for you if the meeting is brought forward; you really want to have something to report about at your board meeting on the 9th. When your partner calls:

1 try to bring the meeting forward to the previous week if you can, but be flexible!
2 suggest that, because your partner is coming from Warsaw, it might be nice to meet in the afternoon, stay overnight in Paris and continue the following morning – the best days for you would be the 2nd to the 3rd, or the 4th to the 5th.
3 be flexible and offer to move some appointments if it helps you to bring the meeting further forward.
4 remember to confirm any arrangements you make before you finish your call.

Check your schedule below and, when you're ready, call your partner to change your appointment.

March

	MON	TUE	WED	THUR	FRI
	1	2	3	4	5
A.M.	Fly to Stockholm for the HR conference	Fly back from Stockholm			
P.M.	Stockholm conference		Staff performance reviews		Leadership training session
	8	9	10	11	12
A.M.	Induction session	Board meeting	Strategy meeting: Teleworking (Paris)	Draft report on Paris meeting	
P.M.					
	15	16	17	18	19
A.M.	Budget meeting			Fly to Riga	Fly back from Riga
P.M.	Teleconference with São Paulo office		Committee meeting: flexitime	Meeting with Latvian team	

Lesson 6.3 > 1B

A colleague has had a disappointment at work. What is **the one most important thing** I can say and/or do to make him/her feel better?

BUSINESS WORKSHOP 3 3A

Student C

Martine's Coffee Shop

Martine Burgess opened her pop-up coffee van last week. 'I'm delighted with the response. During the week lots of people come by here for their morning coffee on their way to work.' Martina was a barista in a large coffee chain before she started her own business. 'People want a top-quality coffee wherever they are today, and I saw an opportunity to be my own boss. With the van and a few tables I can move around the city. It's quick and easy to park and open for business.' She often makes many stops in a day at offices, sports events, concerts and conferences. 'Weekdays I can focus on the office workers and shoppers. Weekends I can park near big events. I'm learning a lot about the different neighbourhoods in the city and finding out the best places to be. I want to have a regular route. Customers like to see a familiar smiling face.'

Lesson 5.3 9A

The Team Tasks Game

The grid below shows some of the key tasks for a project team. Underline five tasks you can do well (it doesn't matter whether you can actually do them well in real life!). These are your comfort zone tasks. ~~Cross out~~ five tasks you can't do at all (again, it doesn't matter if this actually true). These are your danger zone tasks. Leave the other six tasks blank. These are your challenge zone tasks.

LEAD THE TEAM	CONTROL THE BUDGET	DO THE CLIENT RESEARCH	PREPARE THE POWERPOINT
DEVELOP THE PROJECT PLAN	RECRUIT THE PROJECT STAFF	MANAGE THE PROJECT	PROVIDE UPDATES TO THE BOARD
GIVE THE CLIENT PRESENTATION	PRODUCE THE PROJECT REPORT	CHECK THE AVAILABILITY OF RESOURCES	PROVIDE THE TECHNICAL DOCUMENTS
CHAIR THE TEAM MEETINGS	MANAGE THE PROJECT WEBSITE	ESTIMATE THE COSTS	WORK OUT THE PROJECT SCHEDULE

Lesson 4.2 2 and 3

Student A

Read the interview with Kathryn Bishop on this page and put the questions in the correct place. Two questions are not used.

a What is your favourite book?
b What is an average day at work like?
c What is the biggest lesson you have learnt?
d What is the best advice you have ever received?
e What is the worst job you have ever had?

Read your article again and answer the questions.

1. What did Kathryn study at university?
2. Which types of organisations has she worked for?
3. When does she seem busiest – on her teaching or non-teaching days?
4. How many jobs does she have now?
5. In which parts of her life has Deborah Tannen's book helped her?
6. How does she try to organise herself?

FT

Women in Business: Kathryn Bishop

Kathryn Bishop works as a Consultant and is also an Associate Fellow at the University of Oxford's Saïd Business School. She has a degree in English and American literature from Wellesley College in the USA, and a Masters in English Studies from Oxford. She designs and teaches women's leadership development programmes. She has worked for financial services companies and has had a variety of roles in universities and government.

1 ____________

When teaching at Saïd, I am busy from breakfast until after dinner each night: listening, presenting, holding discussions and learning from participants, as well as checking with the administrative staff if there are any practical problems that I need to respond to.

On non-teaching days I might meet with academic colleagues to discuss new ideas or parts of the programme, or talk to people in other departments, such as marketing and business development, who make the programme happen. I have three jobs and two voluntary roles and I enjoy the variety. I regularly learn something in one job that can be useful in the other.

2 ____________

An Intimate History of Humanity by Theodore Zeldin. It has taught me to look at a problem in many different ways. I also recommend *You Just Don't Understand: Women and Men in Conversation* by Deborah Tannen, an American professor of linguistics – a book that has helped me work in boardrooms and also helped my marriage.

3 ____________

There is only so much time in a day and there is always more to do. The advice I have found most useful in dealing with this problem is, 'Only do what only you can do.' I used to manage my time carefully, but now I manage my energy.

Lesson 4.3 › 12A

1 Fitness tracking

Team leader – open the meeting by summarising the following information to the rest of your group.

> As you may know, employers are becoming increasingly worried about the health of their employees. Fortunately, it's now really easy to use modern 'fitness tracking' technologies to check the diet, stress levels, sleep and exercise patterns of staff.
>
> At this company, we feel we have a special responsibility to make sure our employees enjoy healthy, productive lifestyles. So the proposal is that we introduce fitness tracking here.
>
> I'd like to get your input before we finalise anything. So, what does everybody think?

TEAM NOTES

Pros

1 Company performance (healthy employees perform better – a lot of work hours are lost every year because of illness and unhealthy lifestyles)
2 Incentives (staff who score highly on the health checks could be given incentives, e.g. they could pay less into their company health plan)
3 Public relations (fitness tracking would be good for the company's image as a caring employer)
4 Anything else?

Cons

1 Privacy (some employees may not like being 'spied on' in this way – they could lose confidence in us as an employer)
2 Stress (if people feel pressure to perform well on the health checks, they may become *more* anxious and unfit, not *less*)
3 Confidentiality (how can we make sure fitness tracker information remains private?)
4 Anything else?

Lesson 5.5 › 3A

Dear Sir/Madam,

a We look forward to supplying you in the future and thank you for your business.
b Yours faithfully,
c We are sure you will agree that quality is very important.
d Therefore, we must continue to use the best quality raw materials.
e As you know, we have not increased our prices for three years now.
f The increase is only small so that our prices still remain competitive.
g Unfortunately, because of increasing costs, we now need to raise our prices by 5 percent from 1st November.
h Enclosed with this letter is our new price list.

Lesson 3.3 › 9

Situation 1, Student 1 (S1)

You're getting a little nervous about the presentation in Montreal because:

1 there will be a big audience of important people and Canada is a major market for you.
2 you will be using Apple Keynote software for the first time on your new MacBook Pro.
3 the presentation will be in English, but you're not sure if English will be everyone's first language. You've asked S2 to produce the slides in both English and French.

In your meeting with S2 make sure you:

1 find out why he/she's having problems, but try not to blame him/her.
2 ask him/her to suggest some solutions.
3 suggest some solutions of your own.

Here are a few ideas for suggestions you could make.

1 You didn't ask how well S2 knows Apple Keynote – he/she may need some IT support.
2 The situation is urgent, so you're prepared to pay S2 overtime to get the job done.
3 You could also give S2 a one-day extension to finish the slides if you have to, but not more – you fly to Montreal in three days' time!

You start: *Ah, there you are! Have you got a moment? How are you doing with those slides for my presentation?*

Lesson 6.4 › 7A

Student B

You're the note-taker at the meeting. Put all the ideas on a flipchart or a large piece a paper. You also have some ideas yourself:

- Create a special 50th anniversary company logo to put on our website and business cards.
- Organise a 'retro party' for our clients and staff – everyone wears clothes that were popular fifty years ago!
- Provide fifty $1,000 scholarships for students at the local art and design school.

BUSINESS WORKSHOP 2 › 6A

Paul

You are married with two young children.

- You want to move to a smaller city like Tallinn.
- Your wife is from Finland, which is next to Estonia.
- You think Tallinn will be cheaper to live in than Berlin where rents are rising fast.

BUSINESS WORKSHOP 4 > 4B

Finance Manager

You are the Finance Manager. You want no major changes to work patterns if possible. The thing you want most is to keep the split working day.

1 The working hours – You want to keep a split working day from 8.30 a.m. to 2 p.m. and 4 p.m. to 6 p.m. Monday to Thursday and everyone finishes by 3 p.m. on Friday. If employees want or need to work late, they should be allowed to.
2 Flexible hours – You don't think this is necessary. All staff can have one hour off a week for personal business if necessary.
3 The lunch break – A one-hour lunch break is very important in order to have a break from work and a good lunch. On days when you have business lunches this needs to be at least two hours.
4 Working from home – You don't think this is a good idea. It means people get less work done and increases costs.

Lesson 6.3 > 10A

Speaker

Choose one of the two situations below or a real situation you don't mind talking about. Take a few minutes to prepare. When you are ready, explain to the Helper what went wrong step by step. Let him/her make comments and offer support as you speak.

The nightmare presentation

I just gave my worst presentation ever!
It took me weeks to prepare it, but ...
... everything went wrong!
My PowerPoint didn't work properly!
My microphone caught all my breathing!
I was so nervous I forgot my introduction!
Nobody laughed at my jokes!
There were almost no questions in the Q&A!
The applause from the audience at the end was terrible!
Worst of all, my boss was in the audience!

The missed promotion

I didn't get the promotion!
I worked so hard for it, but ...
... my promotion interview was a disaster!
The boss said I always miss my deadlines!
He/She also said I have poor leadership skills!
Customer feedback was terrible – they hate me!
Even my assistant said I'm difficult to work for!
Profits have gone down since I joined the firm!
The atmosphere in the office has got worse, too!
Worst of all, I just heard my assistant got the job!

Lesson 4.5 > 3B

Wednesday 10th October

10.00	Short team meeting
11.00	Meeting with Marco Contini at factory in Milan
13.00	Ask Marco to book taxi to Milan Linate Airport
16.00	Flight to Australia

BUSINESS WORKSHOP 8 > 4A

Pair B

Cloud computing

Current situation: Employees' computers are connected to more powerful computers in Walsh Ryan's offices called servers.

Cloud computing:

- stores data and programs online so the company will not need servers.
- means files and information can be available through a web browser.

Advantages for Walsh Ryan:

- Hardware – Don't need to spend money buying new computers or security systems or keeping them working properly (Savings: approximately €12,000 a year)
- IT staff – Can spend less time making sure the servers work properly and more time on other projects (Savings: approximately €15,000 a year)
- Energy – Less electricity to run the computer servers and cooling and ventilation system for the server room (Savings are difficult to calculate: approximately €3,000 a year)

Cost:

- €90 per user per year, total €36,000 for 400 staff with the ability to store as much as needed

Note: The savings each year are approximately €30,000, which is lower than the cost of cloud computing at €36,000. Many companies find out that cloud computing actually costs them more, not less, than having servers in their offices. Don't say this in your presentation. Do your colleagues notice that this will not save money?

Lesson 7.4 > 5B

Student A

This is only the second time you have attended an online meeting. You don't have much experience of using the technology. The first time you attended a meeting like this there were a lot of technical problems.

Lesson 4.4 7A

Student A

You heard from a colleague this morning that your partner may have to change your appointment. This is actually good news for you because you'd really like more time to complete your research before the strategy meeting. When your partner calls:

1. try to postpone your meeting until after the 10th if you can, but be flexible!
2. suggest that for such an important meeting you really need a whole day – the best days for you would be the 12th, 15th or 17th.
3. be flexible and offer to move some appointments if it helps you to postpone the meeting for longer.
4. remember to confirm any arrangements you make before you finish your call.

Check your schedule below while you wait for your partner to call.

March

	MON	TUE	WED	THUR	FRI
	1	2	3	4	5
A.M.	Fly to Stockholm for HR conference	Fly back from Stockholm	Receive visitors from Riyadh	Management coaching session	Draft feasibility study for Paris
P.M.	Stockholm conference			HR dept. meeting	
	8	9	10	11	12
A.M.			Strategy meeting: Teleworking (Paris)		
P.M.	Complete feasibility study for Paris	New software demonstration		Lunch with editor of *HR Week*	
	15	16	17	18	19
A.M.		Interviewing for new PA		Management coaching session	
P.M.		Teleconference with Tokyo office			Begin quarterly report

Lesson 5.5 3B

Write a letter to all our customers telling them about the following:

price increase 7 percent – 9th September (because of new design)

design = improved product line uses more expensive materials

quality important to customers

prices still very competitive

send price list with letter

Lesson 6.3 10A

Observer

You are going to watch the Speaker and Helper have their conversation. Take notes on the Helper using the observation form below. Take a few minutes to read through the form while they prepare.

Feedback notes

Comments	Evaluation
1 How well does the Helper say how sorry he/she is?	☺ 😐 ☹
2 How well does the Helper show that he/she understands how the Speaker feels?	☺ 😐 ☹
3 How well does the Helper encourage the Speaker to see the positive side (if there *is* one)?	☺ 😐 ☹
4 How well does the Helper encourage the Speaker to try again?	☺ 😐 ☹
5 How well does the Helper share a personal disappointment with the Speaker?	☺ 😐 ☹
6 How well does the Helper advise the Speaker to think of the future and learn from his/her experience?	☺ 😐 ☹

BUSINESS WORKSHOP 4 4B

Vice President

You are the Vice President and lead the meeting. You want to introduce these work patterns if possible. The thing you want most is to make the lunch break shorter.

1. The working hours – You want to stop late-night working in the Madrid office.
2. Flexible hours – You want a system in which employees can start work any time between 8 a.m. and 10 a.m. and finish anytime between 4 p.m. and 6 p.m. They have to work 37 hours a week but can organise how they do that.
3. The lunch break – You want to make this shorter. In Denmark it's usual to have 30 minutes for lunch and bring a sandwich from home to eat in the company lunch room or canteen.
4. Working from home – You think office staff should have the option to work from home one day a week.

Lesson 4.3 › 12A

2 Third-agers

Team leader – open the meeting by summarising the following information to the rest of your group.

> Did you know that, on average, people are living six years longer today than they did in 1990? And, as a result, they expect to work longer, too.
>
> At this company we value the experience of our older employees. And we want our younger staff to be able to learn from that experience. So the proposal is to introduce 'The Silver Scheme' – our way of saying thank you to our retired staff by paying them to coach junior employees on a part-time basis.
>
> I'd like to get your input before we finalise anything. So, what does everybody think?

TEAM NOTES

Pros

1 Intellectual capital (the Silver Scheme is a great way to make sure the combined knowledge of the company is not lost when staff members retire)

2 Economic success (economists predict that GDP will increase by 15 percent if people over 65 continue to work)

3 Innovation (there are a lot of innovative but high-risk projects we can't afford to give to our full-time staff, but ex-employees might enjoy the challenge of these)

4 Anything else?

Cons

1 Peer pressure (a lot of our employees look forward to retirement – they do not want to feel pressure to continue to work)

2 Exploitation (is this just a clever way of continuing to employ older members of staff on lower pay?)

3 Loss of opportunities (isn't keeping older employees on, even on a part-time basis, taking jobs away from younger people?)

4 Anything else?

Lesson 8.4 › 6B

Presenters

During the presentation, you realised that some of the team are against the idea of having an open-plan office. While you understand and have the same worries, you have to respond positively and in line with company policy.

Use strategies from Exercise 1 and expressions from Exercise 4 to manage the Q&A session. Remember to do some of the following to make sure the Q&A session runs smoothly:

1 Invite (more) questions from the audience.

2 Repeat the question so that everyone can hear.

3 Thank the participant for their question.

4 Ask for clarification if necessary.

5 Make sure you have answered the question or say you can't answer the question.

Lesson 5.4 › 9A

1 Did you know that, on average, female managers in the UK earn just over three-quarters of what men do?

77%

2 To put that in context, it means that women work for well over one and a half hours a day for free!

3 Have a look at this diagram, which shows the average salaries of male and female managers.

£30,392 £39,461

£9,069

4 As you can see, women are earning about £9,000 a year less than men – roughly the price of a small family car.

£408,105

5 To give you an idea of just how much that is, it means that during her career a woman will lose more than £400,000 in earnings!

6 To put it another way, women would have to work until their late 70s or early 80s to earn as much as men!

75 76 77 78 79
Retirement age

34% 45–60 yrs
35% 60+ yrs

7 And, as you can see, the gender pay gap for managers in their mid-40s to early 60s is even worse.

8 The key takeaway here is that UK employment laws for equal pay are clearly not working in practice.

UK WORKFORCE
53% 47%

BOARD OF DIRECTORS

9 Now, have a look at this. In the UK, women are approximately half the total workforce.

10 But currently only about three out of ten board directors in the UK are women.

11 Numerous studies show that companies with more women at senior levels enjoy both higher profits and share value. So, in terms of attracting the best talent, unequal pay is not only unfair. It's bad for business!

PROFIT

12 In summary, what we need is UK companies to be open about pay, so that they cannot hide differences in earnings for the same job, and equal pay becomes a reality. Let's work together to achieve this!

Lesson 8.4 › 6B

Q&A session 1

Questioner 1

You work in a creative role and need a lot of space. You often work with freelancers and need space to meet with them. You've worked in an open-plan office before and didn't like it.

Questioner 2

You deal with staff-related issues and need privacy from time to time. You are new to the company and like the idea of working in an open-plan office. However, as you have never worked in this way before, you still have some questions.

Choose 2–3 points from the box or think of your own. Make questions to ask the Presenter.

noisy, difficult to concentrate, not enough storage space, too hot / too cold, difficulty booking meeting rooms, desks are allocated to the people who arrive first, possible problems with private information, makes it easier for people to get sick, not much privacy, reduces the amount of work that gets done

BUSINESS WORKSHOP 3 › 3A

Student B

Angelica's Fashion Jewellery

Angelica Wilson studied art and design at university. She creates her own jewellery and also makes personalised jewellery for customers who want something special. 'I sell my products online as well as in pop-ups in other people's stores, art galleries and temporary exhibitions. I didn't want fixed retail opening hours. I like the flexibility of pop-ups.' Angela promotes her pop-ups on social media to attract her customers to the events. 'This creates opportunities for me and for the other businesses where I have my pop-ups, so everyone wins. Regular customers come to my pop-up events to see me and my new designs.'

Angelica says retail habits are changing and retailers need less space today. 'People are shopping more online and younger consumers want more urban, boutique-style shopping experiences. There is a movement away from big stores and towards shopping small and shopping local. The pop-up store is part of this new retail experience.'

Lesson 7.4 › 5B

Student C

You have a lot of experience of online meetings. You understand how the technology works and aren't worried if there are technical problems. You don't have much patience with people who don't understand technology.

Lesson 4.3 › 12A

3 The human cloud

Team leader – open the meeting by summarising the following information to the rest of your group.

Has anyone heard of the 'human cloud'? It's a global network of freelance digital workers who can be employed by companies just when they need them. Employers go to a special website, where they invite freelancers to compete for projects. The pay is good, but companies save money on recruitment, holiday pay, sick pay and other costs.

The proposal is that we transfer some of the jobs here to the cloud and save some money.

I'd like to get your input before we finalise anything. So, what does everybody think?

TEAM NOTES

Pros

1 Cost savings (the money saved on employing freelancers could be used to create a better work environment for our employees)
2 Flexibility (some employees could decide to work from home)
3 Job security (having freelancers to work for us only when we need them will actually protect permanent staff)
4 Anything else?

Cons

1 Quality (how do we know the freelancers are good at their jobs?)
2 Wages (if the freelancers do a good job for less, wages for permanent staff may go down)
3 Job security (employees may even lose their jobs in the long term)
4 Anything else?

BUSINESS WORKSHOP 5 › 6A

Student C

You are an unemployed builder. You support the **time bank** project for the following reasons:

- It will give unemployed people something to do.
- It will give people with little or no money a way to get jobs done – building work, for example.
- There are no financial costs – no taxes, no fees.

You don't like the other projects for these reasons:

- Local currency: Money is money. If people don't have much, it doesn't matter if it's local currency or 'real' currency.
- Saturday market: People will sell things other people don't really need – art, for example.

Lesson 2.3 > 9A

Group B

Scenario 1: Eco-clean

Candidate Profile Form	TGC THE GALLAGHER CONSULTANCY	
Contract type	[1]*replacement / maternity / new post / temp*	(circle)
Company name	Eco-clean	
Job title	Accountant	
Main responsibility	[2] ______	
Location	[3] ______	
Contract length	[4] ______	
Experience	[5] ______	
Language(s) spoken	English and [6] ______	
Language level	[7]*basic knowledge / working knowledge / fluent*	(circle)
Package offered	[8] ______ / ______	
Business travel	[9]*Yes / No / Negotiate with candidate*	(circle)
Number of candidates for interview	[10] ______	

Scenario 2: Bike-co

Bike-co, which is based in Dublin, organises cycling tours around Ireland.

You want to hire a Marketing Consultant to develop the business internationally and have hired TGC for their recruitment services. You want to do more business in Europe, so candidates must be willing to travel abroad at least once a month. They must be able to speak and write French or Spanish to a high level. Knowledge of html is also necessary.

This is an 18-month contract to begin with and you would prefer a recent graduate. The company is young and dynamic and you are looking for someone with a similar personality who loves cycling.

Interviews will take place 14–16 September in Dublin. You can interview up to 5 candidates. Benefits include lunch vouchers, cheaper Bike-co tours and a free travel card. Explain what you need to the person from TGC (Student A).

BUSINESS WORKSHOP 2 > 6A

Ewa

You like the idea of living and working in Berlin.

- It's just a three-hour drive from your parents, who live in Poznań.
- It's an international and multicultural city.
- It's cheap to live near the centre and to get to work by bike.
- Estonia is a good, cheap alternative to Berlin.

Lesson 6.4 > 7A

Student A

Unfortunately, Marc can't attend the meeting, so you're the chair! But don't worry. All you have to do is:

1 Open the meeting:

'Good morning/afternoon, everyone. Thanks a lot for coming. Unfortunately, Marc can't be here, so I'm chairing the meeting today. As you know, we're here to discuss how we celebrate our 50th anniversary. So I'd like to hear all your ideas. This is a great publicity opportunity for us. Let's make the most of it'.

2 Explain the rules of the meeting:

Rules of the meeting

- Let's have lots of ideas – keep them coming!
- Please let everybody speak.
- Stay positive – don't be negative!
- If you make a negative comment, you'll have to put money in the negative comment box! ☺
- Try to build on other people's ideas.
- If you can see a problem with someone's idea, don't criticise it – ask a question.

3 You also have a few ideas yourself to share with the team:

- Set up a special 50th anniversary website linked to our home page.
- Organise some kind of creative event – perhaps a video exhibition of our best commercials.
- Give our clients personalised 'retro gifts' – gifts which were popular 50 years ago!

4 Close the meeting:

'OK, thanks a lot, everybody. Some great ideas there. Let's stop for today and meet again in a couple of weeks.'

Lesson 7.4 > 5C

Problem cards

Echo	Volume too low	Cutting out
Web cam switched off	Eating during the meeting	______ (your own idea)
Frozen screen	Background noise	______ (your own idea)

Lesson 8.4 > 6C

Q&A session 3

Questioner 1

You are very organised, and everything in your office is always in the right place. You have never wanted to share an office in the past. You feel most people are not tidy or organised and you think this will make it hard for you to work.

Questioner 2

You are new and would prefer to share an office with a more experienced member of the team, such as Questioner 1. You like the social side of work. You have some questions about the open-plan office as this is a new idea for you.

Choose 2–3 points from the box or think of your own. Make questions to ask the Presenter.

noisy, difficult to concentrate, not enough storage space, too hot / too cold, difficulty booking meeting rooms, difficult to adjust temperature to individuals, possible problems with private information, makes it easier for people to get sick, not much privacy, reduces the amount of work that gets done

Lesson 6.1 > 10C

- A new **Sales Manager** – knows the industry well, is a great public speaker but doesn't know the company's products well
- An **Engineer** – knows the products very well, very shy, afraid of public speaking
- A **Vice President** – friendly, good at conflict management, great listener; must leave on a business trip at 12.30 tomorrow
- A **Sales Representative** – knows the products, friendly, loves talking, but sometimes talks too much and changes the topic of conversation
- A **Project Manager** – excellent at planning, cooperation, communication, talented public speaker

Lesson 6.5 > 3A

Before we do anything else, we have to let all our clients know about the move. [1]Alex and Miguel, you should do that?

The IT team are trying to make sure that the new files systems are ready and working on 22/05. [2]You all contact them to transfer your files by Monday 15 at the latest.

Luis, I know you will check that the builders are following the new plan next week. [3]Why don't you update me the next day? [4]Go and send me a meeting invite.

Unfortunately, the painting company we booked cannot do the work now so we will have to find a new company. The deadline for the painting is 15/05. And finally, we need someone to be there for the furniture delivery on 22/05 and put it in the right place. [5]I want anyone to help with these two tasks?

Lesson 8.3 > 9A

Student B

	Employee feedback – Notes
Job title	Marketing Manager
Positive	calm, positive, __________ (add another quality), __________ (add another quality)
Corrective	problems with time management, sometimes says negative things about junior staff members, can sound rude on the telephone
Examples	missed a deadline for the marketing report for AGM, there has been a complaint from a marketing intern

BUSINESS WORKSHOP 2 > 6A

Yelena

You are young, free and single and love travelling.

- You're happy to stay in London or move to Berlin.
- Moving to Tallinn does not interest you.
- You're a digital nomad* so you don't really need a desk in an office.

***digital nomad:** person who uses computers and the internet to work wherever he or she is, for example abroad, coffee shops, public libraries, etc.

Lesson 3.3 > 9

Situation 1, Student 2 (S2)

You're a little worried about meeting S1 because:

1. a colleague has been off work with illness, so you've been extra busy for the last two weeks. You've finished about three-quarters of the slides, but they won't be finished by tomorrow.
2. you've used Apple Keynote before, but you're much more familiar with PowerPoint, so it's taking longer than usual to prepare the slides.
3. S1 asked you to prepare slides in English and French for the Montreal audience, but your French is not perfect and this is holding things up.

In your meeting with S1 make sure you:

1. apologise for being behind schedule.
2. explain the problems you're having, but don't make excuses.
3. try to suggest some possible solutions.

Here are a few ideas for suggestions you could make.

1. PowerPoint works fine on Apple computers – you could convert your work on Apple Keynote into PowerPoint and finish the other slides a lot faster.
2. Because you're having difficulty translating the slides it may be quicker to email them to a colleague in the Paris office, who can check them.
3. If you can have a two-day extension, you're sure you can finish the job.

S1 will start the conversation.

Lesson 7.5 > 3A

Slide 1

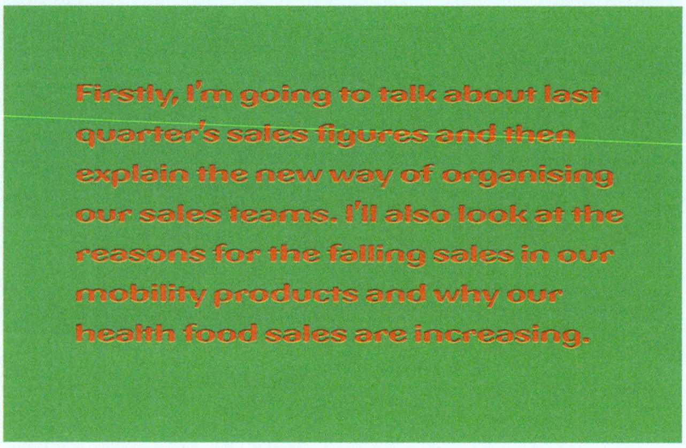

Slide 2

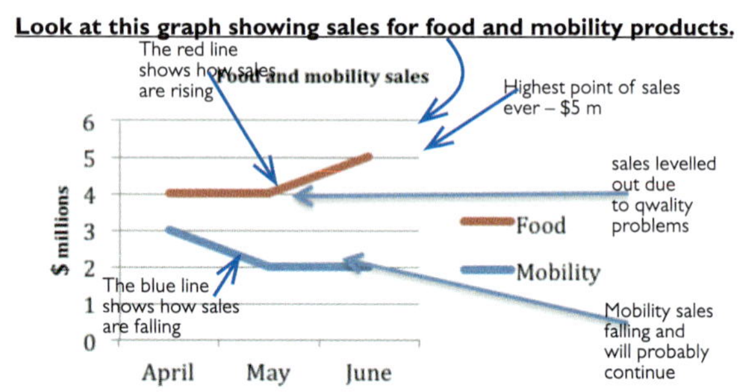

Slide 3

TARGETING NEW MARKETS

Why? – Asian markets, mainly India and Malaysia, are interested in bying our products. We've had a lot of enqueries from there.

- What? –
  doing market research there
  mutlinational focus group
  come up with new design

When? – Market research will finish in 2 months, the focus group is going to have a meeting next month, designers are going to work on a new design after that.

Lesson 6.4 > 7A

Student E

Share as many ideas as you can in the meeting and remember to comment on other people's ideas, too. Here are a few suggestions to get you started:

- Create a wall display in the office telling the story of the agency in words and pictures.
- Ask our design department to create a comic book with staff members as characters in the story.
- Give money to a charity that helps young people interested in the arts.

BUSINESS WORKSHOP 5 > 6A

Student A

You are leading the meeting to decide which project the local government should work on. Guide the meeting through this agenda:

1 Welcome everyone to the meeting and explain its purpose.

2 a Ask: *Who supports the* ***local currency*** *project?* Allow that person to explain why.
  b Ask for arguments against the local currency project.

3 a Ask: *Who supports the* ***time bank*** *project?* Allow that person to explain why.
  b Ask for arguments against the time bank project.

4 a Ask: *Who supports the* ***Saturday market*** *project?* Allow that person to explain why.
  b Ask for arguments against the Saturday market project.

5 Take a vote, including your own. One project needs at least three votes to win. Keep discussing the three projects until one project has at least three votes.

Lesson 8.5 > 3A

Proposal for improving sales

As you know, we trying to improve company sales. We have done research and are we now ready to propose ideas.

Fristly, we are going to sell more green products. This is because many customers tell us that they like our products, but they want to be sure that they are not bad for the environment. Secondly, we also plan to changing our supplier so that we have eco-friendly materials. Finally, we are planning us to launch the new product range next June.

Also, we are going to help some local environmental projects. We are theirfore holding a meeting next week to discuss ideas for these projects. We will also answered any questions you may have.

Lesson 8.5 > 3B

Your manager has asked you to write an update about company changes which will happen next month. Organise the update into three paragraphs.

Here are the most important points:

- moving to smaller offices outside city centre – more eco-friendly
- free company bus to bring staff to work from city centre – more relaxing for staff, less pollution
- working from home – fewer cars on road – full details coming soon
- meeting next Friday to discuss changes

Lesson 8.3 > 9A

Student A

	Employee feedback – Notes
Job title	Personal Assistant
Positive	a good team player, enthusiastic, ___________ (add another quality), ___________ (add another quality)
Corrective	seems negative in some emails, problems with time management, doesn't update online diary
Examples	final report and official correspondence, arrived late three times in last two weeks

Lesson 8.4 > 6C

Q&A session 2

Questioner 1

You work in Finance and often work to tight deadlines. You need an office where you can concentrate. You have a friend who works in an open-plan office and who often complains about it.

Questioner 2

You work in Sales and spend a lot of time on the phone. You like the idea of working in an open-plan office but are worried you may disturb your colleagues.

Choose 2–3 points from the box or think of your own. Make questions to ask the Presenter.

noisy, difficult to concentrate, not enough storage space,
too hot / too cold, difficulty booking meeting rooms,
possible problems with private information,
problems with changing lighting to individual needs,
not much privacy,
reduces the amount of work that gets done

Lesson 6.4 > 7A

Student F

Share as many ideas as you can in the meeting and remember to comment on other people's ideas, too. Here are a few suggestions to get you started:

- Organise sports events for staff, clients and suppliers.
- Ask our writers to create a sixty-second commercial for the agency.
- Create a history of the company video with the person who started the agency.

BUSINESS WORKSHOP 5 > 6A

Student D

You work in an office, but in your spare time you paint pictures. You support the **Saturday market** project for the following reasons:

- It will give people a way to earn extra money from hobbies.
- It will give people an opportunity to buy things locally instead of buying them online.
- It will help young people learn about running businesses

You don't like the other projects for these reasons:

- Local currency: It may make it easy for people to avoid paying tax.
- Time bank: Some people's time is more valuable than others – doctors are more important than builders, for example.

BUSINESS WORKSHOP 4 > 4B

Human Resources Manager

You are the Human Resources Manager. You want to introduce these work patterns if possible. The thing you want most is an intensive working day.

1. The working hours – You want to introduce an intensive working day with employees starting between 7 a.m. and 8.30 a.m. and finishing by 3 p.m. every day.
2. Flexible hours – Employees can start any time between 7 a.m. and 8.30 a.m. and finish any time between 2 p.m. and 3 p.m. on any day Monday to Friday. They can decide their own start and finish time but must work 37 hours a week.
3. The lunch break – There is a 30-minute lunch break with this intensive system. Staff can also take a short coffee break during the morning.
4. Working from home – You don't think this is necessary with the new intensive timetable you want to start using.

1.1.1

N = Narrator A1 = Alex A2 = Alessio A3 = Amira

N: In a global economy, many companies do business overseas. This means that workers often travel to see their colleagues or clients abroad. There are many reasons why people travel for work.

A1: I go abroad to complete projects which are set by my company. Those projects can include setting up certain systems, laptops, docking stations, etc.

A2: I need to travel for work because sometimes the projects I do are based somewhere outside London, where I live, so I've been travelling to France, to Italy, to Spain, to Romania.

A3: I need to travel because we work with big brands and multinationals, and they want to understand different people in the different markets and countries, so we travel across the world.

N: An important part of business travel is organising transportation. When people travel internationally, they often fly, though in some cases taking the train is an option.

A1: I travel for work once or twice a month, on a regular basis. I tend to fly short haul and I use two different airlines.

N: Alex makes the most of his travel time and keeps busy during the flight.

A1: When I'm flying for business I tend to get my laptop out and do some work during the flight, and half an hour before my plane lands I remove my laptop, put it back in my bag, and get ready for the landing.

N: On business trips, you may need to stay overnight. It's important to book accommodation that is suitable for your trip and has everything you need, so you can keep working during your stay.

A2: The accommodation where I like to stay when I travel for work is ... is hotels, usually, but they need to be very close to the place where I need to go to work. What I expect at my location is wi-fi because I need to work most of the time when I'm back in my room. And, of course, parking, because usually I need to hire cars or a vehicle from the airport to the workplace.

N: When travelling for work, you may not know much about the local area and how to get around. Find out about transportation before you go. And when you get there, ask for help if you need it, or ask for directions.

A3: When I have to go from a business meeting to another meeting, I either use public transportation, because it's a really good way to mix with the locals, or I use a ridesharing app. I always worry about getting lost but it's part of the adventure. I carry an online map on my phone and, if I do get lost, I just ask people and they're really helpful.

N: Even if you've planned ahead, things can still go wrong. Your flight could be delayed or there might be a mistake with your hotel reservation. It's rare, however, to find a problem that cannot be solved.

A3: I remember once, I was at the airport lounge waiting for my flight, and I got really confused with timings; and then I get to the gate and it's written in huge red letters 'gate closed', and I start panicking. Thankfully, the staff were really helpful and they helped me through. And they rushed me to the plane through a back door, and I made my flight.

N: Like anybody who's done the same thing several times, regular business travellers have advice they can offer to others.

A2: My top travel tip when travelling for work is to be very efficient in organisation. Because this gives you time also to enjoy the place where you are going, after you've done your business.

1.3.1

J = Jasmine D = Driver G = Graham

J: Is it always this busy?

D: Not always. It depends. So, what are you doing in Dublin?

J: I am starting a new job on Monday. I'm a trainee at TGC. They're an HR consultancy firm. They advise companies on different aspects of their business – recruitment, company strategy, that kind of thing. They've invited all the new recruits to a welcome dinner. And it's happening ... right about now.

G: Jasmine just sent me a text – she's stuck in traffic but she'll be here soon. In the meantime, welcome to TGC. Cheers!

1.3.2

O = Orla A = Azra S = Shaun J = Jasmine

O: Where do you come from?

A: I'm from Turkey. But ... I've lived in Dublin for years.

O: Ah. You're basically a native now. What do you think about this restaurant?

A: It's ... a nice place.

S: Ah, the traveller is here!

J: Sorry I'm late. The traffic was a nightmare.

S: Friday night traffic. Always terrible. It can be like a car park out there sometimes. It can take me hours to get home.

J: Really? So you live outside the city?

S: Not as bad as Los Angeles, though. I was at a conference there last year. The traffic was so bad I arrived late and missed my presentation. The boss was not happy. But that's nothing compared to my flight from Dublin to Bangkok a few years back. Did I ever tell you that story? They lost all my luggage. I tell you, I'm never flying with that airline again.

1.3.3

T = Thiago J = Jasmine Al = Alex Az = Azra

T: Hi. I'm Thiago.

J: Jasmine. Nice to meet you.

T: You too. How long was your trip?

J: About an hour.

T: Shaun says you're American. Where are you from?

J: That's right. I'm from Boston. I went to university there. Do you know it?

T: No, I've never been, but I'd like to.

J: Thiago, that's a Brazilian name, isn't it?

T: It is. My father's from Brazil, but I'm Italian. So ... do you know Orla?

J: Yeah, I met her at the interview. She's really nice. Hey ... What do you know about working at TGC?

T: Not much.

Al: So, I heard you come from Turkey. Whereabouts?

Az: Well, I was born in Istanbul, but my parents moved to London when I was five. We go back quite often to see family. Do you know Turkey?

Al: A little. I went there on holiday about three years ago. Which do you prefer, London or Istanbul?

Az: Hmmm. That's difficult! I love them both.

Al: No more difficult questions, I promise. We're supposed to be relaxing.

Az: No problem.

1.3.4

Let me give you some advice when making small talk. Number one: choose your topic carefully and don't be too negative. Don't talk about personal finances, politics or religion, or more personal topics. Be prepared to listen and remember to show interest in the other person and their opinions. Showing interest is simple. If you're sitting down, move your body forward a little, use eye contact and of course smile as you speak. Watch the other person's body language and if they start to look bored, change the subject. Most importantly, don't dominate the conversation.

Follow the AAA model that Azra used earlier in the video. AAA is a simple formula. Answer the speaker's question, add new information and then ask him or her another question. The conversation will run smoothly if you follow this model. Try it and see.

2.1.1

P = Presenter V = Vaiva Kalnikaitė

P: When a new company launches, or an established company opens, a new branch, there's a decision to be made about where to locate the business.

It's an important decision to get right, and there are a number of factors which could influence it. These might include access to skilled staff, good transport links and reasonable rents for factory or office space.

Dr Vaiva Kalnikaitė launched her company, Dovetailed, in 2010. It's a technology design studio and innovation lab.

V: We tend to work on projects that have human interaction so often it will be projects where we design software or, for example, an app, or it could also be a physical object – for example, we designed a 3D printer for printing food.

P: When Vaiva set up her company, she decided to locate it in Cambridge – a city famous for its university.

V: I was an intern in Cambridge with Microsoft and I really liked Cambridge because it's a very international city, it's a very vibrant city; it's full of really interesting companies from very small start-ups to well-established companies, and that's a really good reason to set up a business in that kind of environment.

P: Dovetailed is now a member of several business networks, which has clear benefits for the company.

V: Being part of these networks, we have access to local investment groups and we've been successful in getting some funding for some of our products.

P: Many companies based in Cambridge are attracted by the chance to connect with the university.

V: We were really interested in working with the university, so we talked to various departments to see if we can collaborate on something.

P: Today Dovetailed is part of a business programme at Cambridge University's Judge Business School and receives advice and support from the school.

V: We also work with, for example, engineering department and we have summer interns who come and work at Dovetailed. It's been really helpful to have an association to Cambridge University because it's given us, as a brand, global recognition.

P: For Dovetailed, locating the company in Cambridge has helped to attract talented staff, who want to work in a lively town.

V: Cambridge is a really nice place to live in, people can cycle everywhere, walk everywhere. My journey to work is three minutes by bike. There's lots of social things happening, lots of interesting cafés opening and it's very close to London.

P: Dovetailed has clients in London, so good transport links are important.

V: It's very important for us to be able to travel to London very quickly. It takes about 50 minutes by train or we can drive to London on a motorway. Again, it takes just over an hour.

P: So how does Vaiva feel about her decision to locate Dovetailed in Cambridge?

V: I'm very happy to have chosen Cambridge as a location to set up my business. I think it's an amazing place to live and work, and it's given us a lot of opportunity to grow.

2.3.1

S = Shaun A = Alex

S: Here it is. Your first assignment. Ready?

A: Yes, I ...

S: Don't worry, you'll be fine. Alright. Here's the situation. We're meeting Nick from Zapna. They're a clothes manufacturing firm with a distribution centre in Poland. Their Assistant Manager is going on maternity leave and they need to find someone to cover. Now, Nick's a nice guy, but he talks too much and he can be unclear about what he wants. I can get impatient with him sometimes. Come on. Let's do this.

2.3.2

N = Nick S = Shaun A = Alex

N: So Marta's post will be vacant soon. And as her post is vacant, we need someone to fill it. We'll need someone for about a year, as that's how long she's away. She's on maternity leave. Did I tell you that? I should also add that we did talk about taking someone on for longer, maybe eighteen months, so they could ...

S: Cover the handover period. Yeah. Great. Understood.

N: That's right. But … is a six-month handover really needed? It's expensive. And …
A: Sorry to interrupt … but I think a handover period is important. But how about two months instead of six?
N: That could work. Or three months, maybe. Shaun?
S: I agree with Alex. So, that's a fourteen-month contract. Can you just confirm that for us, Nick?
N: Yes, I suppose I … fifteen months. Just to be on the safe side.
S: Great. Fifteen months. Now, about the benefits package you're offering …
N: Well … And as you know, I'm really busy at the moment. Also, I'm not a logistics expert, so I don't always know which technical questions to ask. The last time I interviewed …
S: Let me just clarify once more. Alex is your dedicated HR Consultant. Anything you need, he can help you. No need to worry.
N: I really appreciate it. It's wonderful to have you with us, Alex. We've always had an excellent service from your firm. Are you enjoying your time there so far?
S: I'm dying for a coffee. Coffee break? Back here in fifteen minutes.
A: Great.
S: See? On and on. Drives me crazy.
A: I could ask the questions when we go back in.
S: Sure. Be my guest.

2.3.3

A = Alex N = Nick S = Shaun
A: So, Nick, what you're saying is you want someone with logistics experience?
N: Correct, but they also need a diploma in management.
A: Great. And can I just check, you're looking for someone with a good language level?
N: Exactly; fluent in English and Polish.
A: Does that mean you want to hire someone locally?
N: No, not necessarily, but they must be prepared to move.
A: And what would make this appeal to applicants?
N: Well, we're offering an excellent package.
S: Yes, you said that, but could you be more specific?
N: I mean there's a good bonus scheme and a subsidised staff canteen.
S: And there's an international airport not far from Poznań, right?
N: That's right, Poznań has its own airport.
S: And is there a relocation package?
N: What do you mean by a relocation package exactly?
S: Well, you know, help with moving costs …
A: I think what Shaun means is, the best person may not live locally. Are you happy to cover the cost for the right candidate to move to Poznań?
N: Possibly. What I mean is, it's a sensitive topic. We need to keep costs down.
S: Yes, of course. We understand.
A: And you're looking to interview a maximum of six people. Is that right?
N: Six is perfect.
A: So, I think that covers everything. We'll get to work and send you a list of candidates as soon as possible.
N: Great, thanks, Shaun.
S: Nick.
N: Thanks, Alex.
A: Nick.
S: Good work, Alex. Well done.
A: Thanks.

2.3.4

In professional situations, we sometimes meet people, like Nick, who are unclear about what they want. Checking and asking for clarification is a good way to guide the other person so you can understand exactly what they want.
But how do you do this in English? Saying 'What do you mean?' may not be enough to clarify the information you need. Instead, ask 'What do you mean by …?', or 'Could you be more specific?' Alex also rephrases questions to help Nick be more specific. And this works nicely. You can start by saying 'What I mean is …'. Closed questions will then encourage the other person to confirm their needs. Closed questions will force the other person to answer 'Yes' or 'No', or give a simple direct answer. Finally, repeating the other person's words and adding the expression 'Is that right?' is useful to ask if you are still unsure.
And if you are the speaker, notice the body language of the listener. Often, the listener's facial expression will tell you if he or she has understood. So, if necessary, offer to clarify. Use expressions like 'What I mean is …' or 'Let me clarify'.
Remember, conversation is two-way. It's not always your responsibility to understand!

3.1.1

CS = Colin Shenton M = Man W = Woman P = Presenter I = Interviewer C = Customer
CS: We like to describe it as home.
M: You can help yourself to snacks along the way.
W: You really concentrate how much work you can fit in.
CS: Everything in Ziferblat is free, except for the time that you spend.
P: Ziferblat is a café and social space with an unusual business model. You check in and out at a hotel-style desk, stay as long as you want, use the wi-fi and eat and drink as much as you like. Your bill is calculated at 6p a minute, including VAT. The largest branch of this international retail chain is here in Manchester, in northern England.
CS: Ziferblat is a Russian word, it means 'clock face', uh it's the same in German, and it's simply because our pricing mechanism is completely unique. We charge six pence a minute. Start your stopwatch on your iPhone if you like, and work out to the penny what your bill's gonna be.
I: You must get some people who try to abuse the system, 'I've only got 20p in my pocket, I can dash in, wolf down coffee and cake and leave,' does that happen?
CS: It happens and it's absolutely fine. I'm not even sure I'd call it abuse, what we offer is no minimum, no minimum charge, so if somebody feels they want to come in and eat as much as humanly possible – that's absolutely fine.
I: You feel under time pressure because you know that each minute counts.
C: I don't personally worry too much about that, although I, I think it's mounted up a bit this morning.
W: You do think about it after a couple of hours here, but I think it's really good because you concentrate how much work you can fit in.
M: Such a nice creative atmosphere, and the wi-fi is really good, so for uploading things, that's perfect.
CS: I think our smallest spend was three minutes, which is 18p – somebody wanted to go to the loo. Our longest stay was 11 hours, which was a guy based on his laptop who's writing a book. We ask that people respect the space, but this has been a really positive experience in human nature.
P: The business makes a profit. This branch serves 12,000 customers each month.
I: You've got one of these in London, but you've got several in the north – in Manchester and Liverpool – and you're rolling out more. Why is it you're able to expand up here?
CS: One principle reason, which is rent. We could do it in London if we were charging 20 or 25 pence a minute, but that adds up pretty fast, £15 an hour starts to sound expensive.

3.3.1

A = Azra T = Thiago
A: Thiago. Is everything OK?
T: It's just this report I'm doing. For Shaun. It's such a lot of extra work. And I'm nearly a week late with it. If I don't finish the report soon, Shaun is going to kill me!
A: Why don't you ask him for an extension?
T: Shaun? Are you joking? Last time I missed a deadline, he nearly put me on the next flight home to Milan! It's Shaun. You haven't seen me …
A: Shaun …

3.3.2

S = Shaun T = Thiago
S: Ah, Thiago! There you are! Just the person I was looking for! Have you got a moment? Any progress with that report?
T: Er … well …
S: Right. Sounds like there's a problem.
T: I'm just really busy with two other projects, and …
S: Thiago, it's no good making excuses. Time management is part of the job.
T: I know, I know.
S: You're holding everyone up. The report is a week late, and I need it for tomorrow's meeting with the directors. So, what's the delay?
T: Figures. I, er, still need some figures from Accounts, you …
S: Why didn't you ask me to get the figures? Any time over the past seven days? Right, that's enough. I'm bringing in Jasmine.
T: Shaun, I just need a bit more time.
S: You've had time. I'm calling Jasmine now. And I want that report on my desk by 2 p.m. tomorrow. No excuses.
T: Jasmine's going to go crazy when she finds out that we have to do overtime tonight. I guess I'm Mr Popular around here …
S: Was I hard on him? A little. But he has to learn. He can't keep missing deadlines. Anyway, Jasmine should be able to help him out.

3.3.3

T = Thiago S = Shaun
T: Shaun. Do you have a minute?
S: For you, Thiago? I've got two. Now. How are you doing with that report?
T: I'm still having some problems, I'm afraid.
S: Right. You realise I have a meeting with the directors tomorrow afternoon? I wanted it done by then.
T: I'm really sorry. I'm so busy with other projects at the moment. And Accounts didn't get back to me with the figures I need …
S: OK. Let me deal with Accounts. And I'll see if I can get one of the other trainees to share some of your workload. Just for a few days. Does that help?
T: Yes, it helps a lot.
S: Now, what else can we do to get this report finished? What if I bring in Jasmine to help you out?
T: No, no, I can manage.
S: Look, we don't have much time. Let's speed things up. How about asking Jasmine to help you with some of the figures?
T: Yes. OK.
S: Good. I'll give you three more days. But no more. Don't let me down. Of course, this doesn't help me with the directors' meeting tomorrow.
T: Why don't I just write an executive summary of the main points? You can give them that.
S: Alright, yes. Good idea.
I like Thiago's attitude. He definitely has potential. We just need to work out how to improve his time management. Easier said than done, maybe.
T: Result! I can't believe it. I got the extension I needed. Problem solved! Well, until the next one comes along …

3.3.4

When you're trying to solve problems at work, you have two basic options – focus on the problem or focus on the solution.
Now, focusing on the problem can be very effective when it's a simple technical problem. But workflow problems are usually people problems, and they're more complex. In Video A, Shaun made a big mistake. He dealt with a people problem as if it was a technical problem. He focused on what went wrong. He blamed Thiago for not completing the report, so it's no surprise there was an argument.

And when Shaun asked Thiago and Jasmine to do overtime, it was not the best solution.
In Video B, Shaun was much better. He focused on the solution from the start. Instead of asking what went wrong, he asked questions that focused on help: 'What can we do to get this report finished?' and 'What if I bring in Jasmine to help you out?' As a result, we saw Shaun and Thiago working together to complete the report. Shaun also offered to help Thiago get the figures he needed from the Accounts department. And Thiago offered to write a short summary for Shaun to give to the Board of Directors. It was a win-win situation.

4.1.1

P = Presenter S = Sharni L1 = Lauren L2 = Laurie

P: The way we work is changing fast and one clear example of this is our work patterns. This includes the hours people work, the type of contract employees have, and even the number of different jobs they work in. The traditional work pattern was based on permanent employees doing full-time jobs and fixed working hours. The typical office worker in the UK and North America worked from Monday to Friday and had a working day of nine o'clock to five o'clock. Indeed, people talk about 'nine-to-five jobs' to describe traditional office work. However, that is changing. Today's global economy needs more flexible work patterns, not nine-to-five jobs. We talked to some people about their working lives.
S: I'm Sharni, and I'm an Accountant. I work full-time flexible hours, so that means some days I start early and finish early, and some days I start later and finish later. And I'll take breaks depending on what I need to deliver for the day. Some days I work in the office and some days I work at home. I have my office set up at home, so I have everything I need to work as if I was in the office. I like working flexible hours – it gives me the ability to manage my career but also be there for my children. This type of working isn't for everybody. Some people will work better with a fixed schedule and set hours. The advantages for my employer for me to be a flexitime worker means that I'm a much happier employee. I can still maintain all aspects of my personal life and still pursue my career.
P: Some people don't have permanent jobs with one employer but work for employment agencies that find them temporary jobs in different companies.
L1: My name is Lauren. I'm a temporary worker and that basically means that I work for an agency that sends me on different assignments in different companies. I started temping during university, and I am still temping whilst I'm looking for a permanent role. The contracts that I'm assigned on last from around a couple of days to a few months, and this can include a range of different roles, such as clerical as well as reception work. The advantages of being a temp worker are ... it gives you insight into loads of different industries and it allows me to see what kind of permanent roles I'll be interested in. There are some disadvantages to working as a temporary worker and these include lack of job security, and it makes it difficult for career progression. Being adaptable is a very important skill in the job market, and ... erm, temp work definitely allows me to build upon that skill.
P: Freelance work for more than one company at the same time is also more common today.
L2: My name's Laurie. I'm a gig worker. And ... gig working means when you do lots of different types of jobs to earn a living. I work in the television industry, and a typical week for me might involve ... I might write a script, I might direct a film or I might do some camera work. Depending on how many projects I have, I may work 20 hours one week and 40 hours another week. One advantage of being a gig worker is that it allows a lot of variety in my working life. Another advantage is that it allows me to do things, in my free time, that I wouldn't ordinarily be able to do if I had a full-time job. One of the disadvantages to gig working is that there's not that much income security, so you don't always know where your next pay cheque is coming from.
P: It's clear that today there are many more work patterns than in the past. It's also clear that our working lives will continue to change in the future, and we will have to adapt to that.

4.3.1

O = Orla S = Shaun

O: Good meeting with Léana?
S: Great, thanks. She's already spoken to some of the other directors about my idea.
O: What do you call it again? Reverse coaching?
S: Yes. A lot of companies are doing it. I don't know if you've noticed ... but a few of the directors sometimes have problems with office technology. The thing is, we have all these people in junior positions working for us, who practically live their whole lives online. Social media, apps, you name it. So, the idea is they spend some time with the directors who need a bit of help using business apps, social media and so on. It's basically one-on-one coaching.
O: Perfect. What do they think?
S: Well, I'm meeting them later this afternoon. I guess we'll find out!

4.3.2

S = Shaun E = Ethan M = Michael ('Mike') T = Thiago J = Jasmine

S: Ideally, you'd meet with the directors, say, once a week. What do you think? Sounds good? Great. So ...
E: Shaun? Erm, sorry to interrupt, but I thought we were here to discuss this.
S: We are. We're discussing how to do it right. So, Thiago. You're our tech guru. Do you want to work with Léana?
M: So ... we're doing this? You've already made the decision?
S: Well ... yes. Léana has approved it. Come on, it'll be fun! You get to work with the people running the company. It's great for your career!
T: Sorry, Shaun, but how do we find time for this? We're all really busy.
S: It's an hour a week. That's all.
J: Um, Shaun. We're not trained coaches. I'm not sure I'd be comfortable working with people like Léana and Graham.
E: Look, Shaun, let's not rush into anything. We don't have to take an immediate decision on this. Can we go away and think about it?
S: Think about what? These people pay your salaries. They need your help. It's that simple.
T: Will we get paid extra? I'm just asking ...
S: I'm disappointed, guys. Really disappointed. I have a great idea ... and this is how you react! Anyway. I've told Léana about it. It's going ahead. So, you can either like it or learn to like it. Right. Who's going to work with Graham?

4.3.3

S = Shaun T = Thiago J = Jasmine M = Michael ('Mike') E = Ethan

S: Now, we already have the go-ahead from Léana. But I'd like to get your input before we finalise anything. So, what does everybody think? Thiago, you're our tech guru, what are your thoughts on this?
T: Will we have time for it?
S: OK, it's a fair point. We'll figure out a way to fit it into your schedules. Any other thoughts?
J: We're not trained coaches. Are we qualified to be doing this?
S: Hmm, I take your point. How about we arrange some kind of training for you? Just the basics. It shouldn't be too hard. Mike, you haven't said anything so far. I'd like to hear what you think.
M: Why don't we call it 'tech assistance' instead of coaching? It sounds more informal. More comfortable.
S: Mm, you may have a point. Jasmine, what do you think of Mike's idea?
J: I like it. 'Tech assistance' sounds fun.
S: It will be! Does anyone have anything else they'd like to add before we move on?
E: If we're going to be coaching the directors, maybe they could coach us, too? They could teach us a lot about the business.
J: That's a great idea. We're helping them, they're helping us.
S: OK. I'll mention it to Léana. Right, well, thanks for your input, everybody. Now we just have to decide which directors you're working with. Graham, anybody?

4.3.4

In business, it's important to make good decisions. But when those decisions affect other people, it's really important to make sure you involve them before going ahead.
In Video A, Shaun discovered that having a great idea is not enough. You need to persuade your team that it's a great idea, too. Often, the best way to do this is to ask for their input and let them see for themselves how good your idea really is.
Of course, involving others in your decisions can take a little longer. You took time to develop your idea. So your team needs time to think about it, too. And sometimes people don't have much input to give. But by showing them you value what they say, as Shaun did in Video B, you may find they can make your idea even better! In fact, we saw that Michael and Ethan were able to do this. More importantly, your idea will become the team's idea. And because it's now the team's idea, everyone on the team will want to make it work.

5.1.1

I'm here in Mumbai where queues like this outside banks have become a common sight. And that's the story across the country. Last week, the Indian government announced that 500- and 1,000-rupee notes would be completely abolished. So I want to find out how far I can get without a single penny in my wallet.
A lot of people who have suffered from this cash crunch are small businesses who have to buy their goods up front.
Now, businesses like this stall, something that you find on every street corner in a city like Mumbai. Paan is a stuffed betel leaf chewed by millions of Indians.
Thank you.
Great. So, he accepts credit cards, so I don't have to give cash. I've got away with it here. Mobile wallets, where you can load money onto an app, have been around for years and have been gaining in popularity, too. But since the currency announcement has come in, some payment gateways have been seeing a rise of up to 400 percent in customers.
OK, that's great. So he's accepting money via mobile wallets, but vegetables are an everyday item normally paid in cash. So are customers ready to go cashless?
By taking this step, the government is hoping to get more people and businesses into the financial system. And this will also help increase tax revenues.
Cash? So there you have it. I managed to do most of the things without cash. But then I need cash for something that millions of Indians do every day – getting around town. And without everyone willing to turn to technology even in these difficult times, the Indian government's hopes of becoming a hundred percent cashless economy could still be far off.

5.3.1

S = Shaun O = Orla

S: Orla. On your way to the project meeting?
O: Yes.
S: It's the first time this team's worked together, isn't it? No pressure ...
O: Well, we're really just working out team roles today. The client pitch is not for another six weeks. The question is, do I just *tell* them what I'd like them to do or let them figure it out themselves? Part of me wants to let *them* decide. Part of me just wants to tell them ...
S: Well, there are some strong personalities in that team, so I wouldn't give them too much freedom. I'd just *tell* them if I were you.
O: I'll let you know how it goes ...

5.3.2

O = Orla J = Jasmine A1 = Azra A2 = Alex T = Thiago S = Shaun

O: That's the project covered. Now, team roles. Alex, I'd like you to be pitch leader. You've got the most project management experience. Now, Azra, I thought lead presenter for you this time. We've talked about you wanting to develop your presentation skills. Jasmine, I'm going to ask you to be the learning designer.
J: Oh, erm ...
O: Problem?
J: Well, no, it's just quite a lot of responsibility.
O: You're a Learning and Development Specialist, and you're a responsible person. You'll be fine. Finally, Thiago. Tech support. You're so good with technology.
A1: Actually, Orla, I'm really not comfortable presenting. Especially in front of a new client.
A2: I agree. Azra should be the pitch leader on this one, and I can take care of the presentation. And maybe Thiago could help me out. He needs something bigger than tech support.
T: Yeah, why do I always get tech support?
A1: And ... well ... maybe Jasmine also feels like I do. About her role.
J: I am worried. It's a big responsibility.
A2: Perhaps Thiago can help me present and do the slides.
T: Wait a minute. I'm doing the presentation and the slides?
O: Everyone! Please! Your first time together as a team and you're arguing about everything! Let's just think about this.
S: Sounded lively in there.
O: I don't think this is going to be easy.

5.3.3

O = Orla A1 = Azra A2 = Alex T = Thiago

O: OK, you all know each other quite well. So let's decide the team roles among ourselves. Is that OK with everyone? Alex. Azra. I was thinking you could head up the project together as pitch leader and lead presenter. How would you feel about that?
A1: Me as pitch leader?
O: If you don't mind.
A1: Actually, Orla, sorry, but I'd rather not be the lead presenter if that's OK with you. I'm really not comfortable with that role.
O: But ... don't you want to develop your presentation skills?
A1: I do! But one step at a time. I'm quite good at communicating one on one – but presenting to a new client? I'm not sure I'm the best person.
A2: Perhaps Azra and I could swap roles.
O: Well, I did want you as pitch leader, Alex, but if you're both happy to exchange roles, then that's fine with me. Right, Jasmine, I'd like you to be the learning designer. Relax! You have the expertise, and I'll be here to help you out if you need it. Just look at it as a challenge. Now, Thiago, you're our tech expert, so how would you like to do the PowerPoint for us again?
T: I don't mind. But I'd prefer not to do that again if I have a choice.
A2: Actually, Orla, I think Thiago might do a good job as co-presenter with me. Didn't you win a public speaking competition at university or something?
T: I won two of them.
O: Nice idea, Alex, but who's going to do the PowerPoint? No offence, but it's not really your strong point, is it?
A2: Maybe Thiago and I could work together on both? Thiago's a lot better with technology than I am, but I can help him with some of the other stuff.
O: OK. Great. I think we've got the team roles covered. So, just to summarise ...

5.3.4

It's a key question when building a team: do you simply tell people what you want them to do, or do you let them decide? After all, they know what they're best at, and what skills they still need to develop.
In Video A, we saw Orla taking the first approach. And immediately we saw a negative reaction from the team. When Orla gave Alex and Thiago roles she knew they were good at, she didn't consider if they might like to develop new skills. And with Azra and Jasmine, Orla went too far in the other direction. She gave them challenges they didn't feel prepared for.
But both of these problems were solved in Video B. This is because they negotiated their own team roles. Jasmine kept the role Orla suggested, but the others changed or shared roles. In this way, there was room for them to improve their skill set without challenging them too much.
When you're building a team, you want people to do things they're good at, and also excited about. You can trust each team member to know what these things are. And if you show that you trust them to be involved in the decisions about their roles, it gives them confidence, and builds their trust in you. This is the ideal scenario.

6.1.1

P = Presenter R = Roy White B = Brent Jennings T = Team member Dr R = Dr Rick de Decker

P: Whether we play team sports in our free time, work on joint projects or are part of a team at work, most of us have to cooperate with others on a regular basis. But there is one context in which teamwork is especially important ... and that's when danger is involved. At more than 1,000 metres high, Table Mountain towers over Cape Town in South Africa. Easy access from the city makes it very popular with tourists and hikers. But with over eighty rescues a year, it is more dangerous than people realise.
R: Table Mountain is not a simple mountain, it's not an easy mountain.
P: This is why the Table Mountain Rescue team is always ready. If someone has an accident on the mountain, it's the team's job to get them down. This hiker was on his way down from the mountain with a friend when he fell and hurt his leg. He can't walk, so the rescue team has to get him to safety. With the sun going down, the team has to work in the dark. They need to be very careful and very patient or they will put everyone at risk.
B: The main problem is that you don't ever get two people carrying a stretcher. You'll have maybe nine, ten people carrying a stretcher at any one point; and that whole group has got to make its way down safely.
P: By working together, the team has reached the bottom safely. The members of the Table Mountain rescue team have faced many difficult situations together, but it takes more than practice and experience to work well as a team.
B: You can't just expect rescue experience alone to give you what you need in a rescue team.
P: Lots of personal skills are necessary for a good team worker. But being a good communicator – knowing what to say, when to say it, and how to say it clearly – is one of the most important. And connected to that, of course, is the ability to listen to others.
T: Woah, woah, woah, slowly guys!
P: You also need to be reliable, so the rest of the team can trust you.
Dr R: If you get that level of trust with somebody who is on the ledge above you, then you've got a really good team going. But that takes some doing, it takes quite a lot of training to get to that level.
P: Even in experienced teams, people may disagree, so good team members need to know how to deal with arguments, stay calm and help everyone reach agreement – in other words, they need to be good at conflict management. If team members show each other respect, a solution can usually be found. When the work is finished, the team can relax, talk about what went well and get ready for the next rescue.

6.3.1

T = Thiago J = Jasmine

T: Coffee? Hell-o!
J: What? Oh, thanks. Sorry, I'm just thinking about this Miami thing.
T: You're going to Miami?
J: Hopefully, yeah. I put in a proposal for a talk at the Global HR Leadership Conference. Orla said I should give it a try. And ... I don't believe it. That's an email from them. The conference organisers. Ah ... this could be so great for my résumé.
'No'. They said 'no'.

6.3.2

T = Thiago J = Jasmine A = Azra

T: I'm sorry, Jasmine. That's too bad. But ... look on the bright side.
J: What bright side?
T: Erm ...
J: Exactly.
T: Come on, it's no big deal. It's just a conference, after all.
J: Thiago, it's the biggest HR conference in the world! And I should be speaking at it. Now I've got to tell Orla they rejected me.
T. Orla will understand. Come on. Cheer up! Look ... some of us are going for a drink after work. Why don't you come along?
J: You know what? I don't really feel like hitting the pub right now.
T: Harry's Bar. At six. You know ... if you change your mind. And, hey, Orla thinks you're great. We all do. Don't worry so much.
A: Jasmine! Thiago told me your news. You must be so disappointed!
J: Well. Life goes on.
A: Oh, poor you! I know exactly how you feel! Listen, if you need someone to talk to about it, just let me know, OK?
J: Thanks, Azra.

6.3.3

A = Alex J = Jasmine

A: Miami?
J: Thiago. He told you.
A: No secrets in this place. I'm sorry it didn't work out for you. I hope you're not too disappointed.
J: Thanks. Maybe Thiago was right. It's no big deal.
A: It sounds like you put a lot of work into it.
J: Yeah, well ...
A: And I know how important it was to you. So I can understand how you feel. Did the organisers tell you why they didn't accept you? They can be very selective.
J: They said I had an interesting topic, but it didn't really fit this year's theme.
A: So. You had the right topic. You just picked the wrong year. It happens.
J: Looks like it. I didn't really think about the conference theme. Stupid of me.
A: You can always try again. You'll know next time. If it makes you feel any better, I had to apply to engineering school three times before I finally got in. My advice? Put it behind you and move on.
J: I guess I just wanted to impress Orla.
A: Orla likes you. Everyone does. But you haven't been here long. Don't try to run before you can walk. The question to ask yourself is: What can I learn from this?
J: Yeah, I see that now.
A: Look at it this way: you missed out on a trip to Miami, but now you'll be free to help me with the Ferguson pitch.
J: The Ferguson pitch?
A: Yeah. Shaun thinks you're ready to start presenting to clients face to face. So you'll be my co-presenter to start with. What do you think? More fun than talking to a roomful of strangers in Miami?

6.3.4

Business life can have its disappointments as well as its successes. When the presentation doesn't go well, or we don't get the promotion, what do we do? Well, we might turn to the colleague we trust the most for support and advice.
In Video A, Thiago's response to Jasmine's bad news was to avoid it. Then, he tried to change the subject by inviting her out for a drink with the group. He didn't seem to care very much.
Azra did the opposite. She showed too much

emotion, and it was annoying for Jasmine.
In Video B, Alex got the balance right. He said he understood how Jasmine felt, but he didn't pretend to know exactly what she was feeling. He looked for positive things while accepting her disappointment. Most importantly, he was able to empathise – which means to share the experience of another person – and this can make the other person feel better.

7.1.1

P = Presenter S = Simon Lyons

P: Any company offering goods for sale is under constant pressure to improve existing products and to bring new products to market. But any product, whether it's a mobile phone, a new medicine or a washing machine, must go through a period of research and development – R&D – to make improvements to the design, ensure that it's safe, and that consumers will want to buy it. Simon Lyons runs a small design company, Version 22, in Loughborough, a town north of London. In 2016, the company launched a clever product called Nimble.
S: Nimble is a one-finger safety cutter. You put it on your finger tip; it's got a tiny blade at the tip, and you can use it to cut open boxes and parcels that come through the post, food packaging, product packaging.
P: Simon first had the idea when he was studying at university and entered a competition.
S: The brief was to look at these videos of elderly and disabled people describing problems they had at home, and to pick one of those problems and to design a solution. The one problem that kept coming up the most was people with arthritis in their hands, really struggling to open food packaging in the kitchen.
P: After he had the idea, Simon began the research and development process.
S: Starting the R&D process is quite simple – just a pen and paper. So, really rough sketches, coming up with as many different ideas as possible. I then try and make a very, very low-cost prototype. This was the first ever prototype I made of Nimble, which was made out of a finger of a kitchen glove cut off, some plastic from an A4 folder, and the tip of a knife blade.
P: Simon's design won the competition. The prize money allowed him to produce more advanced prototypes.
S: I started doing 3D-printed prototypes of lots of different designs before I got to a final design that I was happy with. One of the main design challenges I had with Nimble was designing it so it could be worn and used by as many people as possible, so having it as a one-size-fits-all design.
P: And how did Simon decide on the colour?
S: Yellow's a brilliant colour for people with visual impairments; and as Nimble's especially useful for people who are blind or partially sighted, yellow was the obvious choice there.
P: Once Simon was confident with the design, Nimble was ready for user-testing.
S: It was important to user-test Nimble to get as many perspectives on the product's usefulness, design and function as possible. I found users to test Nimble by attending a few trade shows, and this way I got about 150 people signed up. I sent out early prototypes of the product to these people, and they used them for about a month and gave me their feedback. Thankfully, the feedback we got from our testers was positive, which meant that we didn't have to make many changes to the design at all.
P: With the R&D stage successfully completed, Nimble was ready to be launched.
S: Nimble's been commercially available for about one and a half years, and it's been selling really well. We've shipped around 30,000 units to about 80 countries around the world so far.
P: So, what's the next product from Version 22?
S: So, the next product we've got coming out is something quite different. It's called Mobu, and it's a tiny little cable clip which will stop your earphones tangling in your pocket, and it works together with another product to keep your cables organised around your desk and around the house.

7.3.1

T = Thiago A = Azra

T: Whose training session are you in? I'm with Shaun.
A: Orla. I'm looking forward to hearing about this new expenses system.
T: Me, too. The current one is so complicated. And I hate having to keep my receipts when I'm travelling. It should be an app – something easy to use.
A: Exactly. Anyway, enjoy the training.
T: I just hope it's not too boring.

7.3.2

S = Shaun T = Thiago C = Caroline

S: What would your ideal expenses system look like?
T: An app?
S: You're in luck. Say hello to *Expenses 220*. A new app – really easy to use. No more Excel spreadsheets. No more paper receipts. Let me take you through the process. So, to create an expense report, you enter the expense item and date, choose the currency and enter the amount, take a photo of any receipts …
T: Are you following any of this?
S: Additional comments in the comment box, and then save it. So, you can go back to your claim as many times as you like … all you need to do is use the drop-down menu …
C: Sorry, Shaun. None of this is clear to me.
T: Yeah, I didn't follow everything either.
S: Come on, guys, it's not that difficult! OK … one more time. Use the drop-down menu to make changes – but make sure your settings are put to the relevant currency. Got it? Of course you have. Now, moving on to …

7.3.3

O = Orla A = Azra T = Thiago

O: OK, so you start by selecting 'Create an expense report'. Do you see that? Then, enter the expense item – like this: 'hotel bill'. After that, enter the date. Don't enter it manually, just select the 'calendar'; because it's the easiest thing to do. Any questions so far? The next step is to choose the type of expense – select this from the menu. You must do this because Accounts need the information for reporting reasons. So, in this case you're going to choose 'Business meal with client'. Right. Once you've done that, choose your currency, and enter the amount. The default setting is euros, so be careful if you need another currency. Then, save your claim and you're almost finished. The last step is to take a photo of your receipt and it'll be saved automatically with your electronic claim. When you have completed all the steps, press 'Submit', and you're done! Any questions?
A: When should we send in our claims?
O: By the end of the month. Oh, and also, the app will remember your data, and that will really save you time! Does everybody understand? Now, it's not perfect and there might be teething problems, but I think …
A: How did it go?
T: Don't ask. You?
A: Great. So I'm guessing you need a lesson from me on how this thing works?
T: I'll buy you a cappuccino! With chocolate!
A: It's a deal.

7.3.4

To explain a procedure clearly, follow these four steps.
Step 1: Speak clearly and make sure you sound interested, even if you're not, or you've already explained the same procedure a hundred times.
Step 2: Divide the stages of the procedure into small parts or pieces of information. It's a lot easier for someone to understand small pieces of information than the whole procedure all at once.
Step 3: Use words like 'first', 'second' and 'next' to order your explanation, just like Orla did. These will help the listener remember the different steps.
Step 4: Use examples where necessary and always invite the other person to ask questions, to check they have understood or need more detail.
There you go – a very simple and effective procedure.

8.1.1

P = Presenter M = Matías Alcalde
J = Juan Pablo Alvarez

P: Punta de Lobos in Chile is one of the best places to surf in South America. In the summer months, 5,000 visitors arrive every day at this popular surf and tourist destination. In recent years, developers have made plans for large construction projects along the cliffs. However, many in the community were not happy about this. The Punta de Lobos Foundation is an organisation created by local people to fight these plans. We spoke to Matías Alcalde, the Foundation's director about why they are against the building projects.
M: Uh, a lot of private projects, uh, real-estate projects – big ones – were wan-, wanted to be developed here, like where we're standing here, there will be uh, houses hanging on the cliffs, uh, four buildings, seven stories high like a surf resort, or not even a surf resort, but huge density of construction and people coming in here. We have a real threatening situation for such a special place like … like this one.
P: The Punta de Lobos Foundation works with other conservation groups, such as Save the Waves. Together, they want to stop private construction on the coast and to keep the cliffs open to the public. They also want to solve other problems caused by the large number of visitors.
M: It was a mess here, if you put a thousand or fifteen hundred cars here, uh, you … you can take an hour, hour and a half to just go a mile out back to the highway. And the second thing is that there were no bathrooms here.
P: The foundation is looking for solutions to these problems. They've already improved the traffic situation and installed eco-bathrooms for visitors. They've also put a fence along the cliff to protect it from visitors' feet. Some local businesses see conservation as important, too. This small hotel is by the beach at Punta de Lobos. Designed to have as little impact as possible on the area, it was built with local and recycled materials. I spoke to Juan Pablo Alvarez, the hotel manager.
J: It's only in the archi-, architecture, we don't want it to be uh, like a big hotel five-star resort, we have 12 rooms, we could have, like, 40, 50, but we wanted to offer something different, something special. This is a very sensitive and special place and spot for us, so we wanted to … to protect it.
P: Matías Alcalde sees Punta de Lobos as an important conservation project for the rest of Chile. It is not only about protecting one favourite surfing location in the country.
M: We're very eager that Punta de Lobos is successful, because it's the example in order to scale this project throughout Chile, uh, there's a need on conservation in Chile, we are a developing country, we're just getting started and we can learn from so many mistakes that, through Punta de Lobos, we can set the example for future developments along the coast.

8.3.1

S = Shaun T = Thiago D = Della

S: You're holding everyone up. The report is a week late, and I need it for tomorrow's meeting with the directors. So. What's the delay?
T: Figures. I, er, still need some figures from Accounts, you …
S: Why didn't you ask me to get the figures? Any time over the past seven days? Right, that's enough. I'm bringing in Jasmine.
T: I'm sorry, Jasmine. That's too bad. But … look on the bright side.
Della.
D: Yes?
T: You sent me a load of emails.
D: The reminder about your expenses claim, yes. I think I only sent two. The first, and a follow-up.
T: No, you sent at least three.

D: Ah. Yes. Three. Well, I was worried.
T: Well, it's quite stressful receiving all these emails. If I didn't respond, there's a reason.
D: Well, I'm sorry you feel that way, Thiago. This is our normal procedure. So ...

8.3.2

O = Orla T = Thiago

O: Come in! Nervous? Don't worry. Let me explain the process. We'll start with the positive feedback, then we'll move on to some areas for improvement. Is that OK with you? So ... you've been with us for six months. How do you feel it's gone so far?
T: I think I'm doing well. I don't think there have been any problems, but I'd be interested to hear what you think.
O: Well, in general, we're pleased with your progress.
T: OK. I'm glad to hear that.
O: You're enthusiastic and you work hard. You're great with technology – that's always a benefit. You're warm and in general you have good interpersonal skills. We saw how you tried to help Jasmine after the Miami conference issue – you were very supportive.
T: That's good to know, thanks.
O: And, of course, you have an excellent sense of humour. However, I have to point out some areas for development. It's important to give what we call 'corrective' feedback. To support you in your professional development.
T: Everyone can improve, right?
O: Exactly.

8.3.3

O = Orla T = Thiago

O: So, there are a couple of areas for improvement ... like your time-management skills. Shaun mentioned that you were late finishing a report for him. And you've missed other deadlines. How do you feel about this aspect of your work?
T: I guess I am sometimes late.
O: You've been late a few times with your expenses claims, too. We think you could improve your admin skills more generally.
T: Yeah, OK, admin's not my strong point.
O: Well, OK, but the reason we're concerned is that it creates problems for other people. The company could miss a deadline with a client. So we really need you to respect all your deadlines from now on. And please remember to submit your expenses claims on time. Now we have the new app, there are no excuses.
T: Sure. Will do.
O: Now ... about your relations with some of the older members of staff ... Della in particular.
T: I get on well with Della.
O: Well, she thinks you're sometimes a little disrespectful.
T: Really? Are you sure she means me?
O: I think it's your tone of voice. So, it's not what you say, it's how you say it. You can sound a bit impolite, even aggressive at times. What do you think? Would that be a fair assessment?
T: Well, I try to respect everyone ...
O: We're worried because the way you communicate could have a negative impact on the team and also on relations with our clients.
T: I never meant to upset anyone.
O: I can see that. But I would like you to pay more attention to this in the future.
T: Yes, yes, of course.
O: And we really love your enthusiasm. So, more of that, please. Do you have any questions about the feedback?
T: No, I don't think so. I appreciate your comments, thanks.
O: OK. So, in summary, we have agreed your goals.

8.3.4

In our professional lives, we all have to receive corrective feedback from time to time and some of us might also have to give corrective feedback. So here's some advice.
First of all, how to give corrective feedback. Here, you can follow a simple model. Prepare the person before giving the feedback and then ask for their agreement. Say something like, 'We need to discuss some areas for improvement. Is that OK with you?' As you give the feedback, give clarification or examples where possible. Then end by inviting the person to assess their own performance. Phrases such as 'Would that be a fair assessment?' encourage the person to remain positive about the feedback.
Secondly, receiving corrective feedback. One of the most difficult things is to stay positive and diplomatic if someone is giving you feedback. 'Your feedback is very useful, thanks.' is a good expression to use. Or when you want to apologise for negative behaviour, say, 'Yes, I accept that is sometimes a problem for me.'
Finally, I would always suggest you thank the person for their feedback. That way you end on a positive note.

1.01

A: Welcome, Alicia. Thanks so much for taking the time to talk with us on *World of Work* today.
B: It's my pleasure, Marek. Thanks so much for inviting me on the show. It's exciting!
A: I'd like to start by asking this: What does an Events Manager do?
B: I manage events ...
A: Oh, right – OK, so the job title says it all: Events Manager.
B: Right. So what that means is that I help people plan events: parties, conferences, corporate hospitality events – that kind of thing.
A: What about weddings?
B: No – not at all. Weddings are *harder* than business lunches and are usually done by people who only plan weddings.
A: OK, so who are your clients?
B: I'd say about ninety percent of my work involves businesses – planning events for corporate clients. I sometimes do parties for individual people, but not very often.
A: OK. So when you plan an event, what do you do? Where do you start?
B: First, I have to find out what the client wants. That means finding out what type of event it is, and also when they want to have it. Because usually, an event is for some reason, like a grand opening, or welcoming new employees or something – so the timing is usually important.
A: OK, I see. And what about money?
B: Yes, of course. We have to talk about budget at the first meeting, because I have to think about the cost for every decision I make. I try to find the best location for each event. I can't choose the most expensive hotel in town for an event for someone with a small budget. For a cheap event, we choose the least expensive venue possible. So we have to choose a venue – a location – carefully.
A: Sure. And for you, are some venues better than others?
B: Definitely. Planning an event outdoors is always the biggest challenge.
A: Because ...
B: Because of the weather. You can't control that!
A: Sure, of course. So after you've talked about schedule, budget and venue, what then?
B: They usually want me to think of something special – you know, to come up with an original idea.
A: Like ...
B: Well, I did a tenth anniversary party for a software company, and we did a circus theme.
A: A circus theme?
B: Yeah – we had clowns, a guy who did magic – and the location was actually a big tent – like a circus tent – in a park. We had about five hundred people there – five hundred guests. It was amazing. Everyone had a great time.
A: Was the circus event more difficult than your usual events?
B: No, not really. We usually have some kind of entertainment, but we also have to arrange food, tables and chairs ...
A: Wow.
B: I usually have to organise a sound system for the speeches and music ...
A: So there are a lot of details.
B: It's all details!
A: Well, that's a good introduction to my next question.
B: OK.
A: What skills are necessary for an Events Manager?
B: Well, we've already talked about attention to detail.
A: What else?
B: Organisation – the ability to organise is super important.
A: Organising what?
B: Everything: Schedules, budgets, food orders, teams of people ... . Getting the right staff for an event is really important – you need the right people.
A: Ah, yes, people. Do you need people skills?
B: For sure. You really need to get on with people – you need to manage people well, because the job is all about people – about making people happy. My top priority is client satisfaction.
A: And for you, are any of the skills more important – or less important?
B: Honestly, I don't think so. You need all of them. If you love people but you can't organise, then you can't do this job. If you pay attention to detail but can't manage a budget – forget it!
A: OK, well, that makes sense. This is really useful for our listeners, thanks Alicia. Please stay with us. We're going to take a short break. When we come back, we'll be asking Alicia about ...

1.02 L = Laura J = Jakob

L: How are you doing, Jakob?
J: OK so far, thanks. I'm looking forward to meeting everyone.
L: Great. So, first, I'll explain the schedule for the day.
J: Sure.
L: So, we'll start with the induction briefing, where you learn about the company. And then you can meet the team. The health and safety training with the other interns is at 10.45. That gives us plenty of time.
J: How many other interns are there?
L: Five. They're mostly from abroad, so it's a really international group this year.
J: Right, OK.
L: And this afternoon you can set up your email account. Our IT technician, Sue, has created a username for you, and temporary login details are on your desk. Sue's really helpful. Just call her if you have any problems.

1.03 S = Sue J = Jakob

S: IT help desk. Sue speaking.
J: Hello, Sue. This is Jakob Davis. I'm ...
S: ... one of the new interns. Hi, Jakob. How can I help you?
J: I'm having problems with the IT.
S: Ah, what kind of problems?
J: I can't connect to the intranet. I don't know how to log on.
S: It should be quite simple. You need to use your login details.
J: I tried my username and password, but ...
S: Can you try logging on again?
J: Er, just a minute ... no, it's not working.
S: OK, no problem. Can I just check your username?
J: Intern82.
S: Are you sure? 82 or 32?
J: Er, it looks like 82.
S: Sorry, it's my writing, it's difficult to read. Try 'intern32'.
J: Ah, that works, thanks. The other thing ... I need to get a company email address. How do I set up my email account?
S: I'll set that up for you. Can you just remind me of your family name?
J: Davis.
S: D-A-V-I-S?
J: That's right. And Jakob is J-A-K-O-B.
S: J-A-K-O-B, thanks. So your email address will be Jakob dot Davis at htm.com. Give me a few minutes and I'll call you back. What's your extension number?
J: Er ... sorry, Sue, I'm having trouble finding my extension number. I was going to ask my colleague for help, but she's just gone into a meeting and ...
S: That's OK. I can help you with that. Just a minute, er, – here we are, Jakob Davis – extension 5182.
J: 5-1-8-2 – got it.
S: I'll call you back in a few minutes to confirm your email address.

2.01

A: Is there enough space in this room for the meeting?
B: Yes, but I think there are too many chairs.
A: You're right! I'll move some next door.
B: And it's too hot in here, isn't it? Let's open the windows.
A: Oh no! There's too much noise from outside. I'll put the air conditioning on.
B: OK! I see there are not enough glasses. I'll get some more from the kitchen.
A: Is there enough time to make some photocopies?
B: Yes! We have lots of time. It's still too early for people to arrive.

2.02 J = Josh S = Samia

J: Hey, it's Josh, how are you?
S: Fine, thanks, Josh. How are you?
J: Good, thanks. Listen, did you get the agenda for this afternoon?
S: Yes. You didn't get it?
J: No.
S: I'll send it to you. And the minutes from the last meeting. Got them?
J: Thanks. Oh, no, Don's chairing again; that means it'll go on and on.
S: Yes, probably. So you're going to present the results of your market survey?
J: Which item is that? Oh, yes, four. It's quite interesting actually.
S: Really? And did you prepare anything for Item 3?
J: The financial report? No, that was an action point from the last meeting for Mike. Anyway, what's Item 5 all about? Micro-kitchen? What's that?
S: Dierdre wants to set up an office kitchen. I think it's quite a good idea.
J: I see you're organising the office party again this year, Samia!
S: Yes, that's me, Item 6 – it's the only item I'm interested in.
J: No surprises. What are you planning?
S: Ah, you'll have to wait and see.
J: Item 8 – Close – that's *my* favourite item ... Do you think we'll leave on time, though, with Don in the chair?

2.03 Don = Don J = Josh E = Ellen S = Samia H = Harry De = Deirdre

Don: Everyone ready?
J: Samia will be a little late. She's on another call.
Don: OK, but I'd like to start on time; it's a full agenda today. Can you tell her what we said, Josh?
J: Sure.
Don: Right, so let's start. Nice to see everyone and welcome back to Ellen.
E: Thanks, it's lovely to see everyone.
Don: So, one reason for meeting is to introduce you all to Harry. He started on Monday and he'll be helping us with our finances.
All: Hello, Harry. / How are you doing? / Nice to meet you.
Don: Does everyone have a copy of the agenda? Does anyone ...
S: Hi, everyone. Sorry I'm late.
Don: Samia, hello. Take a seat. The main aim today is to catch up before the holidays. Does anyone want to add anything to the agenda?
All: Not really. / No. / I'm fine.
Don: We have AOB if anything comes up. Harry, can I ask you to be time-keeper?
H: OK.
Don: And could I have a volunteer to take the minutes? Josh, Ellen?
E: OK, sure. I can do that.
Don: Thanks for agreeing. I know it's a busy time. So, let's look at Item 1, Matters Arising from the last ...
E: Sorry, can we just go back to Item 2? What was the decision? I didn't quite understand it ...
Don: So, moving on to Item 5: this is Deirdre's point, I think. Harry, how are we doing for time?
H: We're on time for the moment.
Don: Great. Deirdre, over to you.
De: Thanks. I'd like to talk about the micro-kitchen we agreed on at the last meeting.
J: Did we?
De: Ah, yes.
S: ... And *you* even agreed to help set it up.
J: Did I? Oh, OK, sorry.
De: Right. The reason I want to discuss this is to agree on a budget. I found some possible suppliers, but of course we need to get some quotes.

H: What did you include in the budget?
De: It seems contractors for micro-kitchens supply everything. I think a maximum of 500 pounds a month is reasonable. What do you all think?

3.01

1
A: We need something for dinner.
B: OK, I'll get some chicken on my way home this evening.
2
A: Where shall we get the presents for the family?
B: I just want to buy everything in one place. You know I hate going around different shops all day.
3
A: You know it'll be Noah's birthday soon. He's five on Thursday.
B: That's right! Let's get him some children's stories for his birthday.
4
A: Are you all right? You look a bit tired.
B: Yeah, I've got a terrible headache. I need to get something for it.
5
A: I should get something to wear for that job interview but I haven't got much money.
B: Try Zara or H&M. Their prices are reasonable.
6
A: Where did you say we're going again?
B: Bluewater. It says on the website that there are 330 stores and 40 cafés under one roof.
7
A: I love that fresh bread you bought in that new place. Let's go there again.
B: Yes, and they have a really nice selection of cakes as well.

3.02

Extract 1
A: Hello, Tony. Did you have a nice holiday?
B: Yes, we had a great time, thanks Sonia.
A: Where did you go? I can't remember if you told me.
B: Istanbul.
A: Ah, yes, that's right.
B: You see my wife went to a conference there last week. And I decided to go with her. Well, I didn't go to the conference. I spent the day visiting the city when Barbara was at work. Then we had dinner together in the evenings. She was working Monday to Friday but she wasn't working at the weekend. We went to the Grand Bazaar on Saturday.
A: Oh, the Grand Bazaar, I heard it's fabulous.
B: Yes, it is. Did you know it's one of the largest and oldest covered markets in the world?
A: Really?
B: Yeah, there are, I don't know, thousands of shops. I mean, we were browsing for hours but we weren't looking for anything specific and we didn't see half of it.
A: Did you buy anything in the end?
B: Yeah, a Turkish carpet. You know, the carpet seller served us tea when we sat down, and then we negotiated the price.
A: Sounds interesting. Did you get a bargain?
B: No, I don't think so, but we really liked the carpet and the experience was fun.
Extract 2
C: Hey! Did I tell you I went to that new shopping mall yesterday?
D: No, what's it like?
C: It's cool. One clothes store had magic mirrors.
D: Magic mirrors? What are those?
C: It's basically augmented reality. So I could try on different styles and colours without putting on clothes. It uses special computer software.
D: Like a video game.
C: Yeah! You know how I really don't enjoy shopping for clothes. The stores are always busy and there are long queues for the changing rooms. Then you spend hours trying on clothes. Then more long queues to pay the cashier. But with a magic mirror I can try different clothes and colours in less time, which makes shopping a bit easier.
D: So, what did you get?
C: Well, there were a couple of nice suits, but I didn't know which style or colour I liked best, so I didn't buy anything. But I have the store's app on my phone.
D: What's that for?
C: Well, when I left the store, they sent me a list of the clothes I tried on to my phone, and I can order online when I decide. Have a look and help me choose.
D: Ah, oh is that the time? What was I thinking? I was talking to Martin earlier and I agreed to help him with something. I'll see you later.
Extract 3
F: Hello, Rafa! Sorry! Did I interrupt you? Were you eating?
E: No, no, I was having a coffee.
F: So, how are you?
E: Very well, and you? How's it going in Shanghai?
F: Not bad, not bad.
E: How's your Chinese?
F: Don't ask! I didn't speak much Chinese when I arrived here a month ago and I don't speak any more today. It's fine in the office because everyone speaks English. But shopping is more of a problem.
E: What about ordering in restaurants?
F: Oh, that's easy. Lots of restaurants here in China have picture menus. They're great!
E: So you can see exactly what you're ordering?
F: That's right! Anyway, the other day I heard about these new automated convenience stores.
E: Automated? You mean with robots? Artificial intelligence?
F: No, not exactly, just self-service with no human staff. I was walking to the metro yesterday when I saw one. When I went in, I chose my food, paid and didn't interact with a single person.
E: How does it work?
F: First you give the company all your personal details. Then you can use your phone to enter the shop with a QR code and you scan the bar codes on products and pay with your phone, too. You also scan another QR code to leave the store.
E: Wow! But don't some people leave without paying?
F: I don't think so. There are security cameras and an alarm system. They're watching you and they have your personal details!
E: Ah! I see. So, it sounds like a good option for you.
F: Well, yes and no. There's not much fresh food, it's mostly snacks and instant noodles. I was looking for something healthy. And my soft drink was warm but I couldn't return it or complain to anyone. I'm not sure I like the future of shopping.

3.03

1 Did you have a nice holiday?
2 ...the carpet seller served us tea when we sat down ...
3 I could try on different styles and colours ...
4 when I left the store, they sent me a list ...
5 I didn't speak much Chinese when I arrived here ...
6 when I went in, I chose my food ...

3.04 T = Tony S = Sonia

T: So, how was work when I was away last week?
S: We were very busy without you. We got another big order from Piotr.
T: Again? Did he pay us for the last order?
S: No, not the full amount. I wrote him an email about it when I received the new order. He rang me immediately and said he'll pay us this week.
T: That sounds good. And did you meet the new Marketing Manager when she started last week?
S: No, I didn't see her. She definitely didn't come to the office. In fact, I think she starts this week.
T: Yes, you're right! I thought it was last week.

3.05 C = Carl I = Inés

C: Right, morning, everyone. Thanks for coming in. OK, let's get started. This is Inés from customer research ...
I: Hello, everyone.
C: Inés has joined us today to help me present the results of last month's customer service survey. As you know, improving customer service is one of our main objectives this year. Now, as you can see, this was a three-stage survey. So, first of all, I'd like to start off by talking about stage one, the customer satisfaction ratings. Secondly, I'll go on to talk about the in-store interviews. And then I'll hand you over to Inés to talk about stage three, the focus group results. Finally, there'll be time for questions at the end. OK? So, let's jump right in. Have a look at this. This is the customer feedback station we now have in all our megastores. Customers simply press the button that shows how satisfied they were with our service. Was it great, good, not good or bad? Then we process their feedback. Here's a full breakdown of the figures by region and store.

3.06

OK, now let's move on to the in-store interviews. First of all, why did we do them? Well, when we sent our researchers into the stores, they noticed that a lot of people weren't using the customer feedback stations at all. So, obviously, these people do not show up in our customer satisfaction figures. Fortunately, plenty of people *were* leaving positive feedback. But *why* were they positive? And how many other people were they telling about us? Again, we had no data for this. So we organised a team of interviewers to stop customers as they were coming out of the store, and this is what we found. First, the good news. Every customer who rated our service as 'great' told us they regularly recommend us to others – on average, *five* other people, which is very encouraging. But, now, the bad news. For every customer who rated our service as 'bad', and explained the reasons, eleven other unhappy customers were not leaving any feedback. They were just going home unhappy. And, frankly, that's a disaster! OK, let's look at the interview data in more detail.

3.07 C = Carl I = Inés

C: So, just to recap on the main points so far. The in-store interviews now give us much more accurate figures for customer satisfaction. But they still don't tell us what we can do to improve our service. OK, that brings me to the end of *my* part of the presentation this morning. Inés, over to you.
I: Thanks, Carl. Well, now, let me try to answer Carl's question. As you know, last month we set up fifteen focus groups in different cities around the country. And one thing we did was ask them to text us ten adjectives to describe the ideal mobile phone Sales Adviser. Here's a diagram of the results. Now, to help them choose a mobile phone, we were expecting people to want a 'knowledgeable' and 'informative' Sales Adviser. But, as you can see, mostly what they wanted was someone 'helpful' and 'friendly'. And that's where some of our sales teams are failing.
So, just to sum up: Too many of our customers are currently leaving our stores unhappy with the service they received. This is not because our Sales Advisers don't have complete product knowledge. They do. It's because they simply don't have the people skills they need to give helpful and friendly service. And that's why I'm recommending that we now make people skills training a priority. OK, let's wrap it up there. Any questions? Yes, Hugo ...

4.01

1
I thought it was a good idea to go part-time at the hospital when my daughter was born, but it's hard work. It sounds nice to say I only work three days a week, but nurses work long hours and a nine-hour shift usually turns into 11 or 12 hours. That's more than most people who work in full-time jobs. And it isn't always possible to take my breaks if there is a lot of work to do.

2
I'm studying for my degree in tourism management and I work for an agency in my free time. Doing temporary jobs is a good way to earn money at weekends and in the holidays. It's the time when hotels need extra staff. If there's a big event or conference on in the city, I miss classes for a few days. But next week I'm starting as an intern with a big hotel chain so I'm leaving the agency work. I know the hotel is a good employer and I hope they'll offer me a permanent contract after my internship.
3
I'm a self-employed driver and I get my work from a taxi service app on my phone. I don't have a fixed schedule and I decide my own working hours. I can work as much or as little as I want and I'm paid for each job I do. But after a ten-hour shift, drivers have to take a six-hour break, by law. But my working day is typically five or six hours. I don't want to work more than that, you see, I retired last year, and this is just some extra money on top of my pension.

4.02

A: Have you ever bought a good business book?
B: No, I've never bought one but I've read a few from the library and I've seen some business experts on YouTube, like Daniel Kahneman. He's written a lot about how we make decisions and how we don't think as clearly as we believe we do.
A: Ah, yes! What was the title of that famous book of his?
B: *Thinking, Fast and Slow*. You know, he's a psychologist but he's won a Nobel Prize for Economics.
A: Really? That's interesting. I've never seen him talk. You know, I've started that book several times, but I've never finished it.

4.03 **L = Lou I = Ian**

L: Hello, Ian?
I: Speaking
L: Hi, Ian, it's Lou.
I: Hi, Lou. What's up?
L: Listen, sorry to bother you. I'm calling about our meeting on Wednesday the 17th.
I: Uh-huh.
L: I'm afraid Sally can't make it.
I: Ah.
L: Yes, it's my fault. I forgot she's in Vienna all week. Do you mind if we fix another time to meet?
I: Sure. Let me just check my schedule.
L: Thanks. I appreciate it.
I: Do you want to postpone the meeting till the following week?
L: Actually, no. That's Berlin Expo week.
I: Oh, right, of course.
L: So, I was wondering if we could bring it forward. How about the week beginning the 8th?
I: Wait a minute, that's next week, isn't it?
L: Yeah, sorry. I know it's a bit short notice. That's why I'm calling.
I: Well, er, let's see. I'm free on Wednesday morning. That's the 10th. Any good?
L: Erm, could we make it the afternoon?
I: Mm, no good, I'm afraid. I've got a staff training session.
L: Well, ... How about Thursday the 11th? After lunch?
I: I'm busy all day Thursday. Friday might be OK ... How does the afternoon suit you?
L: Friday the 12th? No, Friday's out for me, I'm afraid. Oh, dear, I'm really sorry about this.
I: No problem. Look, let me see if I can move the training session and call you back.
L: Good idea.
I: OK, leave it with me. Talk to you later.
L: Thanks, Ian, bye.
I: Bye, now.

4.04 **I = Ian J = James**

I: Hello, James. It's Ian.
J: Oh, hi, Ian. What can I do for you?
I: It's about our training session next Wednesday.
J: Ah, yes, ...
I: Change of plan. We need to change the training to another day, I'm afraid. I've got an important meeting with Lou and Sally from head office and it's the only time we're all free.
J: Oh. Well, it's a bit last minute, but, OK, what day were you thinking?
I: Well, why don't we just move the training to the morning? I think that's the easiest.
J: Wednesday morning? Ah, I think I've scheduled the staff performance reviews for then ... Sorry, I forgot to tell you ... yeah. Performance reviews: Wednesday morning.
I: Well, move those to Friday!
J: Friday. All right. Which is better for you: morning or afternoon?
I: Erm, morning's better. Oh, wait a minute. I've got a meeting with the IT team on Friday morning. OK, that can wait. Let's postpone it till the afternoon!
J: Postpone ... IT meeting ... OK, so that's training on Wednesday the 10th in the morning.
I: Uh-huh.
J: Performance reviews on the Friday morning, the 12th.
I: Fine.
J: IT meeting in the afternoon. And that leaves you free on Wednesday afternoon for your meeting with the people from head office.
I: Brilliant! I knew there was a reason I made you my assistant. Thanks a lot, James.

4.05

L = Lou I = Ian
L: Good afternoon, Lou Klein speaking.
I: Hi, Lou. It's Ian again.
L: Hi, there. Any luck changing your schedule?
I: Yes. We're all set for the 10th.
L: Fantastic. So, just to confirm – we're meeting in your office on Wednesday the 10th at, erm, how about 3 p.m.?
I: Sounds good.
L: That gives you time to set up for the presentation before we arrive. Oh, and I invited Tom Banks to join us. He works for Sally in research. So, there'll be four of us in all.
I: Fine. Hm, with four of us I'd better ask James to book a meeting room. And how about something to eat afterwards? There's a nice restaurant just near the office. I could book us a table if you like.
L: Perfect. Thanks a lot for being so flexible, Ian.
I: No problem. See you on Wednesday.

5.01 **E = Ella D = Dan I1 = Interviewee 1 I2 = Interviewee 2 I3 = Interviewee 3 I4 = Interviewee 4 I5 = Interviewee 5 I5 = Interviewee 6**

E: Hello, listeners, and welcome to *It all adds up!*, the programme that talks about money. I'm your host, Ella Leeson. Today we're going to start with more tips for saving money. Dan Parks went into the street to talk to people and get ideas for saving money on living expenses. Dan?
D: Thanks, Ella. I went to London's Oxford Street earlier this week and asked people how they spend less and save more. Here's what they said.
I1: Make your own food, so you don't spend money on lunch.. If you take your lunch to work, you will save hundreds a year.
I2: I don't have a car now – I sold it! You will save thousands – and become healthier – if you cycle to work instead of driving.
I3: Stop using your credit card. Pay it off. Only spend money you already have – don't borrow it.
I4: Save money every month for emergencies. Then, when you have a problem with your house, or you need a new car, the money will be ready.
I5: Don't buy a new car. If you buy a car that's just one year old instead of a new one, you will save a lot of money.
I6: Go to the cinema on a discount day. My local cinema is cheaper on Mondays. There are special prices online.
D: Smart people out there in Oxford Street, Ella.
E: You're right. Lots of great ideas for spending less and saving more.
D: Right – a little bit here, a little bit there. It all adds up!
E: It all adds up! So, Dan, what can consumers expect in the next few months?
D: Well, the first thing we're looking at is a possible small increase in interest rates.
E: But that's not official yet, is it?
D: No, the government hasn't confirmed it, but it looks very likely.
E: What will that mean for consumers?
D: If interest rates increase, borrowing will go down. People borrow more when loans are cheaper.
E: So if people are thinking of borrowing ... ?
D: They should do it now, before interest rates go up.
E: OK. Anything else?
D: Housing costs will go up – people who own a home will pay a little more each month.
E: So, not great news.
D: No, but it is good news for people with savings. If banks raise the interest rate on savings, savers will earn more. That means it's a great time to start saving, or to increase saving.
E: It all adds up!
D: It all adds up, Ella!
E: Anything else?
D: Just one more thing before I go. International exchange rates. We're watching China closely, because its economy is really strong at the moment. Electronics imports here will be more expensive if China's currency becomes stronger.
E: OK, so if you're thinking of getting a new TV ...
D: ... now may be the time. We'll probably start to see prices go up in a couple of months.
E: Thanks, Dan. Some great tips!
D: Thank you, Ella.
E: That's it on money saving for this show, but now we're going to move on to ...

5.02 **L = Liz M1 = Male 1 F1 = Female 1 M2 = Male 2 F2 = Female 2**

L: Good morning! Could I just ask you to raise your hand if you have children in their late teens or early twenties? You're probably the ones with the largest debts. Hm, quite a lot of you. And that's not really surprising because, like me, you're the right age. Most of us in this room belong to what we call Generation X – the generation born somewhere between the mid-nineteen-sixties and the late seventies. Of course, the younger ones among us, born between the early eighties and the mid-nineties, are Generation Y, also known as the Millennials. You still have teenage kids to look forward to! And it's teenagers and young adults that I'm here to talk about today. Born between the mid-nineties and the early twenty-tens, we call them Generation Z. They are already about a quarter of the total population and they will soon be our biggest customers. Now, when I say Generation Z, what words and phrases can you think of to describe them? Anybody? Yeah ... ?
M1: Live for today!
L: Uh-huh.
F1: Always online.
L: Right.
M2: Don't want to work!
F2: No idea about money!
L: Oh, dear. We're getting a bit negative, aren't we? Well, I think some of the research I'm going to share with you this morning may just surprise you.

5.03

Now, just a moment ago some of you suggested that Generation Z 'lives for today', 'doesn't want to work' and 'has no idea about money'. So let's see if that's true. Have a look at this chart, which shows the results of our survey of the financial habits of people aged sixteen to twenty-one. As you can see, roughly three-quarters of them are already earning their own money through some kind of full- or part-time employment. To put that in context, that's almost the same as the figure for Generation Y. So that shows Generation Z is certainly not afraid of work! You can also see that nearly two-thirds of them have their own savings account. In fact, around one in five has had one since the age of ten. But perhaps the most surprising thing is that over one in ten of them are already saving for retirement! A retirement which may be over fifty years away! Another interesting thing is that just under three out of every ten are strongly against any kind of debt – especially, college debt. Let's not forget that college debt is currently over one and a half trillion dollars in this country and has been a major financial problem for Generations X and Y. The key takeaway here is that Generation Z likes to save, but doesn't like to borrow. Obviously, that's good news for those of you running savings accounts. But maybe not such good news for those of you working in the loans department!

5.04

So, how do we market personal banking services to Generation Z? Well, you were right about one thing. Generation Zers *are* 'always online'. On average, they are currently spending over ten and a half hours a day working or playing with digital content. To give you an idea of just how much that is, multiply it by the total number of Generation Zers in the USA, and it comes to around a billion hours of online activity every day! That's enough time to watch every movie ever made – one thousand times! But here's the really surprising thing. Our studies show that more than half of Generation Z say they actually prefer face-to-face communication. That's over forty million people who want to talk to us in person! So, in summary, if we want to attract this new generation of customers, we need to make sure we connect with them on a personal level. And, in terms of selling banking services, this clearly means that we need to be doing a lot more than just social media marketing.

6.01 **A = Anatol M = Michael E = Erin**

A: Right, I'll get straight to the point. New graduate applications are almost 30 percent down this year. And, as a result, we're not recruiting the number of management trainees we need. Now, we have a good reputation. We pay well. And we offer excellent benefits. So what's happening?
M: It's a new generation, Anatol. Graduates today just don't want to work for big organisations like us anymore. Besides, most twenty-one-year-olds simply aren't interested in insurance as a career.
E: To be honest, it's also a question of the work culture. College-leavers these days prefer the workplace to be informal and ... well, *fun*!
A: *Fun?* We're an insurance company, Erin. What do you want? Music on the TV and pinball machines in reception?

6.02 **A = Anatol M = Michael E = Erin**

A: OK, so, let's get some ideas written up on the flipchart. 'How ... do... we ... attract ... new ... graduates?' How about attending more careers fairs?
M: No, that's a complete waste of time. Students can find out all they need to know about us online.
A: More talks at universities, then?
E: No, there's no point. Michael's right. Job-hunting's all online these days. Now, a video promotion on YouTube – that might be more effective.
M: We tried that before and it didn't work.
A: We're not doing very well, are we? Erm, let's look at what more we can offer as an employer. Erin, any ideas?
E: Well, most of the people I interview tell me they expect training.
M: Yeah, but we're already doing that.
E: *Real* training, Michael. Like sponsored diplomas, MBAs.
M: You want us to pay for *trainees* to do *MBAs*? We don't have the budget for that!
A: OK, look, there's far too much negativity in this meeting. I suggest we go away and think about this a bit more and meet again in a couple of days.

6.03 **A = Anatol E = Erin M = Michael**

A: So, Erin. Let's start with you.
E: OK, well, we all agree that our biggest problem is getting new graduates to think about insurance as a career. So I suggest we introduce twelve-month internships. Believe it or not, it's actually harder to get a paid internship these days than to get a job! I think we'll find it easier to recruit students *before* they graduate rather than after.
A: Mm. I really like that idea. And twelve months is long enough for them to learn something about our business.
E: Exactly. And while we're on the subject of learning the business, why don't we provide personal coaching as well? Teach them the professional skills they don't learn at university.
A: Good idea. Of course, there *is* the problem of cost. What can we do about that?
E: Couldn't we just spend more on student internships and less on graduate recruitment?
A: You know, that might not be such a bad idea. Now, Michael, you're looking at how we market ourselves to graduates. What have you got so far?
M: Yes, well, the first thing is: we need to go mobile with our advertising. Most students prefer to use their mobiles to look for work. So, this is the perfect way to reach them as soon as we have job opportunities.
E: What a good idea! And doing that means we could also make job offers a lot faster – direct to the applicant's phone. Did you know that at the moment, a quarter of the people we offer work to have already taken another job by the time we contact them?
A: Really? But that's terrible ...
E: OK, as we know, another difficulty we have is our size. So the question is: how do we make our large company feel like a small one? And I think the answer is to put our trainees into smaller project teams.
A: Actually, I think that's a great idea. And if we do that, perhaps we can also create a bit of friendly competition between teams. Might make things more ... *fun*. As you say, Erin, that seems to be important nowadays.
M: Mm, it's a nice idea, Erin. I'm just wondering about the amount of reorganisation it'll need. How can we manage that?
A: Mm, good point. Let's see what the board thinks.

7.01 **S = Sam A = Andrea**

S: ... So, on behalf of the team, I'd like to thank Andrea for such an informative presentation. Thank you very much, Andrea, it was really interesting – I learnt a lot.
A: No problem.
S: Now, we've got about fifteen minutes for questions, but before we go into the question and answer session, I just want to mention a few ground rules. Firstly, could you just give your name and division before you speak, so that we know who you are? Can you keep your questions brief, so everyone has the chance to speak? Also, please help your colleagues by speaking slowly and clearly ... and loudly enough. And lastly, don't forget to use the mute button when you're not speaking, to stop any background noise.
All: Yeah, no worries. / Sure, yeah, no problem. / Yeah.

7.02 **S = Sam D = Donna P = Paul K = Karl L = Lena**

S: Right, is everyone ready? Donna, have you switched on your webcam? I can't see you. Your screen is blank.
D: Sorry, my camera doesn't work properly. I'll switch it off anyway because it slows down my internet connection.
S: Oh, OK. That's fine.
P: Hello ... can, can I ask ... easily, and ... so that's a problem if ...
S: Paul, Paul? Paul, you keep cutting out.
P: Sorry, what ... say ... Sam? ... hear you ... well.
S: You keep cutting out, Paul.
P: OK, ju ... moment. Is that ... better now? ... I ... can hear, hear ... you.
S: We still can't hear you properly. The connection is bad. Would you mind hanging up and I'll call you back. Hi, Paul, are you there?
P: Yes. Can everyone hear me now?
All: Yes. / Loud and clear.
K: Karl here, HR. Sam, did everyone receive my notes from earlier?
L: Karl, I'm afraid we can't hear you very well, either. You're very quiet. Could you move closer to the microphone?
K: OK ... Is that better?
S: Not really. If you can just check your volume settings, please?
K: Sure. Any better?
S: Yes, but now there's a bit of an echo. Can you move your mobile phone away from your computer?
K: There we go, how about that?
S: Much better, thanks. I got your notes, by the way, so thanks for those. If we ... Sorry, is someone in a café? I can hear a lot of background noise.
L: Sorry, it's me: R&D. I'm not in the office today.
S: No worries. Would you mind using the mute button? I can almost smell the coffee.
L: Yeah, of course. Sorry, everyone.
S: That's better, thanks. Now, just one last request before we start. I know it's getting close to lunchtime for some of you. So if anyone is hungry, please feel free to eat your lunch as we speak, but just remember to use that mute button!

7.03

Good morning everyone, and thank you for coming. Firstly today, I'm going to answer the question you're all asking – why did we decide to make changes to the product packaging? Now, there are three main reasons for this.
One, we have received a lot of negative customer feedback about the packaging this year. Customers say it looks very old-fashioned and many have suggested they'd like it to be more colourful.
Two, as a result of the issues customers identified, we've seen falling sales over the last twelve months.
And finally – three – we feel we should be using more eco-friendly packaging.
So, what are we going to do? Well, we've already decided to change the colour and to make use of recycled materials for the packaging. And we plan to do all this in just three months.
But, before we look at the details of the schedule, let's look more closely at the colours we're thinking of. Obviously we're keeping the yellow, but we are making it much brighter and we are thinking of adding one or two other colours, such as green or orange, which you can see here on this slide.
So, when exactly is all this going to happen? The first month, we're going to decide on the colours and the designers will produce the final design. We'll also choose the new material. In the second month, we will set up and start production. There'll be a press release, and we'll let everyone know about the launch date. And finally, in three months, we will launch our rebranded product line.

7.04

Today I'm going to talk about redesigning our best-selling product, the walking frame for people who need support when walking. Some people might ask: why change it if it's selling well? Well, everything can be improved so, firstly, I'll talk about the reasons for doing this. New developments in technology have made it possible to make a product which is much lighter and stronger than before. Secondly, new competitors are coming into the market and will begin to take some of our market share if we don't do as well as them.
Now, let's look at the most important parts of this new design. As I said before, the new design means that is much easier for older people or weaker people to move about. They don't have to pick up a heavy object. Also, there's a new non-slip material on the bottom of the frame, which makes it much harder to push over than others on the market.

Finally, I want to look more closely at the sales forecast for next year. As you can see from this graph, we expect sales to increase rapidly once the new product is on sale. In the first quarter we are expecting sales of around £1.5 million, doubling to nearly 3 million by the end of the second quarter. The next-quarter sales may slow down a bit as they always do in summer, but we expect them to reach £4 million by the end of the year.

8.01 **M = Matt K = Kyra**

M: The time now is ten to eight and I'm sure many of our listeners sitting in traffic jams on their way to work will be interested in what my guest today has to say. Kyra Sharma, university lecturer and consultant in public transport, is here with me to talk about her new book, *Travel Chaos*. Kyra, welcome.
K: Thank you, Matt.
M: Kyra, you say in your book that people shouldn't drive in cities. So, why is the car the worst way to get around?
K: Well, a car feels convenient for the person driving, but it's not the most efficient use of space. In busy urban areas there isn't enough space for everyone to drive around. Cars cause massive congestion on city streets, which causes serious air pollution as well as noise problems.
M: You talk in your book about the impact of technology and the transport solutions it offers. For example, electric vehicles, driverless cars, car sharing and software apps to help us get around.
K: Yes, there's a lot of fantastic technology now: electric cars help us to reduce air pollution, satellite navigation helps us to find quicker routes, and software apps allow us to share cars with people doing similar journeys. It's great that technology is giving us more efficient ways to travel and power our vehicles, but these things aren't enough. Our city streets are too crowded for the number of cars we have these days. There is not enough space. We have to reduce traffic on the roads – driverless technology, satellite navigation and electric cars don't solve that problem.
M: Doesn't car sharing reduce car use?
K: If it's real ridesharing with several people sharing a car, not one person hiring a car, then yes, but it's much better to 'rideshare' on buses and trains.
M: So, what is the solution? How should governments plan urban mobility?
K: Well, they should simply spend more on public transport. I mean mass transit systems including urban trains, underground or metro, buses and trams. It's the most efficient way to get around in a big city. As I explain in the book, there are excellent examples in developed countries in Asia: for example, in Hong Kong, Korea and Singapore. Most European cities are now using cleaner energy in public transport, and finding ways to reduce the number of cars on the roads. For example, London has a congestion charge and other cities could use a similar method to reduce the number of cars in the centre. Major cities are now promoting walking as part of a healthier lifestyle, and cycling by having more cycle lanes and public bike-hire schemes. Our cities are growing very fast and we need solutions that improve the quality of life for the people living and working in them.
M: Kyra, thank you for coming to talk to us today. So, that was Kyra Sharma talking about her new book, *Travel Chaos*. Coming up next the latest travel news ...

8.02 **E = Elena S = Steve T = Ted K = Kiera B = Ben**

E: So it looks like we're running out of time and I do want to give you a chance to ask a few questions. If I can answer your questions, I will, but please understand I may have to get back to you on certain points. I hope that's OK. So, does anyone have a question? Yes, Steve.
S: Thanks. I had a question about the open space issue.
E: Sure. What did you want to say?
S: Personally, I don't mind working in an open-plan office, I've done it before. But I know it's not for everyone. Most of our communication with clients is by email, so noise really isn't a problem anymore. My question is about meetings.
E: What do you mean, exactly?
S: Well, I just want to know if there will be rooms provided to hold meetings?
E: I believe so. So, the question is about meeting rooms. Ted, can I pass this one to you?
T: Sure. In the new building there'll be five closed meeting rooms on each floor, as well as some open space for more informal one-to-one meetings. You can reserve the closed meeting rooms using an online booking system. It should work very well. I hope that answers your question, Steve?
S: Yes, it does, thanks.
E: Kiera, do you have a question?
K: Yeah. Can I ask about the timing? When does the move take place?
E: It's a good question, thanks. I didn't mention that, you're right. The final stage of the move is scheduled for the end of May. I'm not sure about the exact dates; it will depend on the team. But you'll be told a long time before you have to move. Does that answer your question?
K: Not quite. You said we'd have to move into temporary office space first.
E: That's right. Most of you will go straight to the new site, but some people will move temporarily to the Oxford Road office while they finish the building work. OK?
K: Yeah, thanks.
B: I have a question, Elena. Can I ... ?
E: Yes, Ben, of course.
B: How do we get to and from the Oxford Road branch? It's quite a long way from here.
E: Thanks for your question. Yes, the company will put on a shuttle bus service between the two sites which should make it easier. I understand it takes around twenty minutes. Does that help?
B: Sure. And do you know who's actually moving over there?
E: So, Ben asked who's moving to Oxford Road, right?
B: Yes.
E: As I understand it, it's only the payroll and finance departments. Anyone who is moving has already been told about this.
B: So I guess I'm not on the list. That's good. I really didn't want to move twice!

8.03 **E = Elena J = Jen T = Ted**

E: OK. Are there any more questions? It looks like we've got time for one more.
J: Yes, I have a question.
E: OK, Jen, go ahead.
J: To be honest, Elena, I'm really not happy about this move and I'm definitely *not* happy about moving from my own office into an open-plan office. Unlike Steve, I can see *lots* of problems with that. Who decides who sits where, for example?
E: Sorry, you're asking how we allocate space. Is that right?
J: Yeah, because I don't see that working very well. I think the best places will all be reserved, anyway.
E: Well, ... I'm not sure I can answer that, but thanks for the question. Ted, can I ask you to respond to this one?
T: Of course. So to answer your question, Jen, we're not talking about hot-desking, ...
J: Oh, right, because that's what I'd heard.
T: No, not at all. Everyone will have their own desk. And these will be allocated fairly; no one will be allowed to reserve the 'best desk'. We're also introducing a clean-desk policy. So this means we need to keep the space as tidy as possible, but everyone will have storage space for their files; we hope that will help.
J: So, not only do I have to share my office with ten other people, but now I can't even choose my own desk. What if I don't like where I've been placed? Who can I speak to about that?
E: I'm sorry, I'm not sure what you mean.
J: Well, basically, I want to know who I can complain to ...

BW1.01

A: Hi, Junko.
B: Hello, Sam.
A: We need to go over a couple of the details of your visit next month before we finalise the arrangements.
B: Sure, OK.
A: You want to arrive in Sydney on the second of June, right?
B: Yes, that's right. I'm flying from Osaka to Sydney on the second.
A: OK, good. And for the hotel, how many rooms do you need? Are you coming on your own?
B: Yes, that's right – it's just me this time. So I need a single room.
A: No problem. There's a great hotel downtown – it's next to our offices in the city centre. We'll book one room for two nights.
B: Great. Thanks.
A: Now, after we've had our meeting in Sydney and seen some of the venues here, we can visit one other city. We need to choose either Melbourne or Brisbane.
B: OK, well ... what's the difference?
A: Well, Melbourne is bigger than Brisbane ...
B: OK ...
A: But for us, Brisbane is slightly better.
B: Why is that?
A: The venues we use in Brisbane are better than the ones we use in Melbourne. We use the two most popular live music venues – medium-sized live music venues. We have a great community there. Don't misunderstand me – our venues in Melbourne are good, but in Brisbane, they're the best.
B: OK, I see. So ... are Brisbane audiences smaller?
A: Ah, well, that's a great question. Brisbane audiences may be a bit smaller, but they really love music. Honestly, for me, Brisbane is probably the best place to start.
B: That sounds fine, Sam. Let's go to Brisbane.
A: OK, great. Now, in Brisbane, you have a couple of choices of places to stay. I can recommend a hotel in the city centre very near one of our music venues, but it's a bit expensive. If you want a cheaper place – maybe a bit quieter – we can arrange a bed and breakfast. There's one we like in Spring Hill.
B: Oh, let's see – actually, maybe the quieter option? The B&B?
A: OK, that's fine. And finally, when are you returning to Japan?
B: Well, I want to depart on June fifth, but I'm not going back to Japan. I'm going to Singapore.
A: Oh, great. OK. I'll make a note of that.
B: Sure. Is there anything else?
A: I don't think so. We're really looking forward to seeing you!
B: Yes, me too.

BW1.02

1 Sam, there's a serious technical problem at Sydney airport. Our flight is going to land at Canberra, not Sydney! The problem may continue until tomorrow!
2 Hi Junko. I got your message. Yes, I saw it on the news. It's a computer problem. Don't worry! We can make new arrangements for Canberra. I'll send you another message soon!

BW2.01 **E = Ewa M = Mark**

Extract 1
E: Now, I've done an online search and spoken to some estate agents and I've made a selection of three places we can see on our trip to Berlin this week.
M: OK! Great! Good work!
E: So, take a look at the photo of this first office. It's empty at the moment so you have to imagine it with furniture. We'd need to buy office desks, chairs, and everything.

M: Yes, those old wooden floors, doors and window frames look lovely. Where is it?
E: It's in Prenzlauer Berg. It's a fashionable neighbourhood in northeast Berlin. It's in a beautiful old building and various creative and media start-ups are already using the building.
M: How big is it?
E: The space is 120 square metres, and that includes two meeting rooms, a kitchen and two toilets. Oh, and the agent says there's a nice park in front of the building; we could sit and relax in the lunch break. And lots of cafés, bars and restaurants are within walking distance.
M: What about transport links?
E: The location is close to public transport. Actually it's never really a problem in Berlin. All these offices I'm showing you are well connected and easy to reach from the main train station and airports.
M: Sounds good. And the rent?
E: That's 2,600 euros a month. There's a deposit to pay of 7,800 – that's three months' rent. Then there's a six-month minimum period to rent the place, with a three-month cancellation period.
M: Um! It's quite expensive. Maybe we don't need so much space. We could probably find something somewhere in the UK for that price ...

Extract 2
E: Well, wait a minute ... I've looked at properties in other parts of Berlin, too – what do you think of this one?
M: I love it. Nice big windows, the office looks very bright in the photo. And this one has furniture!
E: The place is a co-working space in an old factory building in Kreuzberg. That's a trendy neighbourhood in the south of the city.
M: How big is it?
E: In total it's 400 square metres on two floors. Freelancers pay to rent workstations and there's space for around 40 people. Lots of independent creative workers are based there.
M: Workstations?
E: It means desks. And there is a room we can book for free for private conferences and meetings. We also get high-speed internet, use of the printer and also a shared kitchen with free coffee and water.
M: And it would be easy to talk to people we might want to work with.
E: That's right!
M: What can you tell me about the neighbourhood?
E: Very multicultural with exciting arts events. Lots of graffiti on the walls and bohemian cafés, that sort of thing.
M: Sounds like a nice place to live, too. I could walk or cycle to work every day. And the rent?
E: It costs just 300 euros per workstation, per month.
J: So, as there are four of us, we could have a shared work space for just 1,200 euros a month, and we could rent more workstations as the team grows.
E: Yes, it's an option with lots of choices. There's no deposit to pay, a two-month minimum period to rent a workstation and just one month cancellation.

Extract 3
E: So ... That brings me to the third option. Here's the photo. It's an 'office room'. Basically, that means a company is offering a separate room on the tenth floor of their company offices. It's in the heart of the city, the Mitte district – that means 'in the middle' and it's where all the main tourist sights are – the Brandenburg Gate, the Potsdamer Platz and lots of big companies.
M: Sounds like a prestigious location for the company address.
E: Yes! This one is in a big modern office building with lifts and views over Alexanderplatz. The office room is 25 square metres, so it's probably big enough for five or six people.
M: But there isn't a separate meeting room?
E: No, but I thought of that. They also have a 15-square-metre office room for rent on the same floor, so we could rent two rooms and use one as a meeting room. The rent includes furniture, internet, cleaning service and use of the company's shared kitchen and bathrooms.
M: So, how much is the rent?
E: For the big office room it's 1,200 euros a month and there's a 1,200-euro deposit to pay. There's a three-month minimum period only to rent the place and just one month cancellation.
M: So, the same price as the co-working office. And if we rent the two rooms?
E: That's another six hundred a month. So, for two rooms we're talking about 1,800 a month rent and 1,800 deposit.
M: Could we just rent the small office and the four of us work in there for a few months instead?
E: No way Mark! Don't be crazy!

BW2.02 E = Ewa M = Mark

E: OK, so let's make a list of the pros and cons of each office and see if we have a clear winner.
M: OK, I'll start with the Mitte office. It's in a great location, prestigious address but the company there is in finance, so we have nothing in common with them. It'd be better to be in a place with other new creative companies I think.
E: True! Being around other start-ups makes more sense for us. I wouldn't rent a flat in that area either. It's too expensive. Though that's not a major problem because the public transport network is so good. I love the idea of working in the city centre.
M: What about the Prenzlauer Berg office? Great old building! It would certainly give us room to grow. Having a big office would be expensive now, but we could save money in the future if we didn't have to move again soon.
E: True! I liked the office, but it was a bit darker than I expected. That concerns me. I like a bright space to work in.
M: I guess we could buy some bright lights. There's no lift though and it's three flights of stairs up – not all our clients might like that.
E: And the co-working space in Kreuzberg? There were certainly a lot of fun people there and I loved the terrace. Great to have some outside space.
M: Yes, but I wonder how much work we'd get done. It would be easy to get distracted and spend all day chatting in that office!
E: And I'm worried about the lack of privacy. I mean, our projects are confidential. I don't think clients would feel happy about us being in a co-working space. And trying to book that one meeting room when we need it could be difficult.
M: Still, it is the cheapest option, and we'd make friends quickly in Berlin. We should decide soon. Rents are rising fast in the city. But do you really think Berlin is the place for us? I'm still not sure about this move abroad and I'm not sure what Paul, Yelena and the rest of the team are going to say about it ....
E: I'm sure they'll love the idea! Berlin is really multicultural. It has a real buzz about it.
M: I'm not sure. I think I'd miss London, you know. Oh ... time to go or we'll miss our flight.

BW3.01

Extract 1
A: Just one last question. What kind of stores do you want to see in this area?
B: Well, I don't really go to stores much. I do most of my shopping online. But I think this area needs some more nightlife. There are places to go in the evening after work but some of them are really expensive and the others get really busy. We're a young group in my office and we like to socialise around here after work sometimes, but when you leave the office in the evening, it's hard to find somewhere to go in the local area.

Extract 2
A: I just want to ask you one final thing. What type of store does this neighbourhood need, in your opinion?
B: Well, I don't live around here, I work in an office over there but I like to go shopping in my lunch hour. You know, last week, I wanted to buy some personal care products, like shampoo and deodorant, but couldn't find anything I liked. I prefer to buy products that are 100 percent natural. It's something that I don't mind paying extra for if the quality is good. There are a few stores around here but there isn't much variety.

Extract 3
A: Thank you for your time. Can I ask you one final question? Is there any particular kind of store missing from this area?
B: Erm, well, I'm a big fan of small fashion boutiques and good-quality second-hand clothes. I go all over the city to find stores that I like. I prefer not to shop in big chain stores and shopping malls because I don't want to see the same shirt I'm wearing on someone else. I like to browse for original clothes, things that you can't buy anywhere else. And I like to mix and match styles, I don't want to just wear the fashions and colours that are popular right now.

BW4.01 C = Clara Olsen A = Álvaro Martínez

C: So, at this point I'd like to talk about the work culture of Holsted Pharmaceuticals. There are four main areas I want to mention.
First of all, I want to talk about the working hours at Holsted. The usual working week is 37 hours from Monday to Friday. That's typical of Denmark in general. You aren't expected to work long hours.
As for the working day, the timetable at Holsted is quite flexible for most employees. Staff can decide their start times, finish times and lunch breaks depending on their individual needs.
We understand when employees need to collect children from school or have to leave early for personal reasons, like a dentist's appointment. It's completely acceptable to do that. Whenever possible we give employees the opportunity to adapt their working hours to their family's needs. Our company work culture is very relaxed but effective.
Secondly, I want to talk about how we organise work and the relationship between managers and staff. There is a tradition that employees have a lot of individual responsibility for how they organise their own time and work. It is not generally the manager who decides how employees do their work. It is very important that staff meet deadlines and do their job well, but exactly how employees organise their time or projects is their responsibility.
And a third important point to mention is that all employees in Holsted are encouraged to tell us their ideas and opinions. This is very important because a level of staff participation and openness helps us to make better decisions.
And finally, I should say a word about meetings. It's very important at Holsted to arrive on time to meetings. It shows you are professional and organised.
A: Sorry, sorry I'm late. I've just come from another meeting. So, what have I missed?

BW4.02 C = Clara Olsen M = Marina Beltrán A = Álvaro Martínez

C: So, Marina, can you tell us more about the research your department has done?
M: Yes, well, you can see from this bar graph: the working day is very long here in the Madrid office. On an average day only half of our employees leave work by six o'clock. At seven o'clock twenty percent of the staff are still here in the office and ten percent are still at their desks at eight in the evening.
C: That's incredible! When do they spend time with their families? What time do they have dinner?
M: Yes, these working hours are obviously a disaster for family life.
A: Well, it is fairly normal to do this in Spanish companies. And people have dinner late. We have a 'split' working day where we start at 8.30 and go for lunch about two o'clock. We have two hours for lunch so you get back to work at four.
It's a good time to be sociable with co-workers, or go home for lunch if you don't have to travel far, or have business lunches. A long lunch break means finishing work late. It's always been part of our work culture.
M: I agree with Álvaro. It is traditional but I think many employees would prefer a shorter lunch break and the opportunity to go home an hour earlier.

A: I don't think so. It's the way we do things. People like to have a good lunch, not have a sandwich at their desks like they do in other countries.
M: Perhaps, but a lot of our employees are probably tired because of the long working hours and they won't get so much work done late in the day. Long hours can also be a cause of accidents at work and sick leave.
C: Has that been a problem here?
M: I don't know about our company, but international studies show people do more work within shorter hours. I mean, just look at Germany.
C: Yes, that's true. Who has ever done their best work when they're very tired?

BW5.01

Welcome, everyone. We're really happy to see so many people here, so much interest in making our town a better place. The purpose of today's meeting is to discuss practical ideas and real solutions. We've had discussions with quite a few of you already, and there are five main ideas we'd like to discuss today. So I'll introduce the ideas, and then after that, we'll have about ten minutes to discuss each of them.
So, here we go. The first idea is to get more tourists here. We would hire an advertising agency and advertise nationally or internationally about our great town. Tourists would come and spend money here.
Two. Create a local currency. Towns and cities all over the world have done this. It doesn't replace our national currency – it's money you can spend in local businesses. This encourages people to shop here in town.
Three. A time bank. In a time bank, anyone can offer their skills – a doctor, a car mechanic, a cleaner. If you work for someone for two hours, then you get credit for it, and you can ask someone to work for you for two hours.
Four. An online exchange – probably on social media – for second-hand goods. There are a few marketplaces that people use online, but we could have our own, just for people in this area, and people could trade things for other things.
Five. Start a Saturday market for local goods in the town centre. This could be vegetables, things you make at home, possibly second-hand items. We could do this every Saturday, or maybe once a month.
So, those are the main ideas to discuss today. Now we'll take about ten minutes for each idea, and after that we'll vote and choose three that we think are the ones that are the best ...

BW5.02

OK, so now we've counted the vote, and we've decided to consider the following three options more seriously. First, we'll look at creating a local currency. Second, we'll see about setting up a time bank. Finally, we'll consider the idea of a Saturday market in town. Thanks a lot, everyone. We'll contact you all by email before the next meeting.

BW5.03 E = Ellen D = David

E: So, what do you think of the proposed projects?
D: They're interesting ideas.
E: Yeah. Will you vote?
D: Sure, yeah. But I haven't decided yet – I think they could all be useful. The local currency idea is definitely interesting. It would be good for local business.
E: Do you think? It seems kind of a strange idea to me – kind of weird – and I know other people who think it's strange, too. But maybe we're just old-fashioned.
D: You may have a point there!
E: I like the sound of the Saturday market. That's just a good, honest idea that everyone can understand. People will see it as a social event.
D: Yeah, maybe. But I think it's a bit boring compared to the other two. I mean – it's easy to sell old stuff, right? Why not just sell it online? Don't you think the time bank could be good? I mean, you're an accountant. If you join a time bank, people will definitely want your services.
E: Maybe that's what scares me! I have a job – I'm too busy for extra work.
D: I'm with you. I'm the same. I'm not sure I want to trade any of my skills. Sometimes it's easier just to pay people.
E: Yeah, definitely.
D: I think if we create a local currency, local businesses will definitely get a boost.
E: Maybe – but I'm not so sure.
D: Well, I think that one's going to get my vote.

BW6.01

I studied maths at university, but I didn't really think about what kind of job I could get. Everyone thinks if you study maths, then accounting is a natural job to do afterwards. So that's why I'm doing this now. But you know what? It isn't the numbers that I love – it's solving problems. When you study maths at university, you realise that actually, it's a very creative subject – almost like some kind of art, or poetry. And for me, accounting just isn't very creative. So I'm not that happy in my work, but I just don't know what I should do – what job I want to get. But something needs to change.

BW6.02

I love the work I do – I love design. But in my last job, I was part of a team. Now, in this company, I'm the designer – I work alone. One good thing is that I can concentrate – because everyone is busy doing their own job – no one bothers me ... or talks to me. Natalya can't afford another designer. But to have good, creative ideas, I really need to talk with someone – share my ideas – see what other people think about my work. That's what was great about my last job. I'm not sure what we can do, though. The company isn't going to hire a new employee now.

BW6.03

It isn't easy running a small company. I'm very lucky to have João and Leila working for me. They work hard and they care a lot – but I know they aren't completely happy. The truth is, I'm not completely happy, either. I started this company because I wanted to make and sell amazing chairs, not because I wanted to be a full-time manager. Every day there are problems to solve with suppliers, emails to write, phone calls to make. I need help, but I can't afford to hire a new employee.

BW6.04

I had some great news today – we've made a big sale to a hotel group – two hundred and twenty chairs in the next year. That's wonderful, because it will give me enough money to hire someone part-time to help me manage the business. I really need someone to get things organised – someone who can deal creatively with the suppliers and schedules and all that.

BW7.01 S = Sofia O = Oscar

S: That factory tour was really interesting, Oscar. Thanks.
O: You're welcome. I think we've got a great team here. And our customers are some of the biggest international companies. They must have quality.
S: I can see that you're giving them that. But what's your production time?
O: From our three production lines, we can do 3,000 pairs in twelve weeks. That's a high-quality shoe with nice details.
S: You mean twelve from order?
O: Yes, usually. Maybe a bit longer.
S: OK. Well, I think we can probably make some savings there – speed up production time and cut down on costs – you know, find ways to lower them – spend less in general.
O: Well, maybe. What do you suggest?
S: I think there are some new machines you might be interested in. More automation could increase your rate of production by maybe twenty or thirty percent.
O: I was afraid you were going to say that.
S: What?
O: More automation. We take pride in working with our hands. We really value our workers' skill. I'm not sure we're ready to make any big changes there.
S: OK, well, that gives us something to talk about!

BW7.02 S = Sofia M = Mario O = Oscar

S: Before we decide on your shoe designs, we need to know how you're going to make them.
M: Sure.
S: So if you're going for a more handmade style, production will be slower, and there will be less automation. I'm not sure I'd recommend it at this point. It may not be very cost-effective. I think more automation is the best thing to do. Oscar, do you agree with what I am saying?
O: Well, OK ... . But these machines aren't cheap. If we don't improve the factory, we could probably take on a few more workers. And that will only cost us money if we really need to increase production.
S: Sure. I think we're probably talking about the highest quality footwear in that case. And to make it work financially, I'm pretty sure you're going to need to be able to deliver more shoes more quickly.
O: OK, I understand that. Mario – what are you thinking?
M: The designs I'm working on are definitely very high quality – with some really nice details that are finished by hand.
S: They sound great, Mario, but I think breaking into the market – you know, starting to sell a new product – may be harder with a really high-quality shoe ...
M: Yeah, I understand that. But it's like this: Zapatos Trujillo S.A. have made other people's shoes for forty years, and we're good at it. Now we'd like to make some shoes that we are all really proud of – something we can take to the big trade shows, the big fashion footwear shows – you know, Paris, Berlin – and really show people what we can do. Those are the shoes we want to make.
S: OK, that's clear. So let's see how we can make it happen.

BW7.03 S = Sofia J = John

S: Hi, John.
J: Sofia, hello. How's everything going in Mexico?
S: Good, mostly. Zapatos Trujillo S.A. are doing a lot of things right already, so I feel good about the company ...
J: But something's bothering you.
S: Well, I really think automation is the answer here. If they want to increase their annual production, they really need to buy some machines.
J: But they want to keep making handmade shoes.
S: Right.
J: Well, from our own experience, we can offer plenty of success stories about automation, right? I mean, most shoe makers who finally try it agree afterwards that it's helped their business. So maybe you need to tell them about some of the other companies we've worked with.
S: Yeah, that's a good idea. I haven't tried that, but I will.
J: And give them some options. You can show them exactly what automation can do for their profit, but the final decision has to be theirs. In some cases, it really isn't about the money, and that's OK.
S: Yeah, you're right. OK, well, I'll get back to working out some of these numbers. Always good to talk to you!
J: Good luck Sofia. I'm around if you want to talk again.

BW8.01 P = Patricia D = Davy J = Joe

P: Now that we've measured our energy use and waste, we can use that to help us plan the GO project and decide what our priorities are.
D: Yes, it's very important to have this data. Obviously, I can see lighting is a big cost at the moment but the LED lights in the new building will help reduce costs there.
P: And the new motion sensors they're installing.
D: Motion sensors?

P: Yes, these can detect movement in certain areas and switch the lights on and off without anyone having to touch them. Places like the toilets, corridors, storerooms, the stairs and in the car park. But the new building will have them everywhere.
D: Good idea. That's the lighting cost reduced. What else can we do?
P: Well, as you can see from the pie chart in my report, the computer servers are costing us quite a lot of money. First of all there's the cost of the electricity to run the machines and second, there's the cost of cooling and ventilation to keep the server room at the right temperature. Are there any possible savings there?
D: What about 'cloud computing'? I mean, do we need servers in the office now? It's possible to use a cloud computing service.
P: Do we know what the options are? What are the security risks? And the costs of the service?
D: I understand there are fewer risks with cloud computing than having our own servers. I'll talk to the IT department, Patricia. We'll look into the options and the costs and tell you what we find out.
P: Thank you. Now what about waste, especially paper use? I know that paper itself is not very expensive for the company compared to other costs, but everyone is printing too much. The current printers are old, always break down and some employees complain they have to print documents three or four times because the print quality is so terrible.
J: They are terrible! When you think about the paper and toner we waste because of this, then it is clear they are not cost-effective. I think we need new multifunctional machines that print, photocopy and scan.
P: I agree! There'll be costs to upgrade, obviously, but we will save money, too. Joe, would you find out more about those for us? Get some prices and see how we could do this?
J: OK, Pat, I'll do that.
P: Right, so Davy, you'll find out more about cloud computing, Joe, you'll work on the printers and I want to look at a new recycling scheme to find out how we can recycle more of our waste. I mean, two kilos of waste per person per day is not good. I know we won't make big savings, but it is important for our image and our reputation as a green company to help protect the environment. Sorry. Hello! Really? OK, I'll come down. Sorry, we'll have to end there. There's a problem at reception.
D: OK, sure
J: No problem. See you later.

P4.08

1 I've never bought any good business books. But I have read a few.
2 I've read a few, too. I read some when I was a student.
3 I've heard of Daniel Kahneman. I think he's won a Nobel Prize.
4 Yes, he has. He's written a lot about how we make decisions.
5 Have you read this book? I started it once or twice, but I've never finished it.
6 I've just finished it. I liked it.

P6.02

/ɪ/ give busy city issue simple
/iː/ feel believe complete metres people
/aɪ/ price climbing high hiker reliable
/ɪə/ near clearly experienced realise zero

P6.07

1 Do you have everything you need?
2 Print out an extra copy.
3 I've looked everywhere for it.
4 A copy of the report and a pen or pencil.
5 I'm glad you're all here.
6 Just ask if you need help.

P7.02

1 I can't open my door with my key card.
2 You can use the check-in kiosk.
3 You can't go directly to the gate.
4 Can I check in without my ID?
5 This robot can't talk, can it?
6 Yes, it can!

P8.04

1 We could catch a bus or get a taxi.
2 We shouldn't wait here any longer.
3 Do you think I should walk more?
4 Yes, and you could, easily.
5 They should spend more on public transport.
6 Yes, they definitely should.

- The codes [C] and [U] show whether a noun, or a particular sense of a noun, is countable (*a customer, two customers*) or uncountable (*accommodation*).
- The codes [I] (intransitive) and [T] (transitive) show whether a verb, or a particular sense of a verb, has or does not have an object.
- The symbol ↔ means that the object of a phrasal verb can come before or after the particle.
- The codes *AmE* and *BrE* show whether a word or sense of a word is used only in American or British English.

Go to MyEnglishLab for an extended, printable version of the Glossary.

Unit 1

abroad *adv.* in or from a country that is not your own
accommodate *v.* [T] to have enough space for a particular number of people or things
accommodation (*also* **accommodations** *AmE*) *n.* [U] a place that you can live or stay in
arrival *n.* [U] when you get to a place you were going to
bed and breakfast (*also* **B&B**) *n.* [C] a house or small hotel where you pay to sleep and have breakfast when you are travelling
book *v.* [I,T] to arrange to stay in a place, eat in a restaurant, etc. at a particular time in the future (= **reserve** *AmE*)
booking *n.* [C] an arrangement that you make to have a hotel room, a seat on a plane, etc. at a future time
budget[1] *adj.* very low in price (= **cheap**)
budget[2] n. [C] the money that is available to an organisation or person, or a plan of how it will be spent
client *n.* [C] someone who pays a person or organisation for a service or advice
comfort *n.* [U] when you feel physically relaxed and happy, and nothing is hurting you, making you feel too hot or cold, etc.
conference *n.* [C] a large formal meeting in which people discuss important things
confirm *v.* [I,T] to tell someone that an arrangement is now definite
delayed *adj.* late, usually because of a problem (*opposite* **on time**)
delegate *n.* [C] someone that a country or organisation chooses to do something for it, such as speak or vote at a meeting
departure *n.* [C,U] the action of leaving a place, especially at the start of a journey (*opposite* **arrival**)
enquire (*also* **inquire** *AmE*) *v.* [I,T] to ask someone for information
event *n.* [C] something that has been organised, such as a party, show, etc.
events management *n.* [U] the job of organising large events such as conferences and concerts
expire *v.* [I] if something expires, the period of time in which you can use it ends
extension *n.* [C] one of the telephones that is connected to a central system of telephones in a building
facilities *n.* [plural] rooms, equipment or services that are available in a place
flight *n.* [C] a journey in a plane, or the plane that is making the journey
formal *adj.* a formal event is important, and people who go to it wear special clothes and behave very politely (*opposite* **informal**)
freeze *v.* [I,T] if a computer freezes, it suddenly stops working and the screen will not change when you use the keyboard or mouse
gate *n.* [C] the place where you leave an airport building to get on the plane
induction *n.* [C,U] the process of helping someone in a new job by giving them the information about the job and the company
informal *adj.* an informal event is relaxed and friendly (*opposite* **formal**)
intranet *n.* [singular] a system for sending computer messages between people who work for the same company or organisation, which is similar to the internet but smaller
landing *n.* [C] the action of bringing a plane down to the ground after being in the air (*opposite* **take-off**)
local *adj.* near to the place where you live or to where you are staying
location *n.* [C] the place or position where someone or something is
lock someone ↔ out *phr. v.* [T] to stop someone from being able to use a computer or from seeing information on a computer
log on (*also* **log in**) *phr. v.* [I] to start using a computer, for example by typing in your name or password
log-in details *n.* [plural] your name, password or other information that you need to start using a computer
long-haul *adj.* a long-haul flight, etc. is over a very long distance (*opposite* **short-haul**)
look forward to *phr. v.* [T] used at the end of a formal letter to say that you hope to hear from or see someone soon, or that you expect something from them
lounge *n.* [C] a room in a hotel or airport, where people can sit and relax
luxury *adj.* expensive and having a lot of beautiful or comfortable things
network *n.* [C] a system of computers that are connected with each other
on time *adj.* happening at the time or on the date that was planned
public transport (*also* **public transportation** *AmE*) *n.* [U] buses, trains, etc. that anyone can pay to use
reservation *n.* [C] an arrangement that you make to have a hotel room, a seat on a plane, etc. at a future time
ridesharing app *n.* [C] a way of getting a taxi using your phone or tablet
set (something ↔) up *phr. v.* [I,T] to do things that make something ready to be used
short-haul *adj.* a short-haul flight, etc. is over a short distance (*opposite* **long-haul**)
stay *n.* [C] a period of time that you spend somewhere
take-off *n.* [C] when a plane moves off the ground and into the air
theme *n.* [C] the main subject or idea in a book, film, party, etc.
tip *n.* [C] a useful piece of advice
transport (*also* **transportation** *AmE*) *n.* [U] cars, buses, trains, etc. that people use to travel from one place to another
trip *n.* [C] when you go to a place and back again, especially when you only stay in the place for a short time
vehicle *n.* [C] a thing such as a car or bus that is used for carrying people or things
venue *n.* [C] a place where a meeting, concert, etc. takes place
youth hostel *n.* [C] a place where people who are travelling, especially young people, can stay cheaply

Unit 2

access *n.* [U] the chance or ability to use something
agenda *n.* [C] a list of the things that people are going to discuss at a meeting
AOB (*abbreviation for* **any other business**) something that needs to be discussed but is not included on the agenda
ASAP (*abbreviation for* **as soon as possible**) at the earliest time that you are able to do something
attract *v.* [T] if a place or thing attracts people, it makes them want to go there or see it
BTW (*written abbreviation for* **by the way**) used before saying something that is not related to the main subject you were discussing, in a text message or email
cabin *n.* [C] a small house, especially one built of wood in an area of forest or mountains
car park *n.* [C] a place where people can leave their cars
close to *adj., adv.* not far from something
COB (*abbreviation for* **close of business**) the time when the people in a business or company usually stop working for the day
competition *n.* [U] a situation in which people or organisations compete with each other
conservation project *n.* [C] a set of planned activities to protect nature
convenient *adj.* close to you, or easy for you to use
eco-resort *n.* [C] a place where people go on holiday, that tries to reduce the harm the buildings and activities do to the environment
eco-tourism *n.* [U] the business of organising holidays to natural areas, so that people can learn about the environment and the animals and plants that live there
endangered species *n.* [C] an animal or plant that may soon no longer exist, because there are not very many of them
EOD (*abbreviation for* **end of day**) the time when the people in a business or company usually stop working for the day, or midnight
ETA (*abbreviation for* **estimated time of arrival**) the time when a person, plane, ship, etc. is expected to arrive
experience *n.* [C] the things that you do or that happen to you, that you learn from or remember
shopping/dining/visitor etc. experience the way that shopping, eating or visiting a place makes you feel or affects you
unique experience something unusual that you do or that happens to you, that does not happen at other times or in other places
facilities *n.* [plural] rooms, equipment or services that are available in a place
factory *n.* [C] a building in which a lot of goods are produced using machines
FYI (*written abbreviation for* **for your information**) used when you are telling someone something they need to know, in a short text, note or email
headquarters (*abbreviation* **HQ**) *n.* [plural] a company's main or most important office
lab *n.* [C] (=**laboratory**) a special room or building in which a scientist does tests
locate *v.* [T] to put or build something in a particular place
location *n.* [C] the place or position where someone or something is

logistics *n.* [U] the business of transporting things such as goods to the place where they are needed
motorway (*also* **freeway** *AmE*) *n.* [C] a very wide road for travelling fast over long distances
operator *n.* [C] a person or company that runs a particular business
port *n.* [C] a place or town where ships arrive and leave from
public services *n.* [plural] services, for examples buses and trains, schools or health care, that a government provides
relocate *v.* [I] to move to a new place
rent *n.* [C] money paid every month to use office buildings, flats, etc.
resort *n.* [C] a place where a lot of people go for a holiday
salary *n.* [C] the pay you receive from the organisation you work for
sophisticated *adj.* very modern, and using many new ideas and styles
species *n.* [C] (*plural* **species**) a type of animal or plant
stopover *n.* [C] a short stay somewhere between parts of a journey, especially a plane journey
studio *n.* [C] a room where an artist, photographer or designer works
TBA (*abbreviation for* **to be announced**) used to show that a time, place, etc. will be given or decided later
TBC (*abbreviation for* **to be confirmed**) used when the time or date of something is not sure yet, to say that someone will let people know when it has been decided
transport link *n.* [C] something that makes it possible to travel between two places, for example a road or railway
warehouse *n.* [C] a large building for storing materials or things that will be sold
WFH (*written abbreviation for* **working from home**) used to say you are working at your home instead of in the office

Unit 3

assist *v.* [I,T] to help someone ↔ to do something
background *n.* [C, U] the information or events that explain why something happens in the way it does
bakery *n.* [C] a place where people make or sell bread, cakes, etc.
bazaar *n.* [C] a market or area where there are a lot of small shops, especially in India or the Middle East
bill *n.* [C] a list showing how much you have to pay, for example for food you have eaten in a restaurant
bookshop (*also* **bookstore** *AmE*) *n.* [C] a shop that sells books
branch *n.* [C] one local business, shop, etc. that is part of a larger business
bring *v.* [T] **that/this/which brings me to ...** used when saying that something is the next thing that you want to talk about
browse *v.* [I,T] to spend time looking at things in a shop without buying anything and without hurrying
build *v.* [T] **build a relationship** to develop your friendship or knowledge about someone over time
butcher's *n.* [singular] a shop that sells meat
chain *n.* [C] a number of shops, hotels, etc. owned or managed by the same company or person
charge *v.* [I,T] to ask someone for a particular amount of money for something you are selling
client *n.* [C] someone who pays a person or organisation for a service or advice
competent *adj.* good at your work or able to do a job well
convenience store *n.* [C] a shop where you can buy food, alcohol, magazines, etc., that is often open very late at night
cost *v.* to have a particular price
customer *n.* [C] someone who buys things from a shop, company, etc.
department store *n.* [C] a large shop that sells many different types of things
efficient *adj.* working well, without wasting time or energy
estimated *adj.* an estimated amount, time or size is not known for sure, but is guessed based on information you have
experience *n.* [C] **retail/shopping/dining/visitor etc. experience** the way that shopping, eating or visiting a place makes you feel or affects you
fall behind *phr. v.* [I] to not make as much progress as other people
feedback *n.* [U] things people say or write about how well or badly you have done something
focus group *n.* [C] a small group of people that a company asks questions in order to find out what they think about a product, idea, etc.
hand (something) over to *phr. v.* [I,T] to give someone the responsibility for doing something that you were doing before
high street *n.* [singular] the main street of a town where most of the shops and businesses are
hold someone/something ↔ up *phr. v.* [T] to make someone or something late (= **delay**)
informative *adj.* giving many useful information
in-store interview *n.* [C] a situation in which someone is asked questions while they are shopping in a store

jump in *phr. v.* [I] to suddenly say something in a conversation or discussion
location *n.* [C] the place or position where someone or something
look at something *phr. v.* [T] to study and think about something
memorable *adj.* very good and likely to be remembered
move on *phr. v.* [I] to start talking about a new subject
offer *v.* [T] to have something that people need or want and be willing to give it
order *v.* [I,T] to ask for food or drink in a restaurant
overview *n.* [C] a short description of something that gives the main ideas
people skills *n.* [plural] the ability to deal with people well
pharmacy (*also* **drugstore** *AmE*) *n.* [C] (*plural* **pharmacies**) a store where you can buy medicine
point *n.* [C] **main point** the most important fact or idea in something
bad point a problem, mistake, or difficulty in something
good point something useful, interesting, or good in something
professional *adj.* showing that someone has been well trained and is good at their work
profit *n.* [C] money that you gain by selling things or doing business, after your costs have been paid
rate *v.* [T] to say how good or bad you think someone or something is
rating *n.* [C] a measurement of how good or popular something or someone is
recap *v.* [I,T] to repeat the most important information or ideas from something you have already said
recommend *v.* [T] to tell someone that something is good or enjoyable
retail *n.* [U] the activity of selling things to people in shops
retailer *n.* [C] a person or company that sells things to people in shops
review *n.* [C] a report about something such as a restaurant, film, book, etc., that says whether it was good or bad
satisfaction *n.* [U] the happiness you feel when you succeed or get what you want
self-service *adj.* relating to a shop or restaurant in which you get goods or food for yourself, rather than someone bringing them to you
serve *v.* [I,T] to help customers in a shop, restaurant, etc., especially by bringing them the things that they want
service *n.* [U] the help that people who work in a restaurant, hotel, shop, etc. give you
shopping centre (*also* **mall** *AmE*) *n.* [C] a group of shops that are built together in one area, often inside one large building
spend *v.* [T] (*past tense and past participle* **spent**) to use time doing something
sum (something ↔) up *phr. v.* [I,T] to give the main pieces of information from something you have said or written, in a short statement at the end
try something ↔ on *phr. v.* [T] to put on a piece of clothing in order to find out whether you like it, especially before buying
value *v.* [T] to think that something is important
VAT *n.* [U] a tax added to the price of things in the UK and the EU
workload *n.* [U] the amount of work that a person has to do
wrap something ↔ up *phr. v.* [T] to finish a job, meeting, etc.

Unit 4

advice *n.* [U] when you suggest what someone should do
agency *n.* [C] (*plural* **agencies**) a business that arranges services for people
appreciate *v.* [T] to understand that someone has done something good for you, and feel grateful (=want to thank them)
arrange *v.* [I,T] to make plans so that something can happen
attend *v.* [T] to go to a meeting, school, event, etc.
bring something ↔ forward *phr. v.* [T] to change the time or date of something so that it happens earlier than you planned before
confirm *v.* [I,T] to tell someone that an arrangement is now sure to happen
consultative *adj.* asking for advice from other people
contact *v.* [T] to telephone or write to someone
convenient *adj.* good for a particular situation and easy to do
decision-making *n.* [U] the things you do when making important decisions
delighted *adj.* very pleased about something
democratic *adj.* giving everyone the right to help choose or decide something, usually by voting
employee *n.* [C] someone who is paid to work for another person or organisation
employer *n.* [C] a person, company or organisation that gives people work
executive *n.* [C] an important manager in a company
feel free used to tell someone that they are allowed to do something
finance *n.* [U] activities connected with the spending or saving of large amounts of money
fix *v.* [T] to decide on an exact time, place, price, etc.

fixed schedule *n.* [C] a timetable (=list of times when things must happen) that cannot be changed
flexible hours *n.* [plural] when someone can choose when they start and finish work
full-time *adj., adv.* working for all the hours of a normal week at work, usually 35-40 hours (*opposite* **part-time**)
guru *n.* [C] someone who knows a lot about a particular subject, and gives advice to other people
hands-off *adj.* not telling the people that you are in charge of what to do, but letting them make their own decisions
hands-on *adj.* doing something yourself, rather than telling other people to do it
input *n.* [U] ideas, advice, opinions or work that you give to help something succeed
intern *n.* [C] someone, especially a student, who works for a short time in a job to get experience
look forward to *phr. v.* [T] used at the end of a formal letter to say that you hope to hear from or see someone soon, or that you expect something from them
move into *phr. v.* [T] to change to a different job
nine-to-five *adj., adv.* working every day from nine o'clock in the morning until five o'clock in the evening
out *adj.* if a particular suggestion or activity is out, it is not possible
part-time *adj., adv.* working or studying for less than the usual number of hours (*opposite* **full-time**)
permanent employee *n.* [C] someone who has a contract to work for a long time
point *n.* [C] a fact or idea that is part of a discussion
fair point used during a discussion to say that you think someone has said something true and you agree
take someone's point used during a discussion to say that you understand what someone has said
have a point used during a discussion to say that someone has said something that is important or useful
remote worker *n.* [C] someone who works in a place away from the office
retired *adj.* having stopped working, usually because you are old
self-employed *adj.* working for yourself, and not permanently employed by a company
shift *n.* [C] one of the periods of work during a day, for example at a place such as a hospital where there must be workers all day and night
staff *n.* [U] all the people who work for an organisation
suit *v.* [T] to be useful or all right, and not cause problems for you
take place to happen, especially after being planned or arranged
temporary worker *n.* [C] someone who has a job for only a limited period of time
unable *adj.* not able to do something
unemployed *adj.* without a job (= **out of work**)
unfortunately *adv.* used to say that you feel sad or disappointed about something
view *n.* [C] an opinion or belief about something
work pattern *n.* [C] one of the different ways that someone's hours of work can be organised
working day *n.* [C] the time during the day that people spend doing their job
working life *n.* [C] the part of their life during which someone has a paid job

Unit 5

appreciate *v.* [T] to understand that someone has done something good for you, and feel grateful (=want to thank them)
approximate *adj.* a little more or less than a number or amount, but not exact
approximately *adv.* a little more or a little less than a number, amount, etc., so not exact (= **about**, **roughly**)
bank transfer *n.* [C] the act of moving money from one bank to another bank, usually using a computer
borrow *v.* [T] to take and use money from a person or organisation which you must pay back later
borrowing *n.* [U] the fact of taking and using money from a bank, or the money that you take and use
cash *n.* [U] money in the form of coins and special paper
be short of cash to not have enough money
cash in hand if someone is paid cash in hand, they are paid in paper money and coins
cash on delivery a way of buying something in which you pay for it when it is delivered (=brought) to you
in cash using coins or paper money
pay cash to use coins and paper money to pay for something
petty cash *n.* [U] a small amount of money that is kept in an office to buy things
withdraw cash to take money from your bank account
cash crunch *n.* [U] a time when a bank, company, government or person does not have enough money to work in the normal way
cash dispenser (*also* **cash machine**) *n.* [C] a machine that you can get money out of, using a plastic card (= **ATM** *AmE*)
cash flow *n.* [U] the way that money comes into a business from payments and goes out to pay workers or buy materials
cash register *n.* [C] a machine that is used in a shop to keep money in and show how much customers have to pay (=**till** *BrE*)
cashless *adj.* done or working without using money in the form of coins or paper money
cashless economy *n.* [C] a system of buying and selling things without using coins or paper money
cashless payment *n.* [C] a payment that is made without using money in the form of coins or paper money
client pitch *n.* [C] a presentation you give to make a customer want to buy your product or service
competitive *adj.* similar in price, or slightly cheaper, and still good quality
context *n.* [C] **put something in context** to help someone understand the situation within which something is happening
convenient *adj.* easy for you to use
credit *n.* [U] **on credit** using a system in which you buy things and pay for them later
credit card *n.* [C] a small plastic card that you use to buy things and pay for them later
currency *n.* [C] (*plural* **currencies**) the system or type of money that a country uses
debit card *n.* [C] a plastic card that you use for paying for things in shops. The money is taken directly out of your bank account.
debt repayment *n.* [C] money that you pay because you need to give it back to the person or bank you borrowed it from
deposit *n.* [C] part of the price of something, that you pay when you agree to buy it
enclose *v.* [T] to put something inside an envelope with a letter
exact *adj.* completely correct
exchange rate *n.* [C] the value of the money of one country when you change it for the money of another country
expense *n.* [C] the amount of money you have to spend on something
figure *n.* [C] a number representing an amount
financial system *n.* [C] all the banks and other organisations that help with the transfer of money between people and businesses
housing *n.* [U] places for people to live in
increase *v.* [I,T] to become larger in number, amount, size, etc., or make something become larger
interest *n.* [U] extra money that you pay when you borrow money
interest rate *n.* [C] a percentage (=3%, 4%, etc.) that a bank charges when you borrow money, or that a bank pays you when you save money in that bank
loan *n.* [C] an amount of money that you borrow from a bank
mobile phone payment (*also* **mobile payment**) *n.* [C] the act of paying for something using an app on your mobile phone
mobile wallet *n.* [C] software that stores your bank or credit card information on your phone
mortgage *n.* [C] money you borrow from a bank in order to buy a house
mortgage payment *n.* [C] the amount of money you pay the bank each month, in order to pay back the money you borrowed to buy a house
online payment *n.* [C] the act of paying for something using the internet
payment *n.* [C] the act of paying for something
penny *n.* [C] (*plural* **pennies**) a small unit of money, or a coin worth 1p or 1 cent
pension payment *n.* [C] money that you save for a pension
raise *v.* [T] to increase the amount of something
remain *v.* [I] to continue to be something or to be in the same state
rise *n.* [C] when an amount or level becomes larger or higher (= **increase**)
rising *adj.* becoming larger or higher
role *n.* [C] what one person does in a group or situation
savings *n.* [plural] all the money that you have saved
spending *n.* [U] the amount of money that people pay for things
store card (*also* **charge card** *AmE*) *n.* [C] a card that a particular shop gives you, that you can use to buy things in that shop and pay for them later
suffer *v.* [I] to become worse because of something
supply *v.* to provide people with something they need
summary *n.* [C] **in summary** used before giving the most important information from what you have just said or written
takeaway *n.* [C usually singular] the most important piece of information that you learn from a report, meeting, etc.
tax revenue *n.* [C] the money the government collects from people
term *n.* [C] **in terms of something** used to show what part of something you are talking about

Unit 6

agree *v.* [I,T] to have the same opinion as someone else
agreement *n.* [C] the fact of having the same opinions as someone else
argue *v.* [I,T] to not agree with someone, and often give reasons why you are right and they are wrong, sometimes in an angry way
argument *n.* [C] a time when you do not agree with someone, and often give reasons to show why you are right at they are wrong, sometimes in an angry way
catering *n.* [U] the activity of making and serving food at parties, meetings, etc.
challenge *v.* [T] to do something new, exciting or difficult that you will need to work hard to do
communicate *v.* [I] to talk or give someone information, for example by speaking, writing letters, etc.
communication *n.* [U] the action of talking to people or giving them information, for example by writing a letter or calling
communication skills *n.* [C usually plural] the ability to talk or write clearly, so that people understand you
compete *v.* [I] to try to win something or to be more successful than someone else
competitive *adj.* trying very hard to be more successful than other people or businesses
competition *n.* [U] a situation in which people or organisations try to be more successful than other people or organisations
conflict management *n.* [U] the action of helping people to deal with problems caused by not agreeing with someone
cooperate *v.* [I] to work with someone to achieve something you both want
cooperation *n.* [U] when you work with someone in order to achieve something you both want
deal with *phr. v.* [T] to do the things that are necessary, especially to solve a problem
develop *v.* [I,T] to make a skill, ability, etc. better over a period of time
disagree *v.* [I] to think or say that someone's opinion is wrong
disagreement *n.* [C,U] when you do not agree with someone
experienced *adj.* having a lot of skill or knowledge about something, because you have done it for a long time (*opposite* **inexperienced**)
improve *v.* [I,T] to make something better
inspire *v.* [T] to make someone feel that they want to do or achieve something
invitation *n.* [C] a letter or message asking you if you would like to do something with something
manage *v.* [T] to be in charge of something and the people who work there, and organise the things that will be done
management *n.* [U] the job of organising the work of a company, team, etc., and the people who work there
move on *phr. v.* [I] to start doing things differently or change your life
press release *n.* [C] an official statement giving information to newspapers, radio, and television
product launch *n.* [C] the time when a new product is made available to buy
product support *n.* [U] help or information that a company gives to help someone use a product correctly
put something behind you *phr. v.* to try to forget about something bad that happened and think about the future
reduce *v.* [T] to make the amount or size of something less than it was before
reliable *adj.* always doing what you want or expect
remind *v.* [T] to make someone remember something that they must do
respect[1] *n.* [U] if you have respect for someone, you admire them and have a very good opinion of them
respect[2] *v.* [T] to admire someone and have a good opinion of them
responsible *adj.* if you are responsible for something, it is your job to do it
rise *n.* [singular] when something becomes more important or successful
sign up *phr. v.* [I] to put your name on a list because you want to do something
subject *n.* [C] **on the subject of** used to say what the main thing you are talking about is
support *v.* [T] to help and encourage someone
team building *n.* [U] activities that help people to work and communicate well together
teamwork *n.* [U] when a group of people work well together to achieve something
teamworker *n.* [C] someone who works well in a team and helps other people
tonne *n.* [C] **tonnes (of something)** a lot of something (= **loads**)
triathlon *n.* [C] a sports competition in which people run, swim and cycle a long way
trust[1] *v.* [T] to believe that someone is good and will do what they say, or will do what is right
trust[2] *n.* [U] when you believe that someone is good and will do what they say, or will do what is right
venue *n.* [C] a place where a public event takes place
wonder *v.* [I,T] to think about something you do not know, and want to know it

Unit 7

attract *v.* [T] to make people want to go somewhere, see something, buy something, etc.
blank *adj.* having nothing showing, written or recorded on something
brief *n.* [C] a list of instructions that explain what you need someone to do
cater *v.* [I] to provide a particular group of people with what they need or want
challenge *n.* [C] something new, exciting or difficult that you will need a lot of determination and effort to do
character *n.* [C] the particular qualities that a person, place or thing has
competitive *adj.* trying to be more successful than other businesses
consumer *n.* [C] someone who buys things or uses a service that a company provides
create *v.* [T] to make something happen or exist
cut out *phr. v.* [I] to suddenly stop working
design *n.* [C] the way that something is planned or made, especially the way it looks
designer *n.* [C] someone whose job is to design new things or styles of clothes, cars, etc.
develop *v.* [T] to make a new idea, product, etc. over a period of time
echo *n.* [C] a sound that you hear again
enter *v.* [T] to put information somewhere, such as into a computer or a book
expense *n.* [C] money that you spend when you are doing your job, that your employee then pays to you
expenses system *n.* [C] a method of writing down your expenses, so that your employer can then pay you that money
facilities *n.* [plural] rooms, equipment or services that are available in a place
feedback *n.* [U] things people say or write about how well or badly you have done something
function *n.* [C,U] the purpose that something is made for, or how it works
ground rules *n.* [plural] the basic rules for behaviour during an activity, that everyone agrees to at the start
hang up *phr. v.* [I] to end a conversation on the telephone or on an internet call, by pressing a button or key
hospitality industry *n.* [C usually singular] businesses such as restaurants and hotels, that provide food, drink and places to stay
human touch *n.* [U] dealing with people in a kind, friendly way, and able to understand what they need
improvement *n.* [C] something that is better than the thing that came before it
innovation *n.* [C,U] a new thing, idea or method, or the introduction of new things, ideas, methods
kiosk *n.* [C] a machine or small shop where you can buy things or get information
launch *v.* [T] to make a new product available
mute button *n.* [C] a button or key on a phone or computer that stops other people hearing you
operate *v.* [I,T] to do all the things that are needed to work
operator *n.* [C] a person or company that runs a particular business
procedure *n.* [C] the correct way or normal way of doing something
process *n.* [C] a set of actions that are done one after another, in order to achieve something
product *n.* [C] something that is made and sold by a company
product line *n.* [C] a set of similar products that one company sells
product tester *n.* [C] someone who uses a new product to find out whether it works properly
product testing *n.* [U] the action of using a new product to find out whether it works properly
production *n.* [U] the process of making things, or the amount that you make
prototype *n.* [C] the first form that a new product has
purchase *v.* [T] to buy something
rebranded *adj.* when the name of a product or the way it is advertised is changed, so that people think differently about it
receipt *n.* [C] a piece of paper which shows how much you have paid for something
research and development (*also* **R&D**) *n.* [U] the part of a business that thinks of new ideas, plans new products and improves older products

setting *n.* [C] the position in which you put the controls on a machine or instrument
signal *v.* [T] to say or do something that gives other people information
sketch *n.* [C] a drawing of something that is done quickly and without very many details
solution *n.* [C] the answer to a difficult question or problem
step *n.* [C] one of a series of things that you do in order to achieve something
test *v.* [T] to use something to find out whether it works
unique *adj.* very unusual and special
usefulness *n.* [U] the quality of being useful
version *n.* [C] a form of something that is slightly different from others of the same type

Unit 8

accept *v.* [T] to agree that something is true
admin *n.* [U] the activities that need to be done to manage the work of a company or organisation
allocate *v.* [T] to decide to use something for a particular purpose
appreciate *v.* [T] to understand that someone has done something good for you, and feel grateful (=want to thank them)
arrange *v.* [T] to make plans so that something can happen
assessment *n.* [U] the opinion or judgment you make after examining a person or situation
car sharing (*also* **car pooling** *AmE*) *n.* [U] when two or more people use one car, especially to travel to work
cliff *n.* [C] a high piece of land with a very steep side, usually next to the sea
closed office *n.* [C] an office that has small rooms for people to work in
congestion *n.* [U] when a road is too full of vehicles
congestion charge *n.* [C] an amount of money that you have to pay to drive into a city
conservation *n.* [U] the act of keeping natural things such as animals or plants safe from harm
conserve *v.* [T] to protect something and stop it from changing or being damaged
construction *n.* [U] the process of building something
cycle lane (*also* **bike lane** *AmE*) *n.* [C] an area on a road that only people riding bicycles can use
damage¹ *n.* [U] physical harm that breaks or spoils something
damage² *v.* [T] to physically harm something, so that it breaks or no longer works properly
destroy *v.* [T] to damage something very badly, so that people can no longer use it, or so that it no longer exists
destruction *n.* [U] when something is very badly damaged, so that people can no longer use it or it no longer exists
electric bus *n.* [C] a bus that uses electricity to move, rather than petrol
environment *n.* [singular] the land, water, and air that people, animals, and plants live in
feedback *n.* [U] information about how well you are doing your job, and advice about how you could do it better
  corrective feedback n. [U] information about what you have done wrong or badly, and how you can make it better
foundation *n.* [C] an organisation that gives money for special purposes
great *adj.* **be great with something** to be very good at doing or dealing with something
green *adj.* relating to protecting the environment
  go green to change to using products or methods that protect the environment
hold a meeting to make a meeting happen
impact *n.* [U] a big change in someone or something caused by an event, situation, etc.
improve *v.* [I,T] to make something better
improvement *n.* [U] when something becomes better than it was
intend *v.* [T] to have decided that you want to do something
introduce *v.* [T] to put something into use for the first time
manufacturing *n.* [U] the process of making things using machines in a factory
marine *adj.* relating to the sea and the creatures that live there
open-plan office *n.* [C] an office (=place to work) that does not have walls to make different rooms
originally *adv.* in the beginning
plan *v.* [T] **plan to do something** to have decided that you want to do something, and think about how you will do it
pleased *adj.* happy or satisfied
point something ↔ out *phr v.* [T] to tell someone about a mistake that they had not noticed or a fact they had not thought about it
pollute *v.* [I,T] to make the air, water or land dirty or dangerous
pollution *n.* [U] dirty air, water or land, caused by harmful chemicals and waste
private transport (*also* **private transportation** *AmE*) *n.* [U] cars, bicycles, etc. that are owned and used by people rather than a company or the government
proposal *n.* [C] a suggested plan
propose *v.* [T] to officially suggest a plan
protect *v.* [T] to keep someone or something safe from harm or damage
protection *n.* [U] when something is kept safe so that is it not harmed or damaged
public bike hire scheme *n.* [C] a plan that allows people to pay to use a bicycle in a city, taking a bicycle at one place and leaving it in another
public transport (*also* **public transportation** *AmE*) *n.* [U] buses, trains, etc. that are available for everyone to use
put something into action to start using a plan
Q&A session *n.* [U] (*abbreviation for* **question and answer**) a part of a meeting or talk where people can ask questions
recycle *v.* [I,T] to put things such as glass, paper, etc. through a special process so that they can be used again
recycled *adj.* used again, after being put through a special process
recycling *n.* [U] the process of collecting and changing old paper, glass, plastic, etc. so that it can be used again
reduce *v.* [T] to make the amount or size of something less than it was before
reduction *n.* [U] when the amount or size of something becomes less than it was before
resort *n.* [C] a place where people go on holiday
result *n.* [C,U] **as a result** because of something that happened before
review meeting *n.* [C] a meeting between a manager and a worker to discuss the quality of the work, how well they do the job, and how to improve (=**appraisal**)
site *n.* [C] a place where something is
suggestion *n.* [C] an idea that someone suggests
support *n.* [C] help and encouragement
supportive *adj.* giving help and encouragement
timing *n.* [U] the time when something happens or is planned to happen
traffic jam *n.* [C] a long line of cars, etc. on the road that are moving very slowly
transport (*also* **transportation** *AmE*) *n.* [U] vehicles that people use to travel from one place to another
transport system (*also* **transportation system** *AmE*) *n.* [C] the way buses, trains, etc. are organised in a country so that people can travel from one place to another
underground (*also* **metro**, **subway** *AmE*) *n.* [singular] the railway system that runs under a city
urban *adj.* in a city, or of a city
waste *n.* [U] the parts of something that you have not used and do not need